AF556052

Shaping India's Foreign Policy

People, Politics and Places

IN THE SAME SERIES

India's Nuclear Deterrent: Pokhran II and Beyond

The Peacock and the Dragon: India-China Relations in the 21st Century

Kargil and After: Challenges for Indian Policy

Engaged Democracies: India-US Relations in the 21st Century

Shaping India's Foreign Policy

People, Politics and Places

Editors

Amitabh Mattoo and Happymon Jacob

The Foreign Policy, Peace and Security Series

HAR-ANAND
PUBLICATIONS PVT LTD

HAR-ANAND PUBLICATIONS PVT LTD
E-49/3, Okhla Industrial Area, Phase-II, New Delhi-110020
Tel.: 41603490
E-mail: info@haranandbooks.com/haranand@rediffmail.com
Shop online at: www.haranandbooks.com

Reprint, 2024

Published by Ashok Gosain and Ashish Gosain for
Har-Anand Publications Pvt Ltd

Printed in India

The Foreign Policy, Peace and Security Series

The Foreign Policy, Peace and Security Series (FPPSS) is dedicated to publishing scholarly books on critical issues of international relations, especially those concerning India's security and its foreign policy. The series aims to bring to bear diverse opinions to help generate informed debate on India's relationships with the outside world. The volumes will be analytically rigorous and rich in detail. They will, however, be written consciously for a wider non-specialist audience. As India enters the 21st century, in a world that is both anarchic and integrated, Indians can no longer afford the luxury of ignoring external relations or leaving critical decisions to a small group of experts. The Foreign Policy, Peace and Security Series will, hopefully, help bridge the information and analysis gap between experts on international relations and ordinary interested Indians.

Preface

This collection of essays analyzes and describes the relationship between India's domestic politics and the making of the country's foreign and defence policy. We are grateful to the contributors to this volume, all distinguished intellectuals, for making this book one of the first attempts at investigating the linkage. We wish to thank them also for their patience and understanding while we were putting together this volume. We also recognize that much more work needs to be done in his area, and we hope that this book will serve to generate a debate amongst academics and policy analysts.

In essence, this volume investigates and evaluates the impact that the political, economic, social, religious and cultural diversity of India has had on the making of the country's foreign and defence policy. The rich case studies in the volume suggest that internal factors have played a significant role in the formulation of Indian foreign policy, particularly in the last two decades.

This volume is the first comprehensive work to analyze the domestic aspects of foreign policy making in India. Through the case studies and the theoretical chapters, the book is a contribution to the literature on India's foreign policy and international relations theory. It will be, in our view, useful reading for practitioners and scholars alike, and fills a gap in the understanding of India's engagement with the outside world.

We are grateful to the Canada-based Forum of Federations for permitting us to reprint an article titled "Republic of India" authored by the editors of this book, published by the Forum in Hans J. Michelmann (ed.) *Foreign Relations in Federal Countries*, Montreal and Kingston: McGill-Queen's University Press, 2009.

We are also grateful to Souresh Roy and Aditi Bajpai for their invaluable editorial assistance.

School of International Studies
Jawaharlal Nehru University
New Delhi
January 2010

Amitabh Mattoo
Happymon Jacob

List of Contributors

Amitabh Mattoo is Professor at the School of International Studies, Jawaharlal Nehru University, New Delhi.

A K Ramakrishnan is Professor at the School of International Studies, Jawaharlal Nehru University, New Delhi.

Anuradha M. Chenoy is Professor at the School of International Studies, Jawaharlal Nehru University, New Delhi.

Deepa M. Ollapally is Associate Director of the Sigur Center for Asian Studies, George Washington University, USA.

Happymon Jacob is Assistant Professor at the School of International Studies, Jawaharlal Nehru University, New Delhi.

Jabin T Jacob is currently HERMES Fellow, SPIRIT, Sciences Po, Bordeaux, France and Research Fellow, Institute of Peace and Conflict Studies (IPCS), New Delhi, India.

Kamal Mitra Chenoy is Professor at the School of International Studies, Jawaharlal Nehru University, New Delhi.

Mahesh Shankar is a doctoral candidate in Political Science at McGill University, Montreal, Canada.

Nimmi Kurian is Associate Professor, Centre for Policy Research, New Delhi.

Paul Staniland is Research Fellow, Belfer Center for Science and International Affairs John F. Kennedy School of Government, Harvard University.

Rafiq Dossani is a senior research scholar at Shorenstein APARC, Stanford University, USA.

Reji K Joseph is a Consultant with the Research and Information System for Developing Countries (RIS), New Delhi.

Rekha Saxena is Associate Professor at the Department of Political Science, University of Delhi.

Srinidhi Vijaykumar graduated in history from Stanford University, USA.

T. V. Paul is James McGill Professor of International Relations in the Department of Political Science at McGill University, Montreal, Canada.

Vibhanshu Shekhar is Research Associate at the School of International Studies, Jawaharlal Nehru University, New Delhi.

Contents

Introduction

This volume of essays on domestic politics and India's foreign policy has three principal objectives. It seeks to add to our existing understanding of India's external relations at a time when New Delhi's engagement with global issues is in a critical phase of evolution. By focusing on internal political and social forces, the collection also draws attention to the complexity of factors that are influencing and shaping India's foreign policy and decision-making, particularly during a phase of coalition governments. Finally, for students of international relations (IR) and foreign policy (FP) this book can be read as a dialogue between the main theoretical paradigms in international relations (structural-realism, neoclassical realism, liberal-institutionalism and constructivism) and as a critique of the still dominant school of IR: structural-realism. We know of no other book which covers the same terrain.

This book's genealogy is interesting for historical and personal reasons. The idea first took root when the editors were colleagues at the University of Jammu in 2004-2006 and were engaged with the peace process between India and Pakistan, then at its peak. It became obvious to us that political and social institutions within Jammu and Kashmir were playing a vital role in shaping New Delhi's policies towards Pakistan. We recognized the limitations that structural realism had imposed on us; a school of thought that was seductive in its simplicity, and which privileged international system-level analysis while paying scant attention to the importance of understanding the dynamic forces operating within a country. The initial thoughts for the book thus came as the Srinagar-Muzafarrabad bus road opened and several civil society delegations from Pakistan and Pakistan occupied Kashmir came to Jammu and Kashmir. It seemed to us that these events had at least in part been influenced by political and societal actors in Srinagar, Jammu and perhaps even Muzaffarabad and Mirpur. The Forum of Federations, based in Ottawa, Canada, helped the nascent idea to develop; we were commissioned to write the India chapter in a volume of essays on Federal States throughout the world, focusing on their foreign policy-making. A revised version of the chapter is included in this work. The essay suggested that *de facto*, if not *de jure*, many of the constituent units of the Indian federation were players in decisions critical to India's international relations. For instance, Andhra Pradesh on WTO-related issues, Sikkim on the opening of the Nathu La trade route to China, Tamil Nadu on the problems of Sri Lanka, and West Bengal on the creation of the larger Bay of Bengal Community, all significantly contributed to the government of India's policies, although constitutionally states have no legal jurisdiction over foreign policy.

The idea became a reality following our return to our intellectual home, the School of International Studies, Jawaharlal Nehru University (JNU). We recognized the importance of advancing theoretical knowledge on India's foreign policy even as we multi-tasked as peace activists at the track-two level and as policy analysts. In this volume India is the case study, but we are not making a case of Indian "exceptionalism." In recognizing the need to develop a more comprehensive theoretical framework, or an "eclectic approach" (to use T.V. Paul and Mahesh Shankar's phrase from an essay in the book), we are making an argument that requires further research within our neighbourhood, as well as in other parts of the world. We are hoping that IR scholars will take notice. This is then as much a book about India and its foreign policy as it is about IR theory and the world outside the western hemisphere.

We will use this brief introduction to conduct a short historical survey of IR in India in comparison to China, to underscore the salience of the volume. We will then further elucidate the book's main area of focus, and finally we will summarize the principal findings of each one of the essays.

THE STATE OF IR IN INDIA

We believe that there are few (other) disciplines in India, especially in the social sciences, where the gulf between potential and reality is as wide as it is in the teaching and research of IR and FP at Indian universities. Interest in India and India's interest in the world is probably at its highest in modern times, and yet Indian scholarship on global issues is showing few signs of responding to this challenge and opportunity. In contrast, China, where IR emerged as an independent discipline in the social sciences much more recently, has made remarkable strides.

WHAT IS WRONG?

Few disciplines could have enjoyed a more favourable climate for intellectual growth in the first years after India's independence than IR. There were very few political leaders in Asia with the same breadth of vision, sense of global history and deep commitment to building institutions as Prime Minister Jawaharlal Nehru. It was with Nehru's patronage that the Indian Council for World Affairs (ICWA), founded by Sir Tej Bahadur Sapru in 1943, was instrumental in setting up the Indian School of International Studies (ISIS) in 1955, as a constituent unit of the University of Delhi. In 1961, the ISIS became a deemed university under section 3 of the University Grants Commission (UGC) Act which enabled it to award doctoral degrees. In the 1960s, Sapru House, home of the ICWA (and the ISIS in its initial years) was regarded as one of the "best research libraries in Asia" (Rajan, 2005: pp. 196-203).

In 1970, ISIS became a part of JNU under its new *avatar:* the School of International Studies (SIS). A year after the ISIS was established, in 1956, Jadavpur University founded its own department of International Relations, while a year earlier the Department of African Studies was inaugurated at the University of Delhi. This fortunate climate for the growth of IR did lead to a quantitative expansion of departments offering IR over the next four decades. But not much can be said about the quality.

Today, IR is taught in more than 100 universities in India at the under-graduate and post-graduate levels. A close scrutiny reveals that most of these departments in universities have a shortage of qualified faculty, poor infrastructure, outdated curriculum and few research opportunities. At least 50 percent of the departments have no access to online resources, only limited internet connectivity and meager grants for annual field trips. Even standard textbooks are not available in these departments. For instance, neither Kenneth Waltz's *Theory of International Politics* (an important contemporary work from the West) nor any of the Indian classical texts, such as Kautilya's *Arthashastra,* were found to be available in most state university libraries. A survey of 50 state universities revealed that students were unaware of the principal journals in the field, national or international. Neither did any of the libraries subscribe to the leading international journals of the discipline, for instance *Foreign Affairs, International Organization, International Security* or *International Affair* and none of these were accessible electronically through the applicable online databases. Additionally of course, there are very few good translations into Hindi or other Indian languages of the major works in the subject.

There is no All India International Studies Association despite periodic attempts at creating such a body. As a consequence, there are few annual conferences that students and scholars of IR can participate in or where they can share their research findings. Area studies, a vital part of IR, is facing almost terminal decline. There is no Indian Pakistan expert who can read or write or speak Pashto or Baluchi, and this is not an isolated example. The number of scholars who are proficient in Chinese, Japanese, Arabic, Persian or Dari is also limited. In addition, opportunities to attend overseas conferences and roundtables are alarmingly constrained. Despite all of this, there are institutions that have established themselves as centres of academic excellence. The School of International Studies at JNU is a good example, yet it is one of the few islands of excellence in a sea of mediocrity. Tragically, there is no recognizable contemporary Indian school of IR despite the rich civilizational repository of ideas on statecraft and inter-state relations.

In comparison, China—a late-starter—is doing more than just catching up. As Qin Yaqing of the China Foreign Affairs University put it "International Relations as a discipline began to develop since the late 1970s and early 1980s, when China started to open to the rest of the world. The 30years since 1978 have witnessed rapid development of the IR discipline in China, a remarkable time of learning, exploring and reflecting."

For instance, Renmin University of China pioneered a remarkable programme for the development of IR with the translation of major western IR classics. Between 1978 and 2007, the China People's Public Security University Press, the Shanghai People's Publishing House, the Peking University Press, the World Affairs Press and the Zhejiang Publishing House together brought approximately 86 translated IR books. Today all the major schools of thought in IR (Marxism, Realism, Liberalism and Constructivism) are robust in China. In addition, the Chinese IR community has, after a learning and absorbing stage, in the words of Yaqing, achieved "a long cherished hope: to produce a Chinese IR theory and there is a [now the] real possibility that this will happen as more traditional concepts like Tianxia, Datong, and Zhonyong (middle course) will be introduced to the process of creating a Chinese paradigm."

WHAT WENT WRONG?

The unsatisfactory development of IR is attributable to many factors: systemic, institutional, disciplinary and leadership-related. This is not the place to identify the causes for the lack of Indian theory-building tradition or the dearth of methodological rigour. However it ought to be emphasized that the paucity of resources and infrastructure, which are weak throughout the Indian university system, has had a particularly telling impact on IR, specifically on area studies. Scholars, in order to gain expertise of specific areas, need to develop their linguistic abilities or spend time in the region familiarizing themselves with the polity and the society. In reality, few Indian scholars have the luxury of being able to visit the region they are studying or devote time to learning relevant languages. Not surprisingly, India does not even have many real experts even on its immediate neighbourhood. Similarly, in the absence of an ambitious translation programme, IR has not been mainstreamed as a discipline through the country.

WHAT CAN BE DONE?

Kanti Bajpai argues that "rising powers seem to get the IR they need." But, as even he admits, "there is nothing inevitable about good IR as a response to the growth in national power" (Bajpai, 2009). Much, of course, has to be done by the UGC and Vice-Chancellors yet we believe that Indian academics, along with their peers outside, must pay particular attention to IR and FP theory. No discipline can grow, develop and assume academic respectability without a sound theoretical basis. In India, it is the remarkable absence of sound theoretical studies on India's unique IR and FP that is the hallmark of the discipline. As we noted, departments have proliferated, articles and books have been published, but original contributions to advancing an understanding of India and the world with a sound theoretical basis have remained limited. As Sumit Ganguly pointed out some years ago, "… few scholars from [India] have made any significant theoretical or policy relevant contributions to the study of international relations.

This is especially surprising in the light of other significant contributions made by Indian scholars to the cognate disciplines of anthropology, sociology, history and economics."[1] Or as Bajpai put it more starkly:

> No discipline can progress without theory, indeed it is doubtful that a body of scholarship can claim to be a discipline if it has no theoretical endeavour. Yet this is not conceded by many in India IR who see theory as some kind of cafeteria choice that you either pick up or leave at the serving counter as you move along depending on your preference and mood (Bajpai, 2009).

THE SALIENCE OF THIS VOLUME

We hope that this book can provide one amongst many correctives needed in order to realize the full scope and potential of IR and FP studies in India. It is thus in essence aimed at providing a more comprehensive and nuanced understanding of the making of India's foreign policy.

The relationship between domestic politics and India's foreign policy is a largely neglected area, particularly from a theoretical point of view. This is by itself not surprising. Does domestic politics influence contemporary India's foreign policy? If so, to what extent? And in which areas? The Realist school, preoccupied by system-level analysis, has dominated contemporary IR theory. The assumption has therefore been that in an anarchical international system states will behave like unitary rational actors driven, at a minimum, by their own

Sumit Ganguly, "International Relations in India: A Discipline in Search of Itself," unpublished ms, 2006. For other insightful essays on Indian IS see: Kanti Bajpai and Siddharth Mallavarapu, *International Relations in India* (two companion volumes), New Delhi: Orient Longman, 2004; M.S. Rajan(ed.) *International and Area Studies in India*, New Delhi: Lancer Books, 1997; Ankush B. Sawant (ed.), *Area Studies Programmes in Indian Universities: An Appraisal and Review*, Delhi: Kalinga Publications, 1996; and Navnita Chadha Behera, "Re-imagining IR in India," *International Relations of the Asia-Pacific*, vol. 7, 2007, pp. 341-368.

self preservation and, at a maximum, by the objective of global domination. Most essays challenge this assumption as they repeatedly demonstrate, theoretically and empirically, areas where it is implausible to accept this system-level analysis as providing a satisfactory explanation. They view the realist discourse as far too parsimonious and deductive.

The neglect of India by liberals and constructivists is more glaring. Liberals believe in the importance of "ideas" and the role they play in shaping policies while constructivists, *inter alia*, pay attention to multiple narratives, the building of norms and manner in which dominant discourses are constructed. Unfortunately, even these schools of IR—with a few notable exceptions—have paid little attention to internal forces in India that have shaped policies. This book is thus as much a critique of realism as it is a conversation with liberalism and constructivism.

THE ESSAYS

Deepa Ollapally investigates the role of domestic politics and India's 1998 nuclear tests. She critiques the structural-realist argument, and argues that in order to fully understand Pokhran II, simply focusing on what was occurring at the international level is insufficient. She asserts that the international systems argument, with its focus on security, is inherently problematic because security itself is infinitely stretchable. And, Ollapally suggests, the international systems explanation leaves us without a clear enough guide as to why states chose certain foreign policies over others.

Rafiq Dossani and Srinidhi Vijaykumar, in their focus on border states and foreign policy, argue that these states in India are increasingly playing a role in critical areas. They suggest that it is coalition governance in particular that creates a space for interventions by border states on foreign policy issues.

Mahesh Shankar and T.V. Paul propose that there should not be a choice between systemic arguments and those which focus on domestic policy. Instead what is needed is an eclectic approach that incorporates the structural, the material and the ideational.

Jabin T. Jacob and Vibhanshu Shekhar focus on the responses to the Malaysian and Kenyan ethnic crises by the Indian states of Tamil Nadu and Gujarat respectively. They demonstrate through these case studies that parties with strong regional bases are increasing their say in formulating the country's foreign policy.

Rekha Saxena finds that with the growing regionalization in Indian politics, there is increased pressure from "sub-national governments" to play a role in the treaty-making power of the Union Executive.

Amitabh Mattoo and Happymon Jacob argue that centralized control over foreign policy has begun to weaken and this gentle erosion of central authority is likely to continue in the future.

Nimmi Kurian suggests that the shifting border discourse, in the context of the North East India, provides an interesting template for bottom-up approaches to India's foreign policy.

Paul Staniland believes that domestic politics has always influenced the contours of India's foreign policy but goes on to reflect on the manner in which domestic politics influenced India's foreign policy before the liberalization period, and in the aftermath of 1991.

A.K. Ramakrishnan asserts that Indian foreign policy is becoming a realm of increasing contestations and he attempts to problematize the linkage between culture and India's foreign policy.

Reji K. Joseph focuses on the WTO and the role played by nonstate agents. His paper analyses the contribution made by civil society groups regarding the making of India's intellectual property laws in conformity with the WTO framework.

Kamal Mitra Chenoy and Anuradha M. Chenoy evaluate the role played by the Left parties in attempting to oppose the India-Us nuclear deal, even while they were part of the ruling coalition.

Happymon Jacob uses a neoclassical realist lens to more comprehensively assess and evaluate Indian foreign policy making. He argues that this new theory in International Relations is an excellent conceptual platform to address and understand the 'new' dynamism of contemporary Indian foreign policy.

Ultimately however, this book must not read as the last word on the subject. The essays that follow are hopefully only the beginning of a new Indian engagement with cutting-edge "western" IR theory. We hope also that in the days to come Indian thought on IR, ranging from Ashoka's ideas on war and peace to Kautalaya's theories on statecraft, will also be disinterred for a wider audience.

REFERENCES

Rajan, M.S. (2005), "Golden Jubilee of the School of International Studies: An Assessment, *International Studies* 42, 3&4.

Bajpai, Kanti (2009), "Obstacles to Good Work in IR," paper presented at the workshop on Upgrading International Studies in India, Lee Kuan Yew School of Public Policy, National University of Singapore, March 25-26.

I

Foreign Relations of India: The Federal Challenge

Amitabh Mattoo and Happymon Jacob

Introduction

The Constitution of India gives the Union government virtually exclusive jurisdiction over matters of foreign and defence policy. In practice, too, the central government in New Delhi has exercised overwhelming control over India's external relations since the Constitution came into force in 1950. Constitutional position and historical experience notwithstanding, however, foreign policy making in India ever since the 1990s can be said to be increasingly determined by a host of extra-constitutional factors which have made it possible for the Indian states to influence the formation and direction of the country's foreign policy. This chapter attempts to throw light on the various factors that enable the Indian states to emerge as significant foreign policy players.

The rest of the chapter is organised in the following manner. The chapter starts with a brief section on the historical evolution of Indian foreign policy in order to locate the succeeding sections of the paper in proper perspective. This is followed by a discussion on the various constitutional aspects of foreign policy making in the country. Then, after briefly introducing the issue of competitive federalism (Centre Vs. State) in the Indian context, the chapter looks at the various aspects of intergovernmental relations in foreign affairs and domestic and international manifestations of constituent diplomacy in the country.

This discussion, with adequate empirical data, is followed by a section which poblematises one of the key arguments of the paper and looks at the limits of States' foreign economic diplomacy. The chapter also has a section on the increasingly important aspect of the roles that border states play in nuancing India's foreign and defence policy decisions.

INDIA'S FOREIGN POLICY

Independent India's foreign policymakers had to deal with a host of challenges: partition of the country and creation of a hostile Pakistan, extreme poverty, military weakness, underdevelopment, backwardness in the core sectors of industry, and simmering regional and religious tensions. India's policy toward its neighbours—especially in terms of defining its boundaries—mimicked British colonial policy. New Delhi also pursued an independent approach to foreign policy by choosing to remain nonaligned in the rivalry between the Eastern and Western blocs during the early years of the Cold War. A key characteristic, however, has been the centralization of foreign policy decisions as envisioned in India's Constitution, with New Delhi providing little space for states.

Jawaharlal Nehru, India's first prime minister, was the most influential thinker on foreign policy. Virtually single-handedly, he defined the main contours of India's foreign policy in the first decades after Independence. His control of foreign and defence policy played an important role in strengthening the control of the Union government over the country's foreign and defence policymaking. Nehruvian ideas had a lasting impact on the country's foreign policy. Nehru's grand strategy rested on two pillars: self-reliance and nonalignment. As India was a militarily and economically weak state, he believed it was important to avoid entrapment in Cold War rivalries while simultaneously becoming self-reliant internally. Nehru's nonalignment was, however, far from neutrality. India was active in the movement for disarmament, in decolonization, and in the campaign for more equitable international economic development. Nehru sought to make Indian foreign policy adopt the role of almost being the conscience of the world.

The limits of Nehruvian "idealism" were demonstrated by India's military defeat during the Sino-Indian war of 1962. Gradually, even while the Nehruvian legacy survived in many other ways, the reality of power politics injected itself into Indian policymaking. It was Nehru's daughter, Indira Gandhi, who became prime minister after Nehru's death. She conducted India's first nuclear test in 1974, intervened in East Pakistan to help create Bangladesh, and established a close relationship with the former Soviet Union. It was not, however, until 1998 that *realpolitik* became the defining feature of India's foreign policy. The dominating influence of Nehru and then Indira Gandhi meant that there was limited space for other leaders and even less for individual states to intervene in foreign policy issues.

The watershed in India's foreign policy came in May 1998, when—defying traditional assumptions, analytical predictions, and international opinion—New Delhi conducted a series of nuclear-bomb tests. This was the beginning of what has been widely described as a new phase of realism in India's foreign policy. This decision was, however, taken in secret by Prime Minister Atal Behari Vajpayee and his closest advisers and without the knowledge of even the Cabinet, let alone leaders from the states.

Despite this new phase, India's fundamental foreign policy goals had not changed very much. These objectives formed the bedrock of India's engagement with the outside world. It was primarily India's search for security and stability in South Asia, and its quest to influence international politics—beyond the immediate neighbourhood—through its growing "hard" and "soft" power that formed the mainstay of New Delhi's foreign policy. Faced with the necessity of an accelerated and multifaceted engagement with the outside world, India also sought to retain the autonomy to make decisions on key issues of national interest without capitulating to international pressure or being crushed by globalization. This was most strikingly evident in India's position in multilateral trade talks as well as in New Delhi's unwillingness to support the US-led war in Iraq or to let Indian soldiers be deployed there as part of the multinational force.

THE CONSTITUTIONAL SETTING

The Constitution of India came into effect on 26 January 1950. Federalism, secularism, popular sovereignty, fundamental rights, directive principles of state policy (guidelines in the Constitution to the government of the day on certain things to do and achieve that are, nonetheless, not enforceable), judicial independence, and a cabinet form of government are the basic principles enshrined in the Constitution. Even though federalism is one of the basic features of the Constitution, the word "federalism" is not mentioned in the document. Article 1(1) of the Constitution calls the country "a union of states." Each of India's twenty-eight constituent states has its own legislature (some of them have both upper and lower houses), executive, and judiciary. India's Parliament has two houses: Lok Sabha (lower house) and Rajya Sabha (upper house, or council of states). Because the upper house consists of the representatives of the states and the Union Territories, besides those nominated by the president of India, states can influence legislative proceedings on foreign and defence policy by raising and discussing such issues.

That the Union government has ultimate authority over the foreign relations of the country is evident from the fact that even if a majority of states, theoretically speaking, oppose a particular foreign policy, the Union government is not constitutionally bound to take this opposition into account.

The states have policing powers within their own territory and do not possess anything akin to an organized military apart from the state police, whose senior officers are selected, trained, and called to its service by the central government. Although Parliament has the authority to make decisions regarding foreign and defence policy, in practice the Union Cabinet makes the actual decisions. Parliament can discuss these decisions, review them, and vote against them. If the decisions of the Cabinet were overturned not only would they be reversed but, because of the conventions of parliamentary government, the government would fall. This never happens because the central Cabinet enjoys the support of the majority in Parliament. Parliament also has various committees on foreign and defence policy, but their powers are merely recommendatory and not enforceable. Such committees are comprised of members from both houses, although the majority are from the lower house. The permanent civil service in the foreign office is drawn from the Indian Foreign Service (IFS). Its officials are specially recruited through a federally appointed body, the Union Public Service Commission (UPSC), and their cadre management is with the central government.

On balance, India has a strong central government.[1] The centralizing features of the Constitution are evident from the following powers of the Union government: it has major taxation powers; it has the power to reorganize the states through an act of Parliament, a power it has exercised in the past; state governors, who are appointed by the central government, have the power to delay consent to legislation passed by a state legislature; state governors can play a role in the formation of state governments, and the central government is vested with the power to dismiss state governments by virtue of Article 356;[2] and Parliament can override legislation passed by the states, citing national interests.

Legislative powers under the Constitution are divided into three lists under Article 246 of its seventh schedule, namely the Union list, the state list, and the concurrent list. Only the central government has the authority to pass legislation on items listed under the Union list. State governments make laws on items listed under the state list. The concurrent list contains items on which both the state and Union

[1]India's government has also been called a "quasi-federal system," "centralized federalism," and "the union system of Indian federalism."

[2]Amal Ray, with John Kincaid, "Politics, Economic Development, and Second-Generation Strain in India's Federal System," *Publius: The Journal of Federalism* 18 (Spring 1988): 147-67.

governments can enact legislation. However, in the event of a conflict between a state and the centre on any item under the concurrent list, the writ of the central government prevails. The central government, not the state governments, holds the residuary power. The following powers are all unambiguously part of the Union list and thus outside the jurisdiction of state governments: defence of India; matters regarding naval, military, and air forces and other forces of the country; deployment of any armed force of the country in any state as an aid to civil power; delimitation of cantonment areas; foreign affairs and all matters that bring India into relation with any foreign power; diplomatic, consular, and trade representation; the United Nations; participation in international conferences, associations, and other bodies and implementing decisions made thereof; entry into treaties and agreements with foreign countries; implementation of treaties, agreements, and conventions with foreign countries; war and peace; foreign jurisdiction; extradition and admission, immigration and expulsion, passports and visas; and foreign loans. As regards trade and commerce, not only international trade but even interstate trade are the subject matter of the Union government. Treaties with foreign governments can be concluded only by the Union government, and more important, it does not need to have the treaties ratified by Parliament. Parliament may discuss any treaty or agreement entered into by the executive but may not affect its finality or enforceability. The Constitution, then, gives the central government in New Delhi virtually exclusive jurisdiction over foreign and defence policy. The states have, with some notable exceptions, played little role in formulating or implementing the country's foreign relations.

The Indian government's order of business, in allocating functions to each ministry, invariably contains the rider that anything to do with international relations and foreign affairs is not to be dealt with by the concerned ministry but by the central Ministry of External Affairs. As regards the bureaucracy, whether working in the central government or in governments of the various states, its members are forbidden to interact with any multilateral or bilateral agency without the formal knowledge and consent of the concerned agency of the central government. In fact, even for private companies, the maximum extent of foreign direct investment (FDI) and the degree of foreign ownership permissible in different categories of private companies are limited by laws of the Union government.

CENTRE VERSUS STATES

Despite a strong central government, the relationship between India's states and the central government has been an evolving one. This process of evolution has gone through various phases of cooperation and confrontation. The period until the late 1960s was characterized by extreme centralization. It was in 1967, three years after the death of Jawaharlal Nehru, that one-party rule in India started breaking down. The rise of regional parties in the 1970s and 1980s led to demands for the transfer of more powers to the states. The Union government relented by appointing the Sarkaria Commission to review centre-state relations in 1983.

The rise of regional parties to power at the centre had to wait until the general elections of 1989, which saw the establishment of the National Front coalition government led by Vishwanath Pratap Singh. Singh set up the long-awaited Inter-State Council in 1990, a forum for which provision had already been made in the Constitution. Even the Congress government that succeeded the National Front government had to depend on regional parties to gain and remain in power. This became a regular feature after the formation of the United Front government in 1996. In other words, ever since the 1989 general elections, no single party has won a majority in Parliament. Whereas in the 1989 election, 27 regional parties gained seats, 43 did so in the 1991 election. Many of these small parties' agendas are limited to highlighting only state-specific issues.

The demand for decentralization by the states is further augmented by two factors that play themselves out in the Indian political arena: the movement for local governance (through *panchayati raj*[3] and urban local bodies, namely municipalities) and demands for further reorganization of India's states. The movement for local governance is enshrined in the 73rd and 74th Amendments to the Constitution, which were passed by Parliament in 1992. These call for further decentralization of state power to local elected bodies, although this provision is not implemented by many Indian states. The movement for further reorganization of states based on regional identities has already seen results in the recent creation of an additional three states. All these factors appear to have strengthened regional forces asking for more and more decentralization of political power and resources. Although this renegotiation of centre-state relations had no direct implication for foreign relations, it did pave the way for the new assertiveness that the Indian states are showing today vis-à-vis the country's foreign policymaking.

INTERGOVERNMENTAL RELATIONS IN FOREIGN AFFAIRS

The centralized control of foreign and defence policy long exercised by the Union government has begun to weaken over the past decade or so. There are four interrelated reasons for this growing influence of constituent units on foreign relations. First, the special constitutional status given to some states (as in the case of Jammu and Kashmir) may give the states' political leadership a voice in the country's foreign policymaking. Second, the political weight of a leader of a particular state can also influence foreign policymaking, albeit in an informal manner. Third, coalition governments at the centre have provided space for state governments and leaders to exercise greater say on foreign policy issues because coalition Union governments are formed by regional parties, many of which are based exclusively in one state. Finally, although the Constitution has not undergone change, the forces of globalization have created new practices and possibilities that have already given the states a greater role and will continue to do so in the future. This is especially evident in the case of foreign economic

[3] Local self-government institutions.

policymaking. Many international financial agencies and institutions, for instance, are negotiating directly with the state governments in India.

These trends suggest that this gradual erosion of central authority, *de facto* if not *de jure*, is likely to continue over the next decade. The loosening of centralized control of foreign policy is not a conscious or voluntary act by the Union government but a result of the convergence of a number of factors. However, it is necessary here to point out that (1) the central government is not constitutionally bound to consult states on matters of foreign policy, (2) the states do not have any place in foreign policymaking meetings or during negotiations of international treaties and other agreements, and (3) there is not yet any formal structure to consult states on matters of foreign and defence policy. If any state has a concern in this regard, it is usually taken up at the highest political level (the chief minister conveying it to the prime minister). No bureaucratic mechanism exists to channel any such concerns. Rarely are any meetings called even at the political level to discuss foreign policy matters with states. The exceptions are when the prime minister meets with the chief ministers of states to discuss their concerns regarding foreign economic policies. States do not have offices or representatives abroad to pursue foreign policy, economic policy, or even cultural policy. Foreign missions setting up consulates in various parts of India need to liaise with and obtain clearance from the Union government, not from the state governments. It is for the central government to interact with state governments in this regard.

As the Constitution is clear about the centralized control of foreign and defence policymaking, it is necessary to look for evidence outside the constitutional framework to see whether the states have been able to influence such decisions through extraconstitutional means and practices. The following sections look at how globalization and coalition politics have affected the making of India's foreign economic policy and how border states and the political weight of state leaders have affected India's foreign and security policy.

DOMESTIC AND INTERNATIONAL MANIFESTATIONS OF CONSTITUENT DIPLOMACY

The 1990s were of great importance for centre-state relations in foreign policy. The ninth general election to Parliament saw a coalition government come to power, with regional parties, some even single-state parties, playing decisive roles in forming and running the government in New Delhi. This meant political decentralization. The years that followed also witnessed an unprecedented phase of liberalization leading to the opening up of the Indian economy. India's experiment with globalization and privatization meant the gradual abolition of the autarkic "permit-licence raj," characterized by bureaucratic red tape, that had been typical of the Indian economy since independence. This translated into economic decentralization. As Lloyd I. Rudolph and Susanne Hobber Rudolph point out, "economic liberalization, the dismantling of the 'permit-license raj' and an increasing reliance on markets, proved to be an enabling factor for the emergence of the federal market economy."[4] The coming together of these two factors forced a redefinition of centre-state relations in an unprecedented manner. The earlier decades had been characterized by constitutional rigidity, whereas the new era ushered in creative and accommodative federalism. In short, economic liberalization and coalition politics in the country provided the space for the states to confidently participate in the nation's foreign economic policymaking, which earlier had been the exclusive role of the central government.

The states' new role in foreign economic policymaking is demonstrated by the fact that many international financial agencies and institutions, for instance, are directly negotiating with state governments. Independent discussions and negotiations are held between international agencies and organizations—such as the World

[4]Lloyd I. Rudolph and Susanne Hoeber Rudolph, "The Iconization of Chandrababu: Sharing Sovereignty in India's Federal Market Economy," *Economic and Political Weekly*, 5 May 2001, 1542.

Bank, the Asian Development Bank, UNICEF, and the United Nations Development Program (UNDP)—and the various state governments, even though the state governments require permission from the centre to conclude agreements reached in this fashion. If these organizations wish to approach the various state governments, they must do so through the Ministry of External Affairs and the Department of Economic Affairs of the Ministry of Finance. However, if the states approach them, they can do so independently, but a memorandum of understanding (MOU) would require the approval of the Union government. This means that the central government does have the wherewithal to control such negotiations if it wants to do so.

However, on many occasions, the central government is constrained from controlling such activities due to the compulsions of coalition politics. The states of Andhra Pradesh and Maharashtra, among others, have World Trade Organization (WTO) departments to deal with WTO-related issues, and their functioning has been rated innovative. With the southern Indian states becoming the hubs of software development and focal points for foreign investment, the Union government has to consider their policy preferences in making foreign economic policy. Moreover, with the competition for FDI increasing among the states, top state officials often travel abroad to negotiate terms and conditions for such investment with the organizations concerned. Antiglobalization movements in various parts of the country too have exhibited the power to influence the terms and conditions of investment and production in particular regions.

Political and economic structural changes have led the states to become increasingly involved in the world economy. State officials have signed a range of agreements with foreign economic institutions for purposes of collaboration and financial borrowing. There have been visits abroad by state leaders as well as visits of influential political and corporate leaders such as Bill Clinton, Bill Gates, George W. Bush, Yoshiro Mori, and Li Peng to various state capitals. No longer can the central government's prerogative or acts of favoritism determine the destination of FDI. Not only do the states understand that the central government is no longer an all-powerful entity that can bail them out of any financial problems, but they also understand that they need to compete with each other to get investment if they are to survive in the era of economic globalization. State representatives undertake missions abroad to advertise to the world that attractive investment opportunities exist in their states and that the states provide infrastructural support such as roads and low-cost power, capital and interest subsidies, and a stronger enforcement of law and order. Sometimes incentives take the form of special economic zones, software technology parks, reformed labour policies that permit downsizing and more flexible hiring and dismissal practices, tax concessions such as tax-free zones, and more relaxed environmental laws. As early as 1993, this new activism of the states was demonstrated by a deal struck between the Government of Maharashtra and the Enron Corporation to build a 2000-megawatt power plant, with the government of India providing financial guarantees to Enron. This was the first agreement of its kind in the history of independent India.

As the states established their standing among the country's important economic actors, the state chief ministers became the new role models of the new India's economic strength and development. State leaders such as Chandrababu Naidu (former Andhra Pradesh chief minister), S.M. Krishna (former Karnataka chief minister), and to some extent, Buddhadeb Bhattacharjee (presently West Bengal's chief minister) transcended their traditional role—which had been limited essentially to maintaining law and order and managing the state—to aggressively woo investment and capital. It was Naidu who started off this process by negotiating with the World Bank for a loan. Some chief ministers have even participated in the World Economic Forum meetings in Davos, Switzerland. Naidu has visited many foreign capitals to woo investment. In August 2002, for example, he visited Singapore to attract investments in the Special Economic Zone set up in Vishakapatanam in Andhra Pradesh.

In subsequent years, many state governments signed agreements with international economic institutions and aid agencies such as the Asian Development Bank and the World Bank. This is in addition to the many deals that various states struck with multinational companies. Important also are the negotiations conducted by state governments with foreign firms and governments to set up "smart cities" in the high-tech area in their states in order to promote international collaboration and attract investment. Recently, the Government of Kerala negotiated with a Dubai-based firm to set up such a smart city in Cochin. It is pertinent to note that in all these initiatives by the states, the Union government tried to facilitate only due to coalition pressures and because these initiatives were seen as part of its overall economic-development vision.

There have also been differences of opinion between the Union government and the states on a variety of issues. One of the major issues of concern for many states was the signing by the central government of the WTO agreement. Many states claimed that by signing the WTO agreement on agriculture, for example, the Union government had in fact usurped the states' power over agricultural policy. Some state governments took "the GOI [government of India] to court demanding a reinstatement of the constitutionally mandated division of powers between the central and state governments, in which agriculture is categorized as a subject."[5] In another instance of confrontation between states and the central government, the Government of Chhattisgarh opposed the Union government's plans to sell a publicly owned enterprise to a private firm, the Bharat Aluminum Company (BALCO). The state government approached the Supreme Court, but it ruled in favour of the central government. Such aggressive actions by state governments have forced the Union government to consult with them, as did Atal Behari Vajpayee, who

[5]Rob Jenkins, "How Federalism Influences India's Domestic Politics of WTO Engagement (and is itself affected in the process)," *Asian Survey* 43, no. 4 (2003): 598-621, at 607.

held a meeting of state chief ministers in 2001 to discuss with them their concerns regarding the WTO and its impact on agriculture.[6]

THE LIMITS OF STATES' FOREIGN ECONOMIC DIPLOMACY

The new activism of the states has not been without the imposition of many constraints and limits by the various central governments that have come to power. Rob Jenkins, having looked closely at what has become known as foreign economic diplomacy, argues that the newfound activism of the states has not been very successful. Jenkins claims that states' encounters with external actors "do not constitute 'foreign economic policy' so much as domestic policies with implications for the possibility of transacting business with transnational capital and international financial institutions."[7]

Jenkins points out that the central government has not been particularly accommodating of state participation in the decision-making process in the country's foreign economic policy. He writes that "the general trend is the ability of central government officials responsible for the implementation of trade policy to remain substantially impervious to the entreaties of state governments representing key trade-affected constituencies."[8] This has been amply evidenced in the fact that the central government, heedless of repeated requests from many states, did not raise tariffs on certain imported commodities despite evidence that their import had an adverse impact on domestic agricultural producers. Jenkins also points out that the Government of India has not even included the states in the discussions under the WTO-mandated Trade Policy Review Mechanism (TPRM), in which the states' involvement would have served them well.[9] The WTO does not provide any mechanism that allows states to influence

[6]P.K. Vasudeva, "Chief Ministers' Conference on WTO Mixed Results," 2 July 2001, http://members.tripod.com/israindia/isr/july3/vasu.html (accessed 1 February 2008).

[7]Rob Jenkins, "India's States and the Making of Foreign Economic Policy: The Limits of the Constituent Diplomacy Paradigm," *Publius: The Journal of Federalism* 33 (Fall 2003): 63-81, at 69-70.

[8]*Ibid.*, 79.

[9]*Ibid.*

agreements signed with the Union government. Furthermore, the complexities of the behind-the-scene politics of most international financial organizations are well beyond the reach and understanding of the state governments. Most of the WTO cells established by state governments have not been able to contribute much to the states' involvement in decision making about foreign economic policy[10]—this despite the fact that the central government has encouraged the states to set up such bodies.[11] One of the reasons for this is that these cells are often headed by civil servants who are reluctant to undertake initiatives on their own; a second is that their agenda has been limited. A cursory glance at the objectives of the Andhra Pradesh WTO cell, for example, demonstrates that there is nothing radical in its action program.[12]

Moreover, the central bureaucracy has not been very positive about the states' participation in the decision-making process of the country's foreign economic policy even as the political leadership seems to be more open and encouraging. In fact, the central bureaucracy does everything to ensure that the states do not bypass the interests and influence of the Union government when negotiating with international organizations and agencies. Even though politically there may be a willingness to demonstrate greater flexibility, the bureaucracy is unwilling to share turf or to change the status quo. In any case, structural problems inhibit states from taking loans from international organizations, agencies, and states because the central government

[10]WTO cells are set up by state governments to assess the impact of the WTO regime on their economies. Andhra Pradesh, West Bengal, Madhya Pradesh, Karnataka, Delhi, Tripura, Nagaland, Haryana, and the Union territory of Dadra and Nagar Haveli have established WTO cells so far. Punjab has also constituted a high-powered committee to look into the impact of the WTO regime.

[11]"Centre to continue talks with states on WTO," 20 March 2001, http://www.rediff.com/money/2001/mar/20wto.htm (accessed 1 December 2007).

[12]The key objectives are: preparation of the WTO Strategy Document for Agriculture in Andhra Pradesh; regular documentation of WTO impacts on agriculture and allied sectors; advice and guidance to senior management of the concerned departments on WTO-related strategies; determining the communication strategies to advise stakeholders, especially farmers, on WTO-related aspects; and keeping the agriculture sector in Andhra Pradesh in pace with the changing world in the wake of the WTO. See http://agri.ap.nic.in/wto.html (accessed 1 December 2007).

often has a decisive say in such transactions. A good example is World Bank loans. These always identify the central government as the principal borrower even when the loan is to go to a state government. The central bureaucracy, more often without the explicit consent of the political leadership, also tries to place legal impediments in the way of independent state negotiations with international organizations. Therefore, organizations asked to provide loans almost always try to negotiate with the central government before finalizing the agreement with a particular state. Jenkins puts it well: "Through the considerable leverage it possesses with foreign agencies, the Government of India is able to influence the shape of states' multilaterally funded assistance packages even before the draft programmes are brought to state governments themselves."[13]

Be that as it may, it is now widely recognized that there is increasing collaboration and consultation between the Union government and states on matters of economic diplomacy. On the one hand, the central government recognizes that it is better to be understanding of the demands of states because the stability of the central government in the era of coalition politics depends much on the regional parties. The outlook and attitudes of the politicians at the centre also have changed regarding how far they should accommodate regional views. Today's political leadership draws its power from the regional parties and has a thorough understanding of the demands and aspirations of the country's regions. What perhaps has not changed is the central bureaucracy. The real managers of power in the Union government, the bureaucrats, do not like to delegate their power to the states, especially in the absence of clear legislation requiring them to do so.

BORDER STATES AND FEDERAL RELATIONS

India's border states have special problems, two of which are dealing with illegal migration and cross-border terrorism. Because of these

[13] Jenkins, "India's States," 73.

problems, they have negotiated special treatment with or have behaved differently from other states vis-à-vis the central government. Debates and arguments about illegal migration from Nepal and Bangladesh have been especially strong in India's north-eastern states. Rafiq Dossani and Srinidhi Vijayakumar point out that, "as the state parties have increased their voice in government, they have demanded an increased role in controlling migration into their states. Nowhere is the ambiguity of federal jurisdiction more apparent than in the case of border patrol. In West Bengal, the state police and the Border Security Force [a centrally-controlled paramilitary force] often work together to control the movement of migrants and goods from Bangladesh."[14]

Although the legal power over border control and regulation lies with the Union government, it is often not in a position to carry these out effectively without the cooperation of the state governments. This has prompted the central government to delegate powers to them. In one such instance, L.K. Advani, the then Union home minister, asked the states to take the necessary steps to stop illegal migrants.[15] In another instance, the West Bengal government opposed a move by Maharashtra and the central government to expel some alleged illegal Bangladeshi migrants through the territory of West Bengal.[16]

The border states have also had to deal with cross-border terrorism. States like Jammu and Kashmir have designed their own ways to do so and have at least sometimes come into conflict with the central government. The disbanding of the Special Operations Group (SOG) by the Mufti Mohammad Sayeed government in Jammu and Kashmir, opposed by the central government, is such an instance. Although SOG was a state-run organization and therefore operated by virtue of the policing powers of Jammu and Kashmir state, the Union

[14]Rafiq Dossani and Srinidhi Vijayakuamr, "Indian Federalism and the Conduct of Foreign Policy in Border States: State Participation and Central Accommodation since 1990," Shorenstein APARC Working Paper, Walter H. Shorenstein Asia-Pacific Research Center, Stanford University, 5.

[15]*Ibid.*, 10.

[16]*Ibid.*

government had definite interests in the matter because it affected the country's internal security. The Mufti government also had adopted a "healing touch" approach to the Kashmir problem and had decided to release from confinement many persons accused of indulging in acts of militancy despite the central government's displeasure.

In the recent past, Sayeed was also able to have an impact on India's policy toward Pakistan. Sayeed is widely regarded as the architect, although indirectly, of several confidence-building measures that were introduced between the two countries. These include the resumption of the Srinagar-Muzaffarabad bus service across the volatile line of control that divides Jammu and Kashmir between India and Pakistan, as well as the unprecedented collaboration between Islamabad and New Delhi after the devastating earthquake in Jammu and Kashmir in fall 2005. Since then, a large number of initiatives vis-à-vis Pakistan have been undertaken in Jammu and Kashmir. The Poonch-Rawalkot bus service has already begun, and bus services are proposed between Kargil and Skardu in Pakistan-administered Kashmir and between Jammu and Sialkot, also in that part of Kashmir. There have been many debates in the Jammu and Kashmir Legislative Assembly on the role of Pakistan in sponsoring terrorism in the state. For example, in March 2000, speaking in the state assembly, the then chief minister, Dr Farooq Abdullah, stated that "Pakistan was bent upon destabilizing peace in India. He said he had requested the US President, Mr. Bill Clinton, that he should tell Islamabad, during his ensuing visit, that it should stop exporting terrorists to Jammu and Kashmir. He said that Mr. Clinton should assert his authority and force Pakistan to end its 10-year-long proxy war which had resulted in the death of several thousand people in the State. Dr. Abdullah said the USA should declare Pakistan a terrorist state and impose sanctions against it."[17]

The political weight of a particular state leader can also influence foreign policymaking, albeit informally. This is illustrated by the

[17] "J&K House resolves to banish terrorism," 24 March 2000, http://www.tribuneindia.com/2000/20000324/j&k.htm#1 (accessed 1 December 2007).

example of Amrinder Singh, the chief minister of Punjab, who reached out to Pakistan's Punjab on the basis of a shared cultural tradition, Punjabiyat. This policy received considerable popular support in Indian Punjab. Another such instance occurred in 1964 when the Kashmiri leader, Sheikh Abdullah, went to Pakistan as Prime Minister Nehru's emissary, where he is believed to have even worked out an understanding with President Ayub Khan. This understanding, however, was not translated into action because Nehru passed away while the sheikh was still in Pakistan. Similarly, political heavyweights from the southern state of Tamil Nadu have been able to exercise considerable influence on New Delhi's policy toward Sri Lanka. Indeed, the Tamil Nadu legislature has often in the past passed resolutions on the situation of Tamils in Sri Lanka. On 17 August 2006 the Tamil Nadu Assembly condemned attacks on Tamils in northern Sri Lanka by government forces. When Sri Lanka criticized the resolution, Tamil Nadu's chief minister, M.K. Karunanidi, retorted that "if Tamils condemning the killing of their Tamil brethren was dubbed a mistake, then they [Tamil Nadu Assembly] would continue to commit it."[18] Again, in December 2006, the Tamil Nadu Assembly resolved that "this house is deeply concerned about the travails of the Tamils in Sri Lanka because of lack of protection to life and property. We request the central government to take necessary steps to alleviate the situation to the satisfaction of all concerned."[19]

The forces of regional integration in South Asia have also created opportunities for states to play a role. After the chief minister of Sikkim, Pawan Chamling, set up a study group that strongly recommended the opening of the route, pressure from the Government of Sikkim helped to speed up the opening of the traditional trade links between Sikkim and China across the Nathula

[18]M. Mayilvaganan, "Uncertainty in Sri Lanka and a Possible Thaw in Indian Perception," 12 December 2006, http://www.idsa.in/publications/stratcomments/Mmayilvaganan121206.htm (accessed 15 October 2007).

[19]"Tamil Nadu house passes resolution on Sri Lankan Tamils," 7 December 2006, http://in.news.yahoo.com/061207/43/6a3sj.html (accessed 15 October 2007).

Pass, which was closed in the 1960s. Similarly, West Bengal has supported the Bay of Bengal Initiative for Multi-Sectoral Technical and Economic Cooperation (BIMSTEC), which links South Asia to South East Asia and seeks to create a Bay of Bengal economic community. This would have the potential to make Kolkata (the capital of West Bengal) once again the hub of trade and commerce, as it had been until the early years of the twentieth century.

The Kunming initiative, discussed earlier, will undoubtedly require removing existing bilateral irritants between India and its neighbours. Indeed, linking the northeast of the country with the neighbouring countries would be extremely beneficial for that region, as it would benefit from a sea link as well as trade links with the rest of the region. River-water management, border management, and energy production in the region also require regional collaboration between India, Nepal, and Bangladesh. As far-fetched as many of these developments may be, that there is thinking along these lines is of great significance.

Indeed, the Union government is considering many more such trade and other links, which will strengthen the country's regional engagements and enable the states to have more say in the establishment and management of the country's trade and links with neighbouring countries. The following are some of them. Integrated check points (ICPs) are being negotiated with Nepal, along with upgrading of highways and train links between the two countries. Border links with Bhutan, Bangladesh, and Myanmar are also being pursued seriously.[20] Given the importance that successive Indian governments have attributed to neighbourhood diplomacy over the past few years, it is likely that most of these initiatives will see the light of day. What needs to be noted here is that such links with the neighbouring states will certainly increase the role of the Indian states in policy formulation vis-à-vis their foreign neighbours. However, all these links first have to be approved by the Union government.

[20]Shyam Saran, "Connectivity as India's neighbourhood policy," http://www.himalmag.com/2006/october/opinion_1.htm (accessed 15 October 2007).

It is worth considering what would happen if India gave more freedom to its states to engage the international arena in the same manner as, for example, Canadian provinces, Belgian regions and communities, Swiss cantons, or even US states. Can India take the risk of allowing such freedom? If not, why not? Such counterfactual analysis could provide a clue about the health of India's recent federalism. When the Indian National Congress was the dominant party in Indian politics, a period referred to by many as the "Congress system," giving Indian states more freedom to engage the international arena may not have made much of a difference because the centralized Congress party's high command would not have let the state governments exercise such powers in the first place. However, the state of affairs is different in today's coalition era, when states are vying to influence Indian foreign policy, including foreign economic policy. Regional parties and their leaders, without whose support no Union government can today be formed or sustained, have certainly used such constitutional provisions to influence the country's policies toward its neighbours, and state governments have independently negotiated with foreign governments and firms regarding FDI, joint business ventures,[21] border trade, border patrolling, people-to-people engagements, and matters regarding the Indian diaspora.[22]

States have also been more vocal about expressing their foreign and defence policy preferences to the central government.

However, it may not be in the larger interests of the country and its unity to allow a great deal of freedom to its states given their wide-ranging and at times conflicting interests. A strong central government

[21]The Jammu and Kashmir Bank has been planning to open branches in Pakistan-controlled Kashmir. The matter is pending with the central government in Delhi, which has not yet given permission. If the state government had been invested with powers to negotiate independently with the Government of Pakistan, things would have been different.

[22]One would have to consider the outbursts of the Tamil Nadu government in response to the alleged human rights violations against its Tamil population by the Malaysian government. Only the Government of India can formally lodge a protest with the Malaysian government.

may be necessary to hold together a country that has great diversity and constitutes a subcontinent. It should be said that India is still in the process of state building and consolidation. There are regions and subnationalities in the country that have not yet fully accepted the unity of the country. Under such circumstances, it might be rash to grant constituent units such freedoms. Despite the moderately increasing role of the states in decision making on foreign policy, it is curious that there is hardly any discussion of the need to give a greater role to the state governments in the country's foreign relations.

CONCLUSION

The Constitution of India gives the Union government virtually exclusive jurisdiction over matters of foreign and defence policy. In practice, too, the central government has exercised strong control over India's external relations since the Constitution came into force in 1950. Even before then, there were very marked centralizing tendencies due particularly to the British tradition of a strong central government that did not permit state governments to get involved in defence and external affairs during the period of British rule. Although the states have virtually no direct constitutional jurisdiction over foreign relations, in practice the emerging reality is somewhat different. Since the early 1990s there has been a gradual weakening of the central government's tight grip on the country's foreign relations.

This is being made possible by a variety of factors despite the absence of constitutional change. First, the special constitutional status given to some states, such as Jammu and Kashmir, seems to have accorded their political leadership a voice in the foreign policymaking of the country. Second, the political weight of a leader of a particular state has also influenced foreign policymaking in many cases. Third, coalition politics and its ramifications at the centre have provided space for state governments and leaders to exercise greater say on foreign policy issues. Finally, opportunities provided by opening the Indian economy to globalization have created new practices and possibilities that have given the constituent units a greater role. In fact, the happy coincidence of the opening of India's economy and the arrival of coalition politics in India in the early 1990s paved the way for an increased state role in making the country's foreign and defence policy.

The slow and indirect but steady change that the country is witnessing in its foreign policy formulation is widely welcomed. A diverse, plural country such as India must allow change in its style of policy formulation so that it is really in tune with its heterogeneity. A more consultative, organic, and creative style of foreign policy would be more in line with the needs of the people and could become the basis of a real national consensus.

II

Foreign Policy Making in India: Looking for Theoretical Explanations

Mahesh Shankar and T.V. Paul

Introduction

Developing theoretical explanations for Indian foreign policy behavior is a long overdue enterprise, a task which has generally not attracted the concerted effort of scholars specializing in the foreign policy of India in particular and the international politics of South Asia in general. The lacuna is especially glaring given the consistently active role India has sought to play in international politics from the time of independence, its persistent efforts to achieve major power status, and its participation in some of the most virulent and intransigent conflicts in the history of the modern state system, especially in the post-1945 period. Based on the firm conviction that scholarship on India in international politics needs to move beyond short-term policy oriented work towards a more long-term, theoretical and conceptual approach, we here provide our take on what International Relations (IR) theory has to offer students of Indian Foreign Policy. We specifically argue for an eclectic approach; one that pays attention to factors at both the international system and domestic politics levels. The interaction between factors at these two levels of analysis can account for several puzzles that emerge when one analyzes Indian foreign policy, its goals and outcomes. If we incorporate time horizons, systemic approaches can explain a lot of the constancy and variation in long run foreign policy decisions and outcomes, but in the short run domestic politics appears to intervene in one fashion or other. This insight, for us, can mitigate the drawbacks of some of the either/or approaches that are prevalent in international relations theorizing and foreign policy analysis.

Some key empirical puzzles with regard to Indian foreign policy and behavior that need theoretical answers include: Why had India pursued a non-aligned foreign policy during much of the Cold War era; and since the end of the Cold War, why has it abandoned that policy and attempted a closer strategic relationship with the United States (while trying to improve its relations with second ranking great powers)? In the economic realm of foreign policy, why had India pursued an autarkic policy until 1991 and then converted to a much more liberalized economic strategy? More specifically in the security realm, why did it test a nuclear bomb in 1974, only to hibernate the program until the late 1980s when it launched a weapons program and conducted nuclear tests in 1998? These central puzzles in India's foreign policy show that changes in the international system are indeed affecting India's foreign policy, but the manner in which India has approached them seems to be mediated by domestic political factors. Hence our call for an eclectic approach as the most comprehensive one to explain the vicissitudes of Indian foreign policy behavior over the past decades and in the future.

We find that a broadly systemic approach, which nevertheless builds in the prospect of domestic level constraints on foreign policy behavior, as represented in the fledgling neo-classical realist approach offers the most promising vista in searching for theoretical explanations for Indian foreign policy behavior. Our argument in brief is that Indian foreign policy has always sought to respond to and within the constraints and opportunities offered by the international system, and been cognizant of the basic realist argument that states have the potential to become major powers and would eventually seek that status unless constrained by the peculiar balance of power system that is prevalent at a given time. However, *how* India has responded to the broad systemic constraints in its foreign policy has been shaped at most times by short term domestic level constraints. These constraints have been subject to transformation when stark failures have revealed their pernicious effects on Indian foreign policy, thereby reasserting the primacy of systemic variables to some extent. Moreover, our theoretical argument builds in a temporal dimension. We suggest that over an extended period of time, Indian foreign policy behavior is best explained in keeping with the demands of the international and regional structure within which it finds itself. However, the explanation of short run and specific policies—the staple of daily international politics in other words—cannot be undertaken by relying on systemic variables alone, but needs to build in domestic level variables which mediate between the system and state behavior.

SYSTEMIC BASES OF FOREIGN POLICY

The systemic level encompasses the role that the international system plays in determining foreign policy choices and outcomes. All realist perspectives, be they classical, structural, offensive, defensive, or neoclassical give prominence to the systemic level in explaining foreign policy behavior. A quick look at India's foreign policy shows that the international system did exert a powerful impact on it over an extended time horizon. India became an independent state around the time when the bipolar system was emerging and was immediately under tremendous pressure to join one of the power blocks, which it resisted. India sought to remain an independent actor in light of its potential for a leadership role in the international system. It thus followed a non-aligned policy trying to create a third bloc of newly emerging states in the developing world (Rana, 1969; Mishra, 1981; Appadorai, 1981). While its extant capabilities were limited for a leading role, its pursuit of a great power role (largely using soft power resources) suggests that the leaders of India were aware of its power potential and hence did not want it to become subservient to other great powers (Nayar and Paul, 2003: 123-144). This approach was driven primarily by systemic imperatives and power calculations, although domestic compulsions cannot be discounted.

The structural competition involving the dominant great powers affected India to the extent that when the US formed an alliance with Pakistan and later on with China, India was compelled to gravitate towards the USSR, although in a limited entente. Regional politics indeed played a major role in this transition but India's choices were constrained by the prevailing competition in the great power system. What is interesting, though, is why India did not fully endorse either superpower, even at the height of its need and that it played not a secondary role in its relationship with the USSR, but as an active manipulator to the extent that the Soviets gained very little tangible reward from the asymmetric power relationship. Herein lies the importance of the role of domestic variables in shaping India's foreign policy even under tight bipolarity which renders a prominent interpretation of realism, structural realism (neorealism) problematic in explaining India's behavior accurately.

Realism and Indian Foreign Policy

Realism has for long been the dominant paradigm in theorizing on IR, and the quintessential expression of the systemic argument is found in Kenneth Waltz's variant of 'structural realism' (Waltz, 1979). It begins with the fundamental premise that the international system is structurally anarchic, by which is meant the absence of an overarching central authority to regulate affairs between states. For realists then the anarchic structure of the international system means that states, whose primary interest is that of survival, find themselves in a constant security dilemma which requires them to pursue self-help through either internal military buildup and/or external security alliances. The fundamental uncertainty that characterizes the international system, where intentions of adversaries can change at any time, also means that states are essentially positionalist rather than atomistic, where relative gains concerns determine interactions with other states (Grieco, 1988).

The classical realist position as represented by Morgenthau and E.H. Carr acknowledges the role of prudence and even legal mechanisms up to a point, but the main means by which states secure themselves in an anarchic and self-help system is through arms build up and alliance formation (Morgenthau, 1978; Carr, 1939). Because of the operation of the balance of power mechanism, the system is expected to retain its equilibrium even when that equilibrium is challenged by one great power or other at a given time (Paul, 2004: 4-7). Kenneth Waltz's structural realism, while acknowledging many classical realist canons, makes the argument that structure, defined in terms of the distribution of power in the international system, is a leading determinant of and constraint on state behavior. The bipolar structure then (defined in terms of two central actors) was expected to constrain state choices during the Cold War era.

Classical realism offers much in terms of understanding Indian foreign policy in a long term perspective. Despite its apparently idealist foreign policy (as evident in India under Nehru who initially pursued a policy of peaceful co-existence and nuclear disarmament), India eventually ended up in war with its neighbors, realized its military weaknesses, attempted to gain security though arms and quasi alliances and then exploded nuclear weapons to achieve a deterrent capability as well as status in the international system. The transformation of this Gandhian-Nehruvian state to a normal power-politics oriented actor pursuing national interests defined in terms of realist cannons does impart significant credence to the classical realist position.

However, Indian foreign policy maneuverings during the era suggest that it was at least minimally able to overcome many of the constraints exerted by the bipolar structural competition. For much of the early period it pursued a firm policy of non-alignment and later in fact used the competition to gain the support of the Soviet Union while engaging in the Bangladesh war largely of its own volition while also receiving considerable economic aid form the US, especially in the 1960s. Moreover, even after a humiliating defeat to China, India still pursued a non-aligned policy although it did step up its arms buildup.

In the context of the Nehruvian era especially, systemic realist expectations have been found to be incomplete. Nayar and Paul, for instance, construe Nehruvian foreign policy as broadly realist in its pursuit of a major power role for India through an independent foreign policy, while its seeking an activist role in international politics at the same time violated realist expectations in that its extant capabilities were never adequate to support it (Nayar and Paul, 2003: 115-58). Indian foreign policy especially in the Nehru era and to a certain extent even after the war with China and beyond Nehru can therefore be characterized by strategic thought appropriately termed by Bajpai as Nehruvianism. For Bajpai, the school of thought is based on the premise that while the pursuit of national interest is crucial, communication and contact as well as international law, institutions, and military restraint can help transform the most conflictive of relationships. Much of 'hyper-realist' literature, best exemplified in the works of Karnad and Chellaney is indeed based on scathing criticism of the failure of Indian foreign policy makers in toeing the line of realist logic (Bajpai, 2007: 806-09).

The same failure of Indian foreign policy to follow realist strictures is evident in specific policy areas. India scholar E. Sridharan highlights the inappropriateness of 'neo-realism' in Indian behavior in its nuclear policy. He argues that according to neo-realism we would expect India, given its experience of the border war with China and the latter's nuclear capability, to have armed itself at the earliest with nuclear weapons. However, India's first nuclear test came ten years after China's and even more importantly did not lead to an accelerated nuclear weapons program to provide effective deterrence (in terms of weapons and delivery capability) vis-à-vis China. What's more, even after the 1998 nuclear tests which were justified on the basis of the Chinese threat, India has failed to develop sufficient capabilities rapidly enough to counteract those of China. Again, despite the immediate nuclear threat from Pakistan, India is argued to have pursued an unduly slow process of weaponization and deployment, and an even more inexplicable failure to pursue compellant capabilities. Finally, India's nuclear policy-makers have completely ignored the possibility of disarming counter-proliferation strikes by the established nuclear powers, and appear to 'assume an attitude of acceptance of its nuclear capability....' The very testing of nuclear weapons in contravention of the wishes of the United States, under a near unipolar system dominated by the United States, to an extent might be in violation of structural realist explanations. For Sridharan in fact, India's deterrence behavior 'would appear to approximate a desire for nuclear weapons as a currency of power and for generalized security in the long term rather than one of a state facing a real and imminent threat of nuclear or major conventional attack' (Sridharan, 2005: 105-06).

The major challenge then for realism in both its classical and structural forms has been in explaining why India took so long to understand the systemic forces working for or against it, and why in the short-term Indian foreign policy often fails to adhere to realist dictates? For us, while in the long run systemic constraints might assert themselves, in the short run the system level may need to be supplemented with domestic level variables in explaining state behavior. More specifically, domestic level variables are likely to be crucial in determining the timing of foreign policy choices, even though in the larger picture systemic constraints come across as structuring the policy alternatives available to India.

Furthermore, while for Waltz, states are essentially defensive positionalists, the offensive variant of the structural approach put forward by John Mearsheimer argues that eligible states pursue power, rather than security alone, given that being the strongest power in the international system is the surest way to guarantee ones own security. States therefore maximize power towards the pursuit of hegemony in at least their regional order as a means of guaranteeing security (Mearsheimer, 2001: 1-55). Again however, the extreme slowness with which India attempted to achieve its great power goal, especially in the military sense, and the lack of assertiveness as evident in its abstaining from territorial expansion, belies such offensive realist expectations. Moreover, while India has at times pursued a form of regional hegemony in South Asia, this approach seems to have waned over the years, even when India's relative capabilities have been increasing.

In fairness to neorealism, it can be argued that Waltz does not claim that structure alone matters. For Waltz, while the structure imposes certain constraints on states, how they respond to those constraints and whether such responses will be in keeping with the expectations of structural realism, is not within the realm of international politics (as opposed to foreign policy) theorizing. As he puts it, his 'theory explains why a certain similarity of behavior is expected from similarly situated states. The expected behavior is similar, not identical. To explain the differences in national responses, a theory would have to show how the different internal structures of states affect their external policies and actions' (Waltz, 1979: 22-3). The underlying message of realism for foreign policy theories then would be that domestic policy certainly influences foreign policy, 'but the pressures of [international] competition weigh more heavily than ideological preferences or internal political pressures' (Waltz, 1986: 329).

Structural realism is even more problematic in applying to the case of India (and other such cases) due to its self-acknowledged great power focus. As a regional and a middle power with aspirations for great power status, the structural constraints on India function on both the broad international level, as well as at the sub-systemic, regional level. Any theory of foreign policy which fails to build in regional dynamics is likely to be inappropriate. As a result, purely structural arguments have often been criticized for being underspecified, with alterations building in auxiliary structural factors such as geography, military technology (offense-defense balance), and war-fighting costs which might mitigate or exacerbate the security dilemma.[1] Stephen Walt's modification of the structural realist 'balance of power' argument in his 'balance of threat'

[1]A few of the prominent relevant works include Stephen G. Brooks, "Dueling Realisms (Realism in International Relations," *International Organization*, vol. 51 (3) (Summer 1997), pp. 445-477; Robert Jervis, "Cooperation under the Security Dilemma," *World Politics*, vol. 30 (2), pp. 167-214; Stephen Van Evera, *Causes of War* (Cornell: Cornell University Press, 2001); Robert Powell, "Absolute and Relative Gains in International Relations Theory," *The American Political Science Review*, vol. 85 (4) (December 1991), pp. 1303-1320.

approach is particularly illustrative of the additional structural factors that are important in theorizing foreign policy and international politics. For Walt, states balance against threat rather than power, with the former being determined not just by power, but also by geographic proximity, offensive military power, and perception of intentions as offensive or otherwise (Walt, 1990).

Buzan and Waever incorporate very similar structural factors in developing a theory of what they term Regional Security Complexes (RSCs), with South Asia as their core case. In what is viewed as a modified structural argument they define RSCs 'by durable patterns of amity and enmity taking the form of subglobal, geographically coherent patterns of security interdependence ... where the wars and rivalries of the [South Asian] subcontinent constitute a distinctive pattern...' (Buzan and Waever, 2003: 45-7). As with Walt, the RSC argument attributes great importance to geographic proximity 'because many threats travel more easily over short distances than long ones' (Buzan and Waever, 2003: 45). Given the fact that India's foreign policy has been preoccupied to a large extent by its immediate neighbors, especially Pakistan and China, the argument for the inclusion of geographic proximity in any theory of foreign policy appears to be incontrovertible.

Importantly, these modified structural arguments also correct the explicit rejection by structural realists of the role of ideas in explaining state behavior.[2] While Walt speaks of perceptions of intentions, Buzan and Waever speak of 'patterns of amity and enmity' where 'the specific pattern of who fears or likes whom is generally not imported from the system level but generated internally within the region by a mixture of history, politics, and material condition' (Buzan and Waever, 2003: 47). In both cases, these mutually shared

[2]For a discussion of how ideas matter in explaining foreign policy, see Judith Goldstein and Robert Keohane, eds., *Ideas and Foreign Policy: Beliefs, Institutions and Political Change* (Cornell University Press, 1993. The strong argument for the role of ideas is made in the constructivist literature. See Alexander Wendt, *Social Theory of International Politics* (Cambridge: Cambridge University Press, 1999).

perceptions of the other and the relationship as a whole, are fundamentally structural and yet ideational. By allowing for the building in of history of interactions between states, we are in essence dealing with what constructivists refer to as intersubjective understandings and beliefs created through mutual interactions over time (Wendt, 1992: 391-425). In the context of Indian foreign policy behavior these ideational factors are indeed significant. Concerning Pakistan especially, the relationship between the two neighbors is conditioned not just by material, structural factors, but also by very real ideational issues of national identity and purpose (Nasr, 2005: 178-201). The inclusion of ideational factors such as these also correct for what Schweller calls the 'status quoist' bias in structural realism, in that the approach fails to build in the very revisionist aims that characterize the aims of states such as Pakistan, in contrast to the fundamental status-quoism of India (Schweller, 1996: 90-121).

Finally, a modified structural argument factors in the nature of military power, often referred to in realist literature as the 'offense-defense balance,' in accounting for the foreign policy behavior of states. When the offense is dominant, the security dilemma is expected to be more intense, while when the defense is dominant security is of course plenty and hence foreign policy can consequently be less security driven (Van Evera, 2001; Jervis, 1978). The relevance of this for South Asia and hence Indian foreign policy is clearly apparent in Paul's work on war initiation by weaker power's, an integral finding of which is that weaker states are more likely to initiate wars when they possess a temporary and fleeting advantage in terms of offensive military technology. In the South Asian context Pakistan's initiation of war against India has often occurred in such circumstances and it would be reasonable to expect that India's foreign policy be affected by the nature of military power possessed by geographically proximate states (Paul, 1994: 107-25) Even more significant, the introduction of nuclear weapons into the politics of the subcontinent is undoubtedly the most revolutionary of changes in the military balance of the region, and how the foreign policy behavior of India and its neighbors is affected by this change in the nature of military technology is a question that merits sustained discussion.

It is clear then that while the anarchic structure of the international system is a crucial contextual variable, it alone cannot explain state behavior. Additional system level variables such as geography, or the offense-defense balance might provide additional clarity on the structural constraints acting on states, but in the final analysis an account of foreign policy behavior must move beyond the structure alone and delve into domestic level variables to understand how the systemic level matters, to what extent it matters, and what domestic level variables impinge on how states respond to systemic constraints on states. Realism in its structural avatar has been insufficient in dealing with this issue, a problem that is not resolved even by more nuanced arguments which nevertheless focus only on structure.

How Valid are Domestic Level Arguments?

A typical tendency in rectifying the anomalies which emerge in trying to explain foreign policy through a purely structural approach is to move in a diametrically opposite direction and emphasize domestic politics as the determinant of state interests, foreign policy and consequently international politics. Liberal scholarship especially focuses on this dimension.[3] The most systematic liberal argument propounded by Moravcsik locates the fundamental problem with realism is it's assuming, and not problematizing, state interests. For liberalism in Moravcsik's logic, it is the configuration of state preferences, and policies based on such interests, which determine the course of international politics. State preferences in turn can only be explained by delving into the domestic level of analysis. Individuals and

[3]The liberal approach has been described by Stein as "multifaceted, and what is or is not at its core can be disputed." It has often been generally used to term any argument which counters realism's emphasis on conflict by emphasizing the prospects and potential for peace. For others such as Moravcsik the liberal argument is one that reverses the realist emphasis on structure with that on domestic politics. It is in the latter sense that we use the term liberal here.

groups within states are in this logic seen as the primary social actors (as opposed to the unitary, rational state in realism). These individuals and groups contest for what is determined to be their preferred state policy, and state policy itself is a manifestation of who wins in the domestic contest. The state in essence is not an actor in itself but only a conveyor belt of sorts – domestic interests are reflected in the states' conduct in the international system (Moravcsik, 1997: 513-53). The roots of the foreign policy states therefore can be explained purely based on the social and economic structure of states, ideology, or partisan politics with different scholars emphasizing different characteristics but sharing the common belief that domestic politics determines foreign policy.

An explicit consequence of the liberal argument is that domestic politics is seen as prior to international politics, with theorizing about the latter conceptualized as a two stage process wherein state preferences are accounted for, first through an investigation of domestic politics, and only as a second stage are inter-state relations dealt with. In other words, while for realist explanations the independent variable is the distribution of power in the international system, for liberal arguments theorizing begins at the domestic level. We find such an approach problematic, though given the fact that it almost completely neglects the effects of international structure on state behavior. Structure might not exclusively determine state behavior but it does to a great extent limit the range of options states possess in their foreign policy goals. It also provides the context within which states act. India's policy of non-alignment during the Cold War for instance makes no real sense without placing it within the structural constraints imposed on an emerging state. The same would apply for India's nuclear policy over the years, where the immediate regional and international structural context within which India found itself, shaped the problematic in which it was to function, just as its actions shape the options of its smaller neighbors. The problem with a pure *innenpolitik* argument therefore appears to be the reverse of the problems ascribed to the pure structural arguments: one cannot explain why states with similar domestic structures act differently, while states with dissimilar ones often act alike (Rose, 1998: 148).

The propensity of scholars to immediately discard structural, and resort to domestic level explanations of foreign policy, especially on the leadership's belief systems is reflected in George Perkovich's work on the Indian nuclear program. For him Indian nuclear behavior has proven realism wrong as 'domestic factors, including individual personalities, have been at least as important as the external security environment in determining nuclear policy' (Perkovich, 1999: 6). While this much is correct, in discussing Indian nuclear policy prior to the Chinese nuclear tests, he argues that 'international security considerations played little role...' and that 'the main motivations ... had more to do with Bhabha's and Nehru's beliefs that nuclear technology offered India a shortcut to modernity and major power status' and would allow India to 'transcend its recent colonial past' (Perkovich, 1999: 14-5, 47, 59).

The assertion that India's nuclear policy was internally driven however discards the crucial structural factors which influenced Nehru's approach to foreign policy, apart from the fact that the quest for 'major power status' is itself to a large extent structurally driven. If individual or ideological level factors were central, one would expect Nehru, with his repeatedly stated abhorrence of nuclear weapons and calls for universal nuclear disarmament, to explicitly commit India to non-weaponization. This was hardly the case however, with Nehru's posture at best ambiguous on the weaponization prospects of the Indian nuclear program in view of the possession of nuclear arms by others. With independence looming Nehru stated that: 'Indian scientists will use the atomic force for constructive purposes. But if India is threatened, it will inevitably try to defend itself by all means at its disposal' (Saxena, 1998). More explicitly, after independence he admitted that while he preferred the development of atomic energy for peaceful purposes, 'if we are compelled as a nation to use if for other purposes, possibly no pious sentiments of any of us will stop the nation from using it that way' (Arif, 1995: 358). Perkovich is not wrong of course in stating that domestic level variables mattered, but makes the quintessential reductionist error in over-emphasizing domestic level factors at the expense of structural ones. India's nuclear policy under Nehru may have been motivated by imperatives of modernization, but the military potential of nuclear technology was clearly recognized and the option kept open in a context where other states possessed, or were likely to possess, nuclear weapons in the future. To argue that India's nuclear policy was constrained by domestic politics is different from arguing that it was motivated and determined by them, and it is the latter tendency among many Western and some Indian scholars which is problematic. Nehru's words and actions in fact clearly suggest that regardless of what his personal and ideological proclivities regarding nuclear weapons might have been, the interests of India herself ought to be driving its foreign policy.

Even after the Nehru era, more ideologically-oriented leaders, Lal Bahadur Shastri and Morarji Desai, and to an extent, Rajiv Gandhi attempted to initially sidestep the nuclear issue, only to find themselves retaining the program. Importantly since 1989, six Indian prime ministers had the nuclear file on their table and none chose to pursue nuclear disarmament by abandoning the program (Paul, 1998: 1-11). The systemic constraints powerfully affected their calculations, although we cannot discount domestic level constraints fully in terms of short term decisions. However, to emphasize domestic level factors alone in explaining Indian nuclear policy to us is deeply unsatisfying. It has been argued, for instance, that *electoral politics calculations* of the Atal Bihari Vajpayee government were central in for the decision making leading to the 1998 nuclear tests (Bajpai, Forthcoming). Such a contention we find difficult to sustain, since it can fairly be argued that even a Congress-led government would have engaged in nuclear testing had the 1999 CTBT came into force. Furthermore the Narasimha Rao government's aborted attempt to test nuclear weapons in 1995 was due not to any domestic calculations but rather as a result of tremendous US pressure. The systemic pressure in the form of NPT's extension in perpetuity, the prospect of a CTBT with penalties for not signing it, all were background calculations forcing India towards either culminating its nuclear weapons capability or abandoning its nuclear option altogether. In addition, it can be argued, that the loss of Soviet Union as a powerful ally and the deepening of the nuclear relationship between China and Pakistan provided very real structural pressures towards India's choice, to make a self-help choice as far as nuclear weapons were concerned (Paul, 2003: 1-9). This does not mean that domestic calculations are completely lacking in leaders' foreign policy choices, but the relative significance of variables at the systemic level is what we are concerned with.

Moreover, the structural argument as noted earlier, does not discount the possibility that states might violate the fundamental structural constraints on their behavior. Leaders need not fully comprehend the workings of the internationals system or like heroic figures they could try to transcend it (as Iraq under Saddam Hussein attempted). Over time states are expected to be punished for such behavior, and be socialized into behaving more in keeping with broad realist expectations. For structural realists then, the common perception that India's foreign policy behavior for most of the Nehru-era, owing to its idealist bent, undermines realist theory is therefore incorrect. While whether Nehruvian foreign policy was as idealist as claimed is itself debatable, the fact that it did pursue an activist foreign policy far beyond its capabilities, provoking regional containment from the United States is often viewed as violating the expectations of realism. However, whatever idealism did exist in the practice of India foreign policy was soon punished in the form of the US-Pakistan arms transfer deals, as part of the American containment effort. More glaringly it was the humiliating defeat to China which could be viewed as having socialized India into behavior more in accordance with realist expectations. This is most clearly illustrated in Nehru's post-war thoughts. He lamented the streak of idealism in India foreign policy that had been 'conditioned for 30 years by Mahatma Gandhi and his gospel of peace which had left a powerful imprint' (Nehru, 1964: 403). To Nehru 'we were getting out of touch with reality in the modern world and were living in an artificial atmosphere of our own creation. We have been shocked out of it, all of us' (Gopal, 1976: 223).

The point here is not that domestic level variables do not matter. Neither is it that structural realism offers us great leverage in explaining specific foreign policy choices states make. However, the point is that in the long run explaining foreign policies of states cannot be divorced from the structure within which they function. Moreover, foreign policies are often responsive and reactive to international pressures, and outcomes (such as the outcomes of Nehruvian foreign policy) are fundamentally affected by international structure. If we are to think of Indian foreign policy theoretically, rather than offering singular explanations for singular events or policies, then we cannot possibly ignore the effects of the structure of the international system. Nevertheless, while long-term systemic constraints operate, in the short-run, domestic politics can constrain and influence foreign policy choices. This time horizon will offer us a better pathway in finding a compromise between systemic and domestic level perspectives.

AN ECLECTIC APPROACH

What is required then is a synthesis of the two, an eclectic approach which combines the different levels of analysis, and makes room for cognitive and ideational variables in addition to material ones.[4] In developing such a theory however, one would be best served by beginning with the spare and parsimonious structural argument,

[4]Many scholars in IR are moving in that direction. For instance, see Peter J. Katzenstein and Rudra Sil, "Rethinking Asian Security: A Case for Analytical Eclecticism," in *Rethinking Security in East Asia*, ed. J.J. Suh, Peter J. Katzenstein, and Allen Carlson (Stanford: Stanford University Press, 2004), 1-33; John A. Hall and T.V. Paul, "Preconditions for Prudence: A Sociological Synthesis of Realism and Liberalism," in *International Order and the Future of World Politics*, ed. T.V. Paul and John A. Hall (Cambridge: Cambridge University Press, 1999), 67-77; and T.V. Paul, *Power versus Prudence: Why Nations Forgo Nuclear Weapons* (Montreal: McGill-Queen's University Press, 2000), ch.2.; Jeffrey W. Legro, *Rethinking the World: Great Power Strategies and International Order* (Ithaca, NY: Cornell University Press, 2005).

moving towards greater accuracy by building in influences emanating from the other levels of analysis. As Zakaria argues in critiquing *innenpolitik* theorizing, 'a good theory of foreign policy should first ask what effect the international system has on national behavior, because the most powerful generalizable characteristic of a state in international relations is its relative position in the international system...' This however, does not negate the importance of domestic level factors, and 'a first-cut theory can be layered successively with additional causes from different levels of analysis focusing on domestic regime types, bureaucracies and statesmen' (Zakaria, 1992: 197). In this manner, one can move towards more accurate theories of foreign policy, without losing sight of the broad, general constraints that the structure places on the foreign policy behavior of states.

Neoclassical Realism

Our proposal for an eclectic approach then is based on the intuition that the problems and issues states are faced with, and their basic options in response to them, are determined in the long run largely (but not exclusively) by the dictates of the structure of the international system. However, *how* states act in the short run, within these broad structural constraints is indeterminate without taking into account domestic level factors. Thus, the timing of choices is determined by domestic politics more powerfully than acknowledged in systemic analyses. The domestic level factors then function as intervening variables through which structural problems are filtered, leading to our dependent variable, foreign policy behavior. While structural factors, by their very nature change infrequently, we must also look for domestic level intervening variables which are not subject to rapid change. A theory is only useful if its components are operating somewhat regularly, and therefore a theory dealing with Indian foreign policy must identify domestic variables relevant at least to particular time periods or eras, if not the entirety of its history.

Our proposition is therefore in keeping with the logic of neo-classical realism, with a time element that we incorporate. Neo-classical realists, recognizing the fact that systemic pressures and opportunities often do not evoke similar responses from similarly situated states, argue that 'complex domestic political processes act as transmission belts that channel, mediate, and (re)direct policy outputs in response to external forces (primarily changes in relative power)' (Schweller, 2004: 164). For Rose, this means that 'over the short to medium term countries' foreign policies may not necessarily track objective material power trends closely or continuously ... systemic pressures and incentives may shape the broad contours and general direction of foreign policy without being strong or precise enough to determine the specific details of state behavior' (Rose, 1998: 147). The intervening factors include perceptions of the political leadership, state structure, political ideology, or other socio-economic characteristics. For Schweller then whether states 'balance' or 'underbalance' depends on crucial domestic level variables. States, for him, are more likely to underbalance when they lack: elite consensus, government/regime stability, social cohesion and elite cohesion. The lack of these factors in combination undermines state coherence, which in essence undermines the realist assumption of states as unitary actors, and therefore state behavior in accordance with the dictates of structural realism (Schweller, 2004: 169). The particular intervening variables one identifies (of course) depend on the nature of the specific behavior that is sought to be explained, or the state whose behavior is sought to be accounted for. This might well be the challenge for scholars to explain specific foreign policy decisions and outcomes.

At the structural level, as discussed earlier, a more nuanced conceptualization sees India as constrained not just by the broad distribution of power in the international system, but also by narrower more regional structural imperatives which include not just the distribution of power, but also the ideational structure of enmity in the India-Pakistan relationship and also to a lesser extent in the mistrustful relationship with China post-1962. What domestic level variables however have intervened and prevented Indian foreign policy behavior from reflecting a seamless transmission belt from structure to behavior? We contend that three specific factors have functioned as domestic level constraints during different periods in India's history as an independent state: Nehruvian thinking and strategy from independence up until the war with China, the imperatives of democratic politics and accountability in the context of domestic turmoil from then on, and specifically from the late 1980s and early 1990s the emergence of collation politics and the consequent undermining of elite consensus and cohesion, and with it the unitary character of the state.

Nehru's legacy for Indian foreign policy is ambiguous, precisely because his foreign policy was never intended to be driven by his personal idealistic beliefs. For him, 'the art of conducting the foreign affairs of a country lies in finding out what is most advantageous to the country. We may talk about international goodwill and mean what we say, but in the ultimate analysis, a government functions for the good of the country it governs…' (Nehru, 1950: 233-34). The long-term pursuit of a major power role for India in international politics, which included a seat for itself in the high table at the UNSC, as well as its quest for leadership role in the developing world reflected this strain in Nehru's thinking. The same could be said for his ambitious plans for the socio-economic and technological development of India, which he saw as integral to raising India's stature on the world stage. However, his thinking on how to pursue India's interests at the international level has also to be seen as inextricably linked to his thinking on international politics. Driven by a basic mistrust of power politics, and a firm conviction in the values of communication, military restraint, international law and institutions, India's behavior at the international level reflected solutions to structural issues such as a the Cold War, or its relationship with Pakistan and China which were based on Nehru's world view.

Hence, nonalignment as a response to Cold War was precisely a rejection of the power politics that it represented, in addition to being an expression of India's independent foreign policy. It was underpinned by a fundamental belief in the transformative potential in international politics, with relations of hostility viewed as reflections of misunderstanding more than anything else (Bajpai, 2007: 110). As a result, in its relations with Pakistan, India's initial pursuit of a resolution via the United Nations reflected a belief in the possibility of peaceful resolution of disputes and the utility of international law and institutions. With China, the (in hindsight) almost naïve belief in the possibility of peaceful coexistence as personified in the *panchsheela* was again a manifestation of these same ideational beliefs.

At its core, Nehruvian foreign policy was found wanting in underestimating the centrality of capabilities, especially of a military nature, in supporting one's foreign policy. While Nehru understood the value of pursuing capabilities of a holistic nature in the long term, he discounted the value of short-term military strength in defending its immediate security and supporting long-term internal development. It took an event of structural punishment, the disaster of the 1962 war, for the realization to dawn that international power cannot be divorced from military capability. Nevertheless it would be a great disservice to Nehru's legacy to brand him and his foreign policy as idealist with the accompanying implication that Nehruvian foreign policy deserves an *innenpolitik* argument. Indian foreign policy was driven and constrained to a large extent by structural imperatives. How it responded to the latter was shaped greatly by Nehru's thinking and in a very crucial sense by his antipathy for military preparedness. To the extent that Nehru's thinking was naïve in keeping with realist expectations, it was summarily punished, triggering a readjustment of foreign policy.

The debacle of 1962 and the American and Chinese efforts to contain India through Pakistan, and finally Pakistan's initiation of war in 1965 starkly brought home the lessons of realism for the conduct of Indian foreign policy. The lesson was in essence that 'an image of power has to be a comprehensive one—military, economic, political and social. Economic power alone will not do...' (Subrahmanyam, 1997:

69). From the mid-sixties, security and military preparedness became central to Indian foreign policy behavior, and Indian actions on the world stage became more in tune with its capabilities. The immediate emphasis on military expansion and modernization was an obvious response to the war with China, as well as the burgeoning Pakistani military capability. Even more clearly the realist turn in Indian foreign policy behavior was obvious in its nuclear policy and Cold War stance. In the nuclear arena, with the Chinese nuclear tests India's intentions to keep its nuclear option was concretized to the extent that it was willing to spurn the international community in what it viewed as the discriminatory Non-Proliferation Treaty (NPT), the undertaking of a 'peaceful nuclear explosion,' the launching of a missile development program, and the eventual testing of nuclear weapons in 1998. This 'progressively deepening line of policy development' (Nayar and Paul, 2003: 172) was particularly striking in a world where the superpowers and particularly the US were determined in blocking the Indian nuclear effort because in its view 'as additional nations obtained nuclear weapons, our diplomatic and military influence would wane…' (Gilpatric Committee Report cited in Perkovich, 1999: 102).

A similar concern for security the gradual and subtle abandonment of the platitudinous rhetoric which had characterized India's policy as the self-proclaimed leader of the Non Aligned Movement (NAM). With the imperatives of security increasingly informing thinking on foreign policy, there was a toning down of the pursuit of non-alignment to the extent that all that remained of it was the rhetoric. The Bangladesh Crisis of 1971 and the clear siding of both the US and China with Pakistan convinced India that 'the general international environment, dominated by the US and the Soviet Union, was hostile to the development of India as an independent power center…' (Mansingh, 1984: 55). Finally succumbing to the balance of power game, India signed a semi-military Friendship Treaty with the Soviet Union in 1971, and failed to explicitly condemn Soviet interventions in Czechoslovakia or Afghanistan (Subrahmanyam, 1997: 69).

While clearly there was an adaptation to the realities of power politics during this era in Indian foreign policy (as referred to earlier), there is nevertheless the argument that Indian actions were far from being consistent with the expectations of structural realism. These criticisms are centered mostly on Indian nuclear behavior, and the delays in acquiring nuclear weapons capability. Such arguments though for us are problematic for two reasons. At a theoretical level, we have seen that structural realism does not claim to be and therefore cannot fairly be tested against foreign policy making and behavior. More importantly, such arguments ignore the fact that Indian foreign policy was shaped by both complex structural and domestic level factors. At the regional structural level, there was certainly the incentive to exercise the nuclear option, but what is ignored is that there was similarly a strong global structural constraint in not openly defying the superpowers, in what was an unprecedented effort by the two, in jointly regulating the nuclear arena. Lacking the capabilities to defy the superpowers, it is not clear whether or how testing and declaring herself as a nuclear weapons state would have been in India's national interest. The lack of capabilities in fact bordered on dependence on the superpowers. While the Soviet Union was crucial to India's defense needs, the economic and food crises from the mid-sixties onwards led to a reliance on the US for support. As Kux's authoritative work on Indo-US relations puts it, 'for India the prospect was one more drought, one more year of submission to US demands, one more year of exposure to the world as paupers' (Kux, 1992: 255). Realism is as much about prudence as military preparedness, and therefore the benefits of an instantaneous response often need to be weighed against the potential costs of doing so.

There were also however very real domestic level constraints which prevented an instantaneous response by India to the changing nuclear context in its region and internationally. Therefore, even if we assume as many argue that there were real structural demands on India to go nuclear at the earliest and rapidly develop its weapon and delivery capabilities, domestic level factors intervened to prevent the seamless translation from structure to behavior. At a basic level the constraints were a consequence of the democratic framework under which the country functioned, where the survival of the government is a function of the wishes and well-being of the populace. As Zakaria has argued, a crucial intervening variable in explaining state behavior in the international system is 'state power' defined as 'that portion of national power the government can extract for its purposes' (Zakaria, 1998: 9). When the pool of 'national power' from which a state can draw, is itself small, extractive capability is naturally further compromised, which would undermine appropriate responses to structural demands.

While India's economic development had hardly gone as planned in case of a series of food and economic crises, compounded by the direct and indirect costs associated with the Bangladesh war, and the oil crisis of 1973. The public faced the brunt of these problems with rising inflation, and shortages of essential goods, especially food with their violent reactions undermining the stability of the government, already plagued by the decline of the Congress Party (Punekar, 1977: 107; Nayar and Paul, 1997: 185-86). Given these severe domestic travails that India was undergoing, which would continue to greater or lesser extent into the early 1990s, to expect the government to have engaged in an extremely expensive program of immediate development of nuclear weapon and delivery capability is unreasonable to say the least. Given the constraints of the democratic imperative, and the scarcity of resources, India's restrained yet firm positioning on the nuclear issues is probably the most that could have been expected, whereas a response in accordance with only the structural requirements would have in all likelihood endangered rather than promoted national security. India's foreign policy behavior during this period appears to have been responding, in keeping with our expectations to the constraints of the international and regional structure, though its actions were crucially mediated by constraints emerging from within domestic politics.

Until the early 1990s, India's actions at the international stage were largely shaped by the constraints of the structure, and mediated by the constraints of democratic accountability, and the challenges of socio-economic development. The state itself was for most part unitary in keeping with realist assumptions. The government leadership, especially under Nehru but also under successor regimes had sole responsibility for the conduct of foreign policy and acted in accordance with what was perceived by it to be in the broad national interests of India. Explanation of foreign policy conduct therefore for the most part keeps with our emphasis on structural variables mediated by either ideological or domestic material constraints. With the deepening of the liberalization program in the 1990s and the concomitant rise in the economic fortunes of India, domestic constraints which had crippled Indian foreign policy in the 60s and 70s especially, were relaxed by the late nineties. A confident India was better able to address issues emerging from the international structure, a trend best illustrated in the nuclear tests of 1998 in response to the gradual tightening of noose around the Indian nuclear program by the indefinite extension of the NPT in 1995 and the push for a Comprehensive Test Ban Treaty (CTBT) shortly thereafter (Ghose, 1997: 235-61). At the same time that earlier constraints have slackened, however, there appear to have emerged newer sources of constraints at the domestic level which have and are likely to complicate a theoretical conceptualization of Indian foreign policy.

The most fundamental change in domestic politics in India over the last few decades has been the decline of the Congress Party, the rise of smaller ideologically or regionally motivated parties, and the consequent emergence of coalition politics at the national level. What kind of effect coalition politics has on foreign policy behavior however is very much dependent on the nature of the coalition itself. A coalition where the major partner is strong enough to dominate on foreign policy or where partners think alike on issues of foreign policy is more likely to reflect the unitary actor assumption of realism than a coalition government where there are fundamental differences in priorities or approaches to foreign policy. Schweller has pointed to the relevance of elite consensus and cohesion as an intervening variable between the structure and state behavior. For him 'elite consensus concerns the degree of shared perception about some facts in the world as being problems (vs. not) of a particular nature (vs. some other nature) requiring certain remedies (vs. others)... [It] is a measure of the similarity of elites' preferences over outcomes and their beliefs about the preferences and anticipated actions of others' (Schweller, 2004: 170). More specifically, democratic regimes are expected to have lesser elite consensus and cohesion, and we can expect problems of consensus to be magnified in the case of coalition governments.

To be fair, most regionally or caste based coalition partners are driven more by issues of domestic, rather than foreign policy making and their involvement in the latter is therefore minimal. Nevertheless, the introduction of coalition politics requires the introduction of elite cohesion as a possible domestic constraint on foreign policy making. The potential for issues of elite consensus to constrain foreign policy making has been most clearly manifested in the role of the Communist parties in the conduct of foreign policy as crucial members of coalition governments at the center. The most highly publicized of issues obviously has been the recent efforts at the implementation of a civilian nuclear deal between India and the United States. Driven by a fundamentally different conception of where India's interests lie, an antipathy for nuclear weapons and India's nuclear program, and an ideologically motivated distrust of the US, the Communist members of the United Progressive Alliance (UPA) have done all in their power to undermine the Congress Party led governments foreign policy initiative (Karat, Bardhan, Roy and Devarajan, 2007). The nuclear deal with the United States is in fact a most recent example of how systemic and domestic factors can influence the timing of choices. The nuclear deal was signed with a primary objective of bringing India out of the nuclear apartheid that has been set up around it for its defiance of the nuclear order since 1974. The coalition government of Manmohan Singh attempted to operationalize an agreement, ostensibly to set up a number of nuclear power plants to face the severe power needs of India, but in effect as part of a broader calculation to develop a strategic relationship with the US with the long term aim of containing the rising power China and balance its potentially hostile behavior toward India, in addition to moving towards a recognized major power role in the international system.

The Communists, the outside backers of the minority government, sensed this systemic possibility and opposed the deal precisely because they saw it at as a counterbalancing move toward their ideological mentor, China. The BJP has also rejected the agreement purely for domestic politics reasons. It is very clear, however, that if China emerges as a larger threat to India, India may need to accelerate its arms buildup (which it is already doing in the early 21st century) or form limited coalitions with the US and other powers such as Japan. The possibility of this eventuality is constrained now because the Chinese threat is yet to manifest itself in a profound way, and hence at the domestic level, a lack of consensus on fully embracing America exists. The interaction between systemic imperatives and domestic constraints is therefore neatly characterized in the nuclear deal dilemma.

A similar influence has been exercised on the issue of economic liberalization, which again is ideologically anathema to the Communist parties. Although the issue of the liberalization of the economy is very much an issue of domestic politics and economic strategy, the fact is that increasing globalization has meant a growing focus on economics as part of a country's power and security interests as well as its external relations. Given the foreign policy implications of economic policy, in this as in nuclear policy coalition politics, has affected the speed of implementation (sometimes in a positive direction), if not the policy itself. (Nayar, 2001)

While the impact of coalition politics on foreign policy has been most starkly illustrated in the case of the Communist parties, given their ideologically driven worldviews, one could also conceive a similar role played by regional parties as members of ruling coalitions. While in most issues of foreign policy making these smaller parties can be expected to have little input, they are most likely to be active in policy making on issues which are likely to arouse the emotions of their vote base, or regional populace. While the federal structure of the country itself is likely to involve states in foreign policy issues of concern to them, membership of regional parties in central coalitional governments is even more likely to impart them with influence on such issues. Although the number of issues that could generate such pressures is indeed limited, often such issues involve core regional security interests.

Indian policy towards the ethnic conflict in Sri Lanka for example has clearly been constrained by pressures emanating from Tamil Nadu, where the population is overwhelmingly sympathetic to the cause of their ethnickin in Sri Lanka. Such pressures were abundantly obvious during the 1980s, when the Indian response to the escalating violence in the island nation, and its decision to intervene militarily was partially influenced by Tamil Nadu. The active intervention of India in Sri Lankan affairs following the 1983 riots had much to do with inflamed opinion in the state of Tamil Nadu which was magnified by the fact that the Congress (I) led government had a strong political stake in its regional alliance with the All India Anna Dravida Munnetra Khazagam (AIADMK). This is not to deny of course the role played in the intervention by India's perception of itself as the regional security manager, but it cannot be denied that the domestic context made it more likely that India would intervene to the extent it did (Ispahani, 1992: 214-18). The existence of a Tamil party in a significant role in a central government is therefore likely to magnify domestic pressures and can be expected to shape and constrain how India reacts to events in Sri Lanka as long as the Tamil population in India holds on to a strong sense of identity with the Sri Lankan Tamils. Similarly, how the Indian government reacts to the treatment in South East Asia or other parts of the world of minorities with ethnic kin's in India could often be a function of pressures that might emanate for regionally or ethnically motivated parties in the ruling coalition.

The globalization of the world economy, and the demonstrated benefits of free trade as opposed to the failure of India's attempt at autarkic economic development, have also put very real structural demands on India in the economic field, to which India has responded particularly since the early 1990s. With economic liberalization, the number of foreign policy issues on which individual states and coalition partners have a say have also multiplied. The decision to liberalize the economy and privatize various government owned companies are intense subjects for debate, as in the case with the communist parties. But other pressures concerning the pace, extent and composition of liberalization policies are to be expected from coalition partners representing the interests of individual states or particular sections of society. Parties representing liberalization-oriented states such as Andhra Pradesh, Tamil Nadu and Karnataka have in fact been as much of an influence on central economic policy making as the anti-liberalization parties (such as the Communists), and with the growing importance of economics in the foreign policy of states including India, coalition politics again recommends itself as a crucial constraint on Indian foreign policy making.

Crucial then to the explanation and prediction of Indian foreign policy behavior now and for the foreseeable future would be an assessment of the elite consensus which informs the government leadership. The nature of particular coalitions, the parties that comprise it and the preferences they exhibit are all likely to shape how Indian foreign policy responds to challenges and opportunities in the foreign policy realm. As Indian domestic politics becomes more complicated, so does foreign policy making, and attempts at explaining and predicting the foreign policy behavior of India.

CONCLUSION

Our argument here has been driven by our conviction that scholars on Indian foreign policy need to begin thinking about it theoretical terms. Diffidence about theorizing foreign policy is often due to the fact that driven as it is by both systemic and domestic factors, it is simply too complex to be susceptible to theorizing (Rose, 1998: 145). To exclude foreign policy from theorizing due to its complexity simply impoverishes thinking on international politics. As we have seen, both purely systemic and purely domestic level arguments often prove inaccurate in explaining foreign policy. Theories that rely only on material as opposed to ideational factors and vice versa are similarly inappropriate. What is needed then is an eclectic approach which builds in the structural and the domestic, the material and the ideational. For us the neo-classical realist approach provides such a reasonable framework, and as we have suggested a careful application of it to the particular case of India might give us a better handle over the conduct of Indian foreign policy in the past, present and in times to come. We have also introduced the crucial element of time in understanding Indian foreign policy. Our argument is that systemic forces are at work in the background and they have the most salience in the long run. State behavior that disregards structural constraints and opportunities is eventually punished and leads to foreign policy adaptation. However, domestic level factors are short run variables that often determine the manner in which a state responds to specific international issues or foreign policy questions. We therefore need both to understand foreign policy comprehensively and more accurately, even as we sacrifice some level of rigor in that process. In the end, by compromising a little on parsimony, we might be gaining a great deal in how accurately we can explain and predict foreign policy behavior.

REFERENCES

Appadorai, A. (1981), "Non-Alignment: Some Important Issues," *International Studies* 20: 3-11.

Gen. Arif, Khalid Mahmud (1995), *Working with Zia: Pakistan's Power Politics-1988*, Karachi: Oxford University Press.

Bajpai, Kanti (2007), "Pakistan and China in Indian Strategic Thought," *International Journal*, 62(4): 805-22.

Bajpai, Kanti (2009), "The BJP and the Bomb," in Scott Sagan, *Inside Nuclear South Asia*, Stanford: Stanford University Press.

Brooks, Stephen G. (1997), "Dueling Realisms (Realism in International Relations," *International Organization* 51(3): 445-77.

Buzan, Barry and Ole Waever (2003), *Regions and Powers: The Structures of International Security*, Cambridge: Cambridge University Press.

Carr, Edward H. (1940), *The Twenty Years' Crisis, 1919-1939: An Introduction to the Study of International Relations*, London: Macmillan & Co.

Ghose, Arundhati (1997), "Negotiating the CTBT: India's Security Concerns and Nuclear Disarmament," *Journal of International Affairs* 51: 239-61.

Goldstein, Judith and Robert Keohane, eds. (1993), *Ideas and Foreign Policy: Beliefs, Institutions and Political Change*, Ithaca, NY: Cornell University Press.

Gopal, Sarvepalli (1976), *Jawaharlal Nehru: A Biography.* Vol. III, Cambridge, MA: Harvard University Press.

Grieco, Joseph M. (1988), "Anarchy and the Limits of Cooperation: A Realist Critique of the Newest Liberal Institutionalism," *International Organization* 42(3): 485-507.

Hall, John A. and T.V. Paul (1999), "Preconditions for Prudence: A Sociological Synthesis of Realism and Liberalism," in T.V. Paul and John A. Hall (eds.), *International Order and the Future of World Politics*, Cambridge: Cambridge University Press. pp. 67-77.

Ispahani, Mahnaz (1992), "India's Role in Sri Lanka's Ethnic Conflict," in Ariel E. Levite et al. (eds.), *Foreign Military Intervention: The Dynamics of Protracted Conflict*, New York: Columbia University Press. pp. 209-239.

Jervis, Robert (1978), "Cooperation under the Security Dilemma," *World Politics* 30(2): 167-214.

Karat, Prakash, A.B. Bardhan, Abani Roy, and G. Devarajan (2007), "Left Parties' Statement: On the Indo-US Bilateral Nuclear Cooperation Agreement," *Mainstream* XLV (34). [Online: web] Accessed 5 June. 2008 URL: http://www.mainstreamweekly.net/article277.html

Katzenstein, Peter J. and Rudra Sil (2004), "Rethinking Asian Security: A Case for Analytical Eclecticism," in J.J. Suh, Peter J. Katzenstein, and Allen Carlson (eds.), *Rethinking Security in East Asia*, Stanford: Stanford University Press. pp. 1-33.

Kux, Dennis (1992), *India and the United States: Estranged Democracies, 1941-1991*, Washington, DC: National Defense University Press.

Legro, Jeffrey W. (2005), *Rethinking the World: Great Power Strategies and International Order*, Ithaca, NY: Cornell University Press.

Mansingh, Surjit (1984), *India's Search for Power: Indira Gandhi's Foreign Policy 1966-1982*, New Delhi: Sage.

Mearsheimer, John J. (2001), *The Tragedy of Great Power Politics*, New York, NY: Norton.

Mishra, K.P. (1981), "Towards Understanding Non-Alignment," *International Studies* 20: 23-37.

Moravcsik, Andrew (1997), "Taking Preferences Seriously: A Liberal Theory of International Politics," *International Organization* 51(4): 513-53.

Morgenthau, Hans (1978), *Politics Among Nations*, New York: Knopf.

Nasr, Vali (2005) "National Identities and the India-Pakistan Conflict," in T.V. Paul (ed.), *The India-Pakistan Conflict: An Enduring Rivalry*. Cambridge: Cambridge University Press. pp. 178-201.

Nayar, Baldev Raj (2001), *Globalization and Nationalism: The Changing Balance in India's Economic Policy, 1950-2000*, New Delhi: Sage.

Nayar, Baldev Raj and T.V. Paul (2003), *India in the World Order: Searching for Major-Power Status*, New York: Cambridge University Press.

Nehru, Jawaharlal (1950), *Independence and After*, New York, NY: The John Day Company.

Nehru, Jawaharlal (1964), *Jawaharlal Nehru's Speeches: Volume IV: September 1957- April 1963*, New Delhi: Publications Division.

Paul, T.V. (1994), *Asymmetric Conflicts: War Initiation by Weaker Powers*, Cambridge: Cambridge University Press.

Paul, T.V. (1998), "The Systemic Bases of India's Challenge to the Global Nuclear Order," Non-Proliferation Review 6(1): 1-11.

Paul, T.V. (2000), *Power versus Prudence: Why Nations Forgo Nuclear Weapons*, Montreal: McGill-Queen's University Press.

Paul, T.V. (2003), "Chinese/Pakistani Nuclear/Missile Ties and Balance of Power Politics," The Nonproliferation Review 10(2): 1-9.

Paul, T.V. (2004), "Introduction: The Enduring Axioms of Balance of Power Theory and Their Contemporary Relevance," in T.V. Paul, James J. Wirtz, and Michel Fortmann (eds.), *Balance of Power: Theory and Practice in the 21st Century*, Stanford, CA: Stanford University Press. pp. 1-28.

Perkovich, George (1999), *India's Nuclear Bomb: The Impact on global Proliferation*, Berkeley: University of California Press.

Powell, Robert (1991), "Absolute and Relative Gains in International Relations Theory," *The American Political Science Review* 85(4): 1303-20.

Punekar, S.D. (ed.) (1977), *Economic Revolution in India*, Bombay: Himalaya Publishing House.

Rana, A.P. (1969), "The Intellectual Dimensions of India's Nonalignment," *The Journal of Asian Studies* 28(2): 299-312.

Rose, Gideon (1998), "Review Article: Neoclassical Realism and Theories of Foreign Policy," *World Politics* 51(1): 144-72.

Saxena, A. P. (1998), "Nehru & the Bomb," *Times of India*, July 8, New Delhi.

Schweller, Randall L. (1996), "Neorealism's Status-Quo Bias: What Security Dilemma?," *Security Studies* 5(3): 90-121.

Schweller, Randall L. (2004), "Unanswered Threats: A Neoclassical Realist Theory of Underbalancing," *International Security* 29(2): 159-201.

Sridharan, E. (2005), "International Relations Theory and the India-Pakistan Conflict," *India Review*, 4(2): 103-24.

Subrahmanyam, K. (1997), "India and the Changes in the International Security Environment," in Lalit Mansingh et. al. (eds.), *Indian Foreign Policy: Agenda for the 21st Century*. Vol. 1, New Delhi: Konark Publishers. pp. 58-72.

Van Evera, Stephen (2001), *Causes of War*, Ithaca, NY: Cornell University Press.

Walt, Stephen M. (1990), *The Origins of Alliances*, Ithaca, NY: Cornell University Press.

Waltz, Kenneth (1979), *Theory of International Politics*, New York: Random House.

Waltz, Kenneth (1986), "Reflections of *Theory of International Politics:* A Response to My Critics," in Robert O. Keohane (ed.), *Neorealism and its* Critics, New York: Columbia University Press. pp. 322-346.

Wendt, Alexander (1992), "Anarchy is What States Make of It: The Social Construction of Power Politics," *International Organization* 46(2): 391-425.

Wendt, Alexander (1999), *Social Theory of International Politics*, Cambridge: Cambridge University Press.

Zakaria, Fareed (1992), "Realism and Domestic Politics: A Review Essay," *International Security* 17(1): 177-98.

Zakaria, Fareed (1998), *From Wealth to Power: The Unusual Origins of American's World Role*, Princeton: Princeton University Press.

III

Neoclassical Realism and Indian Foreign Policy

Happymon Jacob

INTRODUCTION

The Hindu, India's leading national English daily, tends to display a keen interest in India-Sri Lanka relations. On 7 October 2008, it published an article that stated (p.7): "(Tamil Nadu) Chief Minister M. Karunanidhi told Prime Minister Manmohan Singh on Monday (6 October 2008) that India should summon the Sri Lankan High Commissioner to India and condemn the genocide of Sri Lankan Tamils in the island nation." A few pages later a separate piece announced, (p.11) "Exercise restraint, Sri Lanka told." It read: "National Security Advisor M. K. Narayanan summoned Sri Lankan Deputy High Commissioner G.G.A.D Palithaganegoda to convey India's concern to him ... New Delhi on Monday asked Colombo to act with greater restraint." *The Hindu* was reporting the unease that Sri Lanka's ongoing civil war (between the Tamil rebel group, the Liberation Tigers of Tamil Elam (LTTE), and the Sri Lankan government) had initiated in the Indian state of Tamil Nadu.

The conflict ought to be solely a foreign policy issue for India, given that it is occurring externally from the state rather than within its own borders. However, what *The Hindu's* coverage clearly demonstrates is the way that the events unfolding in Sri Lanka were intimately linked to New Delhi and Tamil Nadu. Indian domestic politics were, and are, caught in the Sri Lankan crossfire. India's Sri

Lanka policy is a prime example of how sub-national units[1] can influence the foreign policy making of a central government.[2] Accounting for sub-state influences in foreign policy making is comparatively new in IR theorizing and structural realists, the proponents of what is undoubtedly the leading International Relations (IR) theory of the day, have failed to adequately address the phenomenon. However despite this, the history of Indian foreign policy making is littered with examples of the way in which domestic influences have impacted upon it directly and indirectly, materially and ideationally, and on multiple levels.

What goes into the construction of a state's foreign policy? Is 'national interest' something that remains untouched and uncontaminated by the din and noise of domestic politics? It is traditionally believed that the foreign policies of a country are made behind the marble façades of its capital, yet at the same time it appears genuinely naïve to assume that political actors can isolate themselves to this extent. By way of example, India's 'noisy' democracy certainly does not appear to lend itself to this kind of disconnection and segregation. Yet to what degree are the decision makers of any country really subjected to the pulls, pressures, perceptions and preferences of the numerous politicians and interest groups, both informed and uninformed, on foreign policy issues? More specifically, is Indian foreign policy ideationally, ideologically and materially informed by the dynamics of its somewhat raucous democracy and its apparently insuppressible domestic players, or does it remain independent of them? The early 1990s can be understood as a watershed moment in Indian politics when the commencement of coalition politics—which has henceforth come to define Indian politics and government formation—and initiatives of economic reforms introduced an increased number of voices into the process of Indian foreign policy

[1]Sub-national units may be understood to be states, provinces, cities etc. In the case of India, I refer to states which are the federal units of the country.

[2]'Central government' is also termed 'federal government' and 'union government'. In India, the term central government is widely used.

making; but is this correct? Ultimately, the nuances of foreign policy making and the questions posed above beg the all-important question: is the traditional realist unitary-actor model the ideal analytical template for understanding the foreign policy making of today's India?

This study is an attempt to answer these questions and map the fresh turns in Indian foreign policy through making use of the theoretical insights of the neoclassical realist framework. It argues that neoclassical realist theorizing in International Relations is an excellent conceptual platform to address and understand the 'new' dynamism of contemporary Indian foreign policy. At this point however, I must offer a caveat: this being one of the initial attempts[3] at applying neoclassical realism to understand Indian foreign policy, it does not claim to be an exhaustive survey of the relationship between innumerable domestic factors and the country's foreign policy making since its independence. Rather (more modestly), this study will (a) identify certain significant domestic variables that, I argue, influence the nature, content and direction of modern Indian foreign policy; (b) apply those variables in relevant situational contexts to test empirically the hypotheses of the chapter; and (c) chart out a modest research agenda for future inquiries into Indian foreign policy making.

PART I

THE NEOCLASSICAL REALIST UNIVERSE

Neoclassical realism is a theoretical paradigm in IR that is still in its initial stages of advancement. Given its relative infancy, it is pertinent to begin by attempting to shed adequate light on the conceptual development of the theory and its key arguments.

Theoretical origins

As its name suggests, neoclassical realism takes its roots from classical as well as neorealism. This new direction in realist theorizing has

[3]Chapter by Mahesh Shankar and T. V. Paul in this book is one of the initial attempts to understand Indian foreign policy using neoclassical realism.

borrowed certain aspects from both of its conceptual precursors and has merged these aspects with fresh theoretical insights. In doing so it has addressed an area of research in which realist thinking has as yet been unable to satisfactorily explain: the domestic aspects (if not roots) of a country's foreign policy. Specifically, one key question that has challenged neorealism is why states that are structurally similar and located within the confines of the same international system behave differently. While classical realism did address this question to some extent, it did so without the significant insights of neorealism's structural arguments. In a similar vein, while classical realism examines in great detail state motivations, state capacity, and attributes of national power, Waltzian neorealists, as Taliaferro points out, preoccupy themselves with the constraints of the international system on state behaviour and take world polarity as the one and only independent variable for their analysis (Taliaferro, 2006: 476).

Waltz's theory does not concern itself with the internal dynamics of the state, thus states are identical actors. Waltz wrote that "[a] balance-of-power theory, properly stated, begins with assumptions about states: they are unitary actors who, at a minimum, seek their own preservation, and at a maximum, drive for universal domination" (Waltz, 1983: 118). While Waltz focused on the distribution of power in the international system, he did not define the concept of power itself. Initial attempts at refining Waltz's work were executed by Walt and Van Evera who introduced "structural modifiers" to refine the notion of power (Rathbun, 2008: 301). In other words, Waltz's unitary approach to the state assumes several things about it, for instance, that the state is endowed with certain natural features. It is this assumption that neoclassical realists problematise and on which they devote a large share of their research energy.[4]

[4]As Taliaferro points out "Waltz's theory assumes that units have an unlimited capacity to extract and mobilize resources from the domestic society" (Taliaferro, 2006:478-9.

As pointed out above, the intellectual lineage of neoclassical realism can be neatly traced back to classical realism and neorealism. While it adopts the strengths of both, it also tries to dispense with their inadequacies. Schweller writes:

> ... a new school of realism, variously called neoclassical or neotraditional realism, has attempted to place the rich but scattered ideas and untested assertions of early realist work with in a more theoretically rigorous framework.... There are several reasons for the emergence of neoclassical realism. Waltzian neorealism is strictly a theory of international politics, which accordingly makes no claim to explain foreign policy or specific historical events. Recognizing such limitations, a new breed of realist scholars has embraced the richer formulations of traditional, pre-Waltzian realists, who focused more on foreign policy than systemic level phenomena. While not abandoning Waltz's insights about international structure and its consequences, neoclassical realists have added first and second level variables (eg., domestic politics, internal extraction capability and processes, state power and intentions and leaders perceptions of the relative distribution of capabilities and of the offense-defence balance) to explain foreign policy decision making and intrinsically important historical puzzles (Schweller, 2003: 316-7).

While Waltzian realism tends to treat all great powers as like units, classical realism had made two key distinctions between them based on the capabilities and interests of great powers, as well as satisfied and dissatisfied powers (Schweller, 1998: 15). Thus as Schweller argues, "... Waltzian neorealism suffers from a status-quo bias: that it views the world solely through the lens of a satisfied established state" (Schweller, 1998: 20). Neoclassical realism problematises the 'unitary actor model' of neorealism in understanding state as an actor. It argues that "[e]lite consensus or disagreement about the nature and extent of international threats, persistent internal divisions within the leadership, social cohesion, and the regime vulnerability to violent overthrow all inhibit the state's ability to respond to systemic pressures" (Taliaferro et al., 2009: 28).

Neoclassical realism, therefore, begins its theorizing from a structure-informed balance-of-power *weltanschauung* (as laid down by neorealism) but goes on to argue, like classical realism, that power and behaviour vary across states.

In its haste to be parsimonious and form a meta-theory of international politics, neorealism skips the crucial question that many neoclassical realists see as the core of their inquiry: why is there no consistency with regards to similar and dissimilar states producing similar and dissimilar effects and outcomes in the international arena? As Taliaferro et al. point out, "(T)he same causes sometimes lead to different effects, and the same effects sometimes follow from different causes" (Taliaferro et al., 2009: 21).

National power is something that neorealism takes for granted. The theory assures us that national power will automatically come into play when states interact because we live in a neorealist world of structural constraints and incentives. Classical realists, on the other hand, delineate the multiple dimensions of national power; natural resources, military preparedness, geography, national character, population, national morale, and industrial capacity are all considered components of national power by Morgenthau. He further develops the concept of national power from being an end, and as such an immediate aim in the typical Hobbesian sense, to being a means to that end (Morgenthau, 1968: 25). In doing so, classical realists are able to point to circumstances where national power can be influential.

This understanding of national power is picked up by neoclassical realists for further refinement. Schweller argues that:

> Although national power has many bases that vary over time and space, one may conveniently divide them into two dimensions: the material and administration. The first includes familiar elements such as population size, territory, number of armed forces, as well as the type, level of development, and scale of the

> nation's economy. The second and mostly overlooked dimension of national power is the administrative capacity and the political structure of the state—its ability to command the population and to tap their resources: the quality of its institutions of its government; the nature and attitude of political classes which influence its decisions and the elite which takes them (Schweller, 2006: 13).

In other words, according to this strand of theorizing, foreign policy making is not a passive reaction to structural constraints and incentives. It is also a product of:

- elites' preferences and perceptions of the external environment
- which of the elites' preferences and perceptions matter in the policy making process
- the domestic political risks with certain foreign policy choices, and
- the variable risk-taking propensities of national elites (Schweller, 2006: 46).

KEY ARGUMENTS PUT FORWARD BY NEOCLASSICAL REALISM

Linking the three images

Neorealism describes the structural dynamics of the international system and argues that states are socialized and familiarized by systemic dynamics, but in response to nothing other than these systemic dynamics. Neoclassical realism's intellectual vocation springs forth from this critical location of neorealist theorizing which discusses the factors that drive state actions in the international system, while not making claims about "explaining broad patterns of systemic or recurring outcomes." (Taliaferro et al., 2009, 21). Taliaferro et al. further address the important question of national behaviour by incorporating the first, second and third image variables in International Relations.[5]

[5]These labels arise from Waltz's typology of levels of analysis: first image (individual-level causal factors), second image (state-level causal factors), and third image (system-level causal factors). See Waltz, 1959.

By appreciating the links and subsequent interplay between the variables belonging to the three images, neoclassical realism positively complicates and allows for a far more nuanced and multifaceted study to be undertaken by the foreign policy analyst. Its assumption, as pointed out earlier, that states react differently to similar structural constraints and incentives, also works to describe more accurately this often unremarked upon behaviour. Neoclassical realists argue the cause for this variation can be found in the complex dynamics that occur within states. Schweller argues, "... complex domestic structures and political processes act as transmission belts that channel, mediate, and (re)direct policy outputs in response to external forces." "Hence," he says, "states often react differently to similar systemic pressures and opportunities, and their responses may be less motivated by systemic level factors than domestic ones" (Schweller, 2006: 6). Notice the phrase "transmission belts" here. It is significant because neoclassical realism does not claim to analyse domestic variables that do not have a systemic linkage. The pre-existing domestic structures, ideologies, political and strategic cultures, are analysed by neoclassical realism only in so far as they form part of the "transmission belt," not as generating pressures, constraints and incentives on their own. In other words, neoclassical realism takes into consideration only those domestic variables that are intervening variables, not those which are causal variables if and of themselves.

Deconstructing state power

Neoclassical realists deconstruct the term 'power' as we see it in Thucydides' famous observation in the *Melian dialogue*: "The strong do what they have the power to do, and the weak merely accept what they have to accept." Power, for neoclassical realism, is not that which exists within a state's borders somewhat intangibly, in material terms, but rather it is something that can be used productively. Furthermore, the neoclassicalists argue, there is a great gap between raw power and usable power.

Schweller writes,

> ... material factors alone do not determine the actual level of state power or its place in the international pecking order. They do not tell us whether a state will be able to mobilize these resources and do so in a timely manner in order to respond successfully to structural-systemic incentives and opportunities. Nor do they tell us the purpose of state action, that is, whether a state is willing to pursue a dynamic foreign policy or aspires to some form of political hegemony. For this we need to know something about the internal or domestic makeup of the state; more specifically, we need to know whether or not there are constraints on the development and exercise of the state's potential power and whether there is a natural will to amass power (Schweller, 2006: 106).

Taliaferro argues that "neoclassical realism suggests that state power—the relative ability of the state to extract or mobilize resources from domestic society as determined by the institution of the state, as well as by nationalism and ideology—shapes the types of internal balancing strategies a state is likely to pursue." (Taliaferro, 2006: 467). Zakaria too considers the resource extraction capability model (Zakaria, 1998).

In his book, *Unanswered Threats: Political Constraints on the Balance of Power*, Schweller further describes the extraction capability of the state. He discusses four factors at the domestic level that may influence the balancing behaviour of states. These factors can also be looked at while trying to understand the foreign policy choices that countries make. These factors include:

1. *Elite consensus:* Elite consensus is understood to be "a measure of the similarity of elites' preferences over outcomes and their beliefs about the preferences and anticipated actions of others." (Schweller, 2006: 47) According to Schweller the key questions regarding elite consensus with regard to balancing behaviour are:

(a) Do policy elites agree that there is an external military threat?

(b) Do they agree about the nature and extent of the threat?

(c) Do elites agree about which policy remedy will be most effective and appropriate to deal with a threat and protect a state's strategic interests?

(d) Do they agree on the domestic political risks and costs associated with the range of policy options to balance a threat? (Schweller, 2006: 47).

2. *Elite cohesion and elite polarization:* "Elite cohesion refers to the degree to which a central government's political leadership is fragmented by persistent internal divisions. Elite polarization may arise over ideological, cultural or religious dimensions, bureaucratic interests, party factions, regional and sectoral interests, or ethnic groups and class loyalties" (Schweller, 2006: 11-12).

3. *Social cohesion:* One way to gauge a society's cohesion is to observe, for example, whether the general populace considers that "society's institutions as legitimate and appropriate mechanisms to settle disputes among them no matter how profound their grievances" (Schweller, 2006: 51). This can be seen through a number of factors, for instance in liberal democracies, to give just one example, it could be argued that citizens' participation through their observance of the state's laws indicates a level of social cohesion rooted in perceived legitimacy. Schweller lays down five relevant questions that may be asked regarding social cohesion and balancing behaviour:

   (a) Is there a struggle among elites for domestic political power?

   (b) If so, are there opportunistic elites within the threatened states who are willing to collaborate with the enemy to advance their own personal power or to gain office?

   (c) If there are multiple threats do elites agree on their rankings of external threats from the most to least dangerous to the state's survival and vital interests?

(d) Are there deep disagreements among elites regarding the question of with whom should the state align?

(e) Are elites divided over the issue of whether to devote scarce resources to defend interests in the peripheries or the core? (Schweller, 2006: 54).

4. *Regime vulnerability:* A regime that is not vulnerable is one that is able to both mobilize and allocate resources to meet its policy commitments, has considerable leverage over activities and groups in the society, maintains autonomy from pressure groups operational from within and outside, and has legitimacy and the compliance of its people (Schweller, 2006: 108). The foreign policy capacity of vulnerable regimes and weak leaders is severely limited. Undue interference from domestic forces hinders the policing capacity of a state, though concurrently it is true that "a political regime that expresses the interests of only one social group is less autonomous than one that encompasses the interests of several social groups" (Schweller, 2006: 107).

Culture and Foreign Policy

Neoclassical realism is also cognizant of the importance of cultural factors in understanding domestic dynamics that influence states' foreign policy making. Colin Dueck argues that in the context of grand strategy formation, "culture shapes strategic choices in several ways. First, culture influences the manner in which international events, pressures, and conditions are perceived. Second, it provides a set of causal beliefs regarding the efficient pursuit of national interests. Third, it helps determine the actual definition of these interests, by providing prescriptive foreign policy goals" (Dueck, 2006: 15).

Within the neoclassical realist framework, this would mean that cultural factors can help specify and explain the final choices made by foreign policy makers when faced with systemic conditions (Dueck, 2006: 18-19). Dueck further looks at the process that takes place in a neoclassical realist framework by which strategic culture influences strategic choice. He says it is twofold: "First, foreign policy officials need domestic support for any new departure in grand strategy ... And if national culture assumptions regarding grand strategy are either shared or shaped by elite officials, then the beliefs of those officials are a second means by which culture can act as an important influence on patterns of strategic choice" (Dueck, 2006: 19).

Culture directs the formation of nationalism, and cultural nationalism is perhaps more influential in the public parlance than civic nationalism. Given the importance neoclassical realism gives to cultural aspects, it could be argued that a country with high levels of cultural nationalism is more able to respond coherently and dynamically to external circumstances. Schweller argues that fascism worked extremely well as a tool to mobilize national resources for the expansion of Germany (Schweller, 2006: 105). He points out that "... the exemplary mobilizing state was best captured, in practice, by the fascist state. In the modern age of mass politics, fascism provided the necessary political content missing from realism to implement the principle that states should expand when they can" (Schweller, 2006: 105).

The importance of nationalist sentiments/ideology is commented upon by other scholars as well. Taliaferro points out that a state's ability to 'emulate and innovate' can be limited by the absence of nationalist sentiments or the presence of anti-statist ideology. Ideologically 'vulnerable' states, according to him, do not look beyond prominent existing strategies (Taliaferro, 2006: 467). Therefore, he argues, that "particularly during periods of high external vulnerability, leaders have an incentive to inculcate nationalism as a means to extract greater societal resources for the production of military power" (Taliaferro, 2006: 491-2). Taliaferro identifies state-sponsored nationalism and ideology as two important elements of national power. While state-sponsored nationalism increases social cohesion thereby facilitating "leaders' efforts to extract and mobilize resources from society for national security goals," ideology, on the other hand, can both "facilitate or inhibit leaders' efforts to extract and mobilize resources, depending on the content of that ideology and the extent to which elites and the public hold common ideas about the proper role of the state vis-à-vis society and the enemy" (Taliaferro, 2006: 491).

In short, on the one hand, persisting domestic ideational structures can prevent a state from arriving at a proper assessment of the structural conditions, and on the other hand these selfsame pre-existing domestic ideational structures can prevent states from acting in one way or another even if their perceptions of the structural conditions are accurate.

All these arguments make one thing amply clear: cultural factors matter in foreign policy making, even in the realist literature. Neorealism relied a great deal on the conceptual tools of rational choice theory and neoclassical realist scholarship is now attempting to compensate for this over-reliance on rational choice by incorporating cultural factors into its analytical framework.

Democracy's inherent problems

Neoclassical realism also points out that democracies suffer from some significant inadequacies which prevent them from balancing against external threats (and by implication to other structural incentives and constraints) because "non-balancing behaviour is (or should be) the status-quo policy prior to the emergence of a dangerous threat and there are typically many 'veto players' in a democratic policy-making process, that is, individual or collective actors whose agreement is necessary for change in the status quo" (Schweller, 2006: 48). Thus, normal democracies tend to be status-quoist, unless, of course, there are other elements (such as nationalist feelings) that prompt a state to be disruptive.

PART 11

INDIAN FOREIGN POLICY THROUGH A NEOCLASSICAL REALIST LENS

This section attempts to use the insights gathered thus far from neoclassical theoretical thinking, in order to understand how Indian foreign policy making processes are influenced by domestic factors. Needless to say that research in this area is extremely limited, even more so from a theoretical point of view. One of the reasons for this has been the unavailability of hard evidence linking internal factors with the external policies of the Indian government; the other is the general tendency in academia to regard foreign policy as externally influenced and oriented.

This section will look specifically at two Indian foreign policy issues and examine how they have (or have not) been influenced by domestic factors. It will consider whether the insights provided by neoclassical realism can help us expound upon these two issues with increased theoretical rigour and clarity. This will be followed by a discussion on the utility of developing a coherent research agenda. An inclusive list of a number of variables will then be prepared with the objective of furthering research in this area.

India is a large and extremely diverse country. It is neither uniform in its social, religious, ethnic and linguistic make-up, nor univocal in its external outlook, and is a vibrant democracy subject to a multiplicity of competing political and ideological persuasions. Given all of this, it is perhaps unsurprising that one might encounter many of those variables that neoclassical realism looks to in order to explain India's foreign and defense policies. In a sense, therefore, the task is rendered easier by the presence of political polycentrism that one encounters in India. When analysing the making of Indian foreign policy, the following neoclassical realist variables ought to be considered:

- elite consensus or lack thereof
- elite cohesion or lack thereof
- elite polarization or lack thereof
- regime vulnerability or lack thereof
- social cohesion or lack thereof
- influence of nationalism (strong/weak) and other inherent cultural characteristics
- dynamics of democracy

DOES CHENNAI CHARM NEW DELHI'S SRI LANKA POLICY?[6]

Can India's Sri Lanka policy be solely explained by structural factors, i.e. India's alleged aspirations to regional hegemony, its desire to keep other powers from involving themselves in conflicts taking place in 'their neighbourhood' (including the one in Sri Lanka) and, how states react in a realist universe? Or are there factors that are outside the neorealist level of analysis, i.e. domestic politics, which perhaps more effectively explain India's Sri Lanka policy or at least domestic politics tried to influence India's Sri Lanka policy? India's response to the Tamil resistance in Sri Lanka is often regarded as having been significantly impacted by the political situation in Tamil Nadu. Shankar and Paul, among others, have made just such an argument: "[T]he active intervention of India in Sri Lankan affairs following the 1983 riots had much to do with inflamed public opinion in the state of TN [Tamil Nadu] which was magnified by the fact that the Congress (I) led government had a strong political stake in its regional alliance with the All India Dravida Munnetra Khazagam (AIADMK)" (Shankar and Paul, chapter in this book).

Mayilvaganan argues that the historical and ethnic linkages between Tamil Nadu and Sri Lanka, the impact of the Dravidian movement, Tamil nationalism in Tamil Nadu, the disenfranchisement of the plantation (Indian) Tamils in 1948 in Sri Lanka and the subsequent uneasy relationship between the majority Sinhalese and Tamils in Sri Lanka, the anti-Tamil riots of July 1983 in Sri Lanka and

[6]Various writers in the past have chosen to analyse the influence that the political elite in Tamil Nadu has exerted on New Delhi in urging them to adopt a pro-Tamil policy, while dealing with the Sinhalese dominated government in Colombo. See for example: M. Mayilvaganan, (2007) 'The Re-emergence of the Tamil Nadu Factor in India's Sri Lanka Policy', Strategic Analysis, 31:6, 943–964; T.S. Subramanian, 'Sympathy Factors', Frontline, 16(26), December 24, 1999 at http://www.frontlineonnet.com/fl1626/16260390.htm; Ispahani, Mahnaz (1992), "India's Role in Sri Lanka's Ethnic Conflict," in Ariel E. Levite et al. (eds.), Foreign Military Intervention: The Dynamics of Protracted Conflict, New York: Columbia University Press. pp. 209-239; and, Mahesh Shankar and T V Paul, "Foreign Policy Making in India: Looking for Theoretical Explanations," chapter in this book.

the influx of refugees to India (Mayilvaganan, 2007: 944) all combined to spark the Tamil resistance against Sinhalese hegemony on the island nation.

The unequal treatment meted out to fellow Tamils in Sri Lanka caused severe reverberations in India's southern Tamil State. After the 1983 anti-Tamil riots in Sri Lanka, there were widespread demands from Tamil Nadu politicians advocating Indian intervention in Sri Lanka. As a result, New Delhi began dispensing economic and military aid to Sri Lankan Tamil resistance groups. Moreover, Mayilvaganan points out, "India's dropping of humanitarian aid in June 1987 ('Operation Poomalai' or 'Eagle Mission 4') also had a lot to do with the sentiments prevailing in Tamil Nadu" (Mayilvaganan, 2007: 946).

Later, after signing the Indo-Sri Lankan Accord of July 29, 1987, India intervened militarily in Sri Lanka under the auspices of a force dubbed the Indian Peacekeeping Force (IPKF), but withdrew in defeat in 1990. After this setback and following the assassination of former Indian Prime Minister Rajiv Gandhi by the LTTE, New Delhi was confronted by an upsurge of anti-LTTE discourse that forced a temporary halt to any plans the centre had to act in favour of Sri Lankan Tamils.

By April 2000, there were enough structural incentives for New Delhi to intervene in Sri Lanka. However, in May 2000, tempers flared again when fighting between the LTTE and Sri Lankan security forces intensified. Colombo made repeated appeals to the Indian government to intervene and rescue troops trapped by LTTE forces in the LTTE-held Elephant Pass to the north of the country. At this stage, however, the then National Democratic Alliance (NDA) government in New Delhi faced extensive pressure from the Chief Minister of Tamil Nadu and his Dravida Munnetra Kazhagam (DMK) party, the NDA's coalition partner, to refrain from sending troops to Sri Lanka (Mayilvaganan, 2007: 948). Furthermore, a drift in public sympathy toward Sri Lankan Tamils stirred by the influx of refugees that occurred precisely at the time of the 1998 and 1999 Tamil Nadu assembly and parliamentary elections, led to even the moderate parties in Tamil Nadu refusing to support another Indian military intervention (Mayilvaganan, 2007: 948). Forced to remain sensitive to the DMK's vacillations due to a desire to maintain power in the state, and mindful of the sentiments of the population of Tamil Nadu, the NDA acquiesced and did not send in its troops. Indeed, it would have been impossible for it to have done so.

In December 2006, when the Tamil National Alliance parliamentary delegation from Sri Lanka – which faced allegations of LTTE ties – arrived for its first official visit to India, it was given an audience with the Prime Minister as well as several top Indian officials and the National Security Adviser (Tamilnet 2006). This followed the Sri Lankan Prime Minister's visit to New Delhi and an un-granted request for military aid in November 2006; the Indian government was only willing to go so far as extending vague indications of possible alternative forms assistance, which remained largely unarticulated (Sengupta 2006). This inevitably strained centre-state relations (as the arrival of additional Tamil refugees once again engendered sympathy within Tamil Nadu) while simultaneously burdening New Delhi's relationship with the Sri Lankan government. India was, once again, faced with challenging and unpleasant choices.

As recently as October 2008, there was increased pressure from Tamil Nadu demanding that New Delhi force Sri Lanka to ensure the safety of Tamils caught in the crossfire between LTTE and Sri Lankan security forces. On October 14 2008, an all-party meeting in Chennai demanded the Central Government in New Delhi ask the Sri Lankan army to immediately halt its offensive in northern Sri Lanka. This all-party meeting issued an ultimatum to New Delhi: "... [T]ake steps to stop Lankan army's offensive within a fortnight, failing which all Members of Parliament from Tamil Nadu would resign *en masse* (Zeenews 2008)." Moreover, approximately 13 Lok Sabha (Lower House of the Indian Parliament) Members of Parliament, including Party Chief Karunanidhi's daughter Kanimozhi and a number of

DMK MPs from the coalition UPA government, handed over their resignation letters. Immediately following the eruption of the crisis, the Indian foreign secretary summoned the Sri Lankan High Commissioner to India and conveyed New Delhi's concerns over the situation. In response to these developments the Sri Lankan government sent a high level team to India to appraise New Delhi of the prevailing situation in Sri Lanka (Ibid). Interestingly, in the light of increasing protests from Tamil Nadu over the recent standoff between the LTTE and Sri Lankan forces, the Sri Lankan government has begun addressing Tamil Nadu politicians directly (Reddy 2009). Mayilvaganan remarks that "owing to the growing interest in Tamil Nadu over the Sri Lanka Tamil issue, the central government has, of late, approached the issue in a 'cautious' manner. It has also adopted a policy of consulting and sharing its concerns with the state government" (Mayilvaganan, 2007: 955).

For the central government in New Delhi a strategic partnership with Sri Lanka is pragmatic for a number of reasons. It acts to establish India's pre-eminence in region, while preventing other powers from exerting their influence. Additionally, it ensures that India remains the security manager of the sea lanes (of both trade and travel) in the Indian Ocean region. A strategic partnership would also serve as a vehicle for New Delhi to use in its attempts to root out the threat of terrorism (LTTE is an internationally banned terror outfit) from the region, and, to strengthen its ties with Southeast Asian in general. Despite all these systemic and sub-systemic incentives, India has been unable to formulate adequate strategies to engender a true strategic partnership with Sri Lanka due to a fundamental lack of elite cohesion. While it was easier for the government of India to forge a relationship with Sri Lanka in the 1980s—which it did in the form of the 1987 Indo-Sri Lanka Agreement—it is next to impossible to do so today with DMK a partner in the coalition government. The DMK refuses to engage with the government of India on policies that it feels may be detrimental to Sri Lankan Tamils because of its political calculations and social stance in Tamil Nadu.

The LTTE has since been defeated and the tempers have died down in Tamil Nadu. Reports indicated[7] that the Government of India actively helped the Sri Lankan army in defeating the LTTE. This could be considered as going against the argument that Chennai influences New Delhi's Sri Lanka policy. However, even as New Delhi helped, mostly in covert manner, Colombo despite the opposition from Chennai, the fact remains that material evidence points to, first of all, great amounts of historical influence that Tamil Nadu has had on New Delhi's Sri Lanka policy and secondly that New Delhi was prevented from acting the way it wanted to in the past by Tamil Nadu.

India's struggle to find direction and consistency in its relationship with Sri Lanka—in short, its inability to establish a 'thick' strategic relationship—demonstrates how in a multi-ethnic and multi-religious country such as India, it is hard for federal policy makers to ignore religious and cultural factors when framing foreign policy. Similarly, the inherent fragmentation of coalition democracy took its toll on the making of India's Sri Lanka foreign policy, just as neoclassical realism's understanding of the (in)ability of democratic states to make strong foreign policies would predict.

POKHRAN II'S *DESI* INFLUENCES

The Pokrahn nuclear tests that took place in the Thar desert region of Rajasthan in May 1998 raise many questions among international relations scholars. One of the most obvious is that of why they occurred at all. Do long and short term structural constraints imposed on India by the international system explain them adequately, or are there domestic causal or intervening variables that are more useful in describing what took place? A number of scholars have observed and

[7]See for example "Indian Help on on LTTE Reduced World Pressure: Lanka," November 16, 2009. URL: http://news.outlookindia.com/item.aspx?669540; and, "India Behind Lanka's Victory Over LTTE: Book," August 23, 2009. URL: http://news.outlookindia.com/item.aspx?664792.

discussed some of these internal factors. Thanks to their work, it is possible to ascertain the key arguments relating to the interaction between domestic variables and structural constraints in order to further elucidate the arguments that this chapter proposes. There are indeed those who argue that purely systemic factors have led to Pokharan-II, and there are others who argue that domestic factors made Pokhran–II happen. I wish to propose a neoclassical realist argument in this regard: domestic politics, milieu and strategic culture in India (a) mediated between systemic causes and Indian nuclear decisions and (b) created the political context within which structural factors were picked up and 'going nuclear' was made possible.

Sumit Ganguly and Bhumitra Chakma have argued that the tests were essentially a result of structural factors. According to Ganguly, select factors were responsible for the tests: "Fifty years of critical political choices, influenced by ideology and imperatives of statecraft; fitful scientific advances in India's nuclear infrastructure; and an increased perception of threat from China and Pakistan since the end of the Cold War" (Ganguly, 1999: 149). Ganguly also cites the 1995 passing of the Brown Amendment in the US that granted economic and military assistance to Pakistan without any attached conditions, as well as the US' indefinite extension of the Non-Proliferation Treaty, as prompting India to 'go nuclear' in 1998 (Ganguly, 1999: 149).

Chakma argues that the tests were a culmination of a policy process followed by India since the 1960s that "has been primarily guided by and responsive to the existence and gradual intensification of a nuclear security dilemma in the South Asian region" (Chakma, 2005: 404). He argues along the lines of Ganguly:

> [I]ndeed, the Pokhran II was prompted by strategic factors. To the extent India was pushed to the wall on the nuclear issue in the aftermath of the indefinite extension of the NPT and the conclusion of the CTBT, sooner or later it had to make a choice against the backdrop of extreme pressure from the major powers

> to sign the CTBT, India's policy of nuclear ambiguity had gradually become unsustainable in the latter half of the 1990s. The choice was either to accept a non-nuclear status by signing the NPT and the CTBT or to adopt an open declaratory posture by conducting a nuclear test (Chakma, 2005: 402).

Chakma rules out the argument linking the tests with the BJP's rise to power because, he asserts, if the US had not detected the Indian preparations and put extreme pressure on the government of India to stop immediately, the BJP Narasimha Rao government itself would have tested in 1995 (Chakma, 2005: 401).

Some of these arguments are also paraphrased by Kanti Bajpai (forthcoming, 2009). Quoting Raj Chengappa, Bajpai cites R Chidambaram, the former head of India's atomic energy establishment, reportedly said to Prime Minister Vajpayee that "with the CTBT due for review in September 1999, the more we delay, the more the danger grows of India losing its options altogether." Bajpai also writes that the "... nuclear tests were a way of dealing India back into the game of international politics at the highest level after the cold war" (Bajpai). Yet another argument put forward by the proponents of the 'structural factors' argument is that "... Pakistan and China between them were working to hem India strategically. The tests would demonstrate that India had both the capacity and will to defend itself and that its patience was not unlimited" (Bajpai, forthcoming, 2009).

Apart from these structural arguments, scholars have also analysed the domestic factors that led to the Pokhran II tests. Ollapally (chapter in this book) points to the "national sentiment" that prevailed at the time of the BJP's accession to power due to the "perceived international pressure on India during the CTBT negotiations."

While making a general argument about the change of course of the BJP's foreign policy in 1998, alluding to their nuclear strategies,

Sridharan argues that "domestic level determinants, and elite perceptions were far more important in charting a different course action" (Sridharan, 2006: 80).

Bajpai, Ollapally and Sridharan have examined 'pre-disposed political culture' as a possible domestic explanatory variable for the 1998 tests. Ollapally talks about the hardened domestic public opinion that already existed by the time the BJP came to power (Ollapally, chapter in this book). Sridharan argues that the BJP's political culture was pro-bomb: "with the BJP at the helm, a change in nuclear policy was to be expected given that a pro-bomb stance had been one of the party's long-held objectives" (Sridharan, 2006: 82). Bajpai argues that the "political culture of the BJP with its mythos of promise-keeping and the strategic culture of the BJP obsessed with power and prestige were the basic force behind testing" (Bajpai, forthcoming, 2009). Bajpai explains this further:

> At the level of political culture, the BJP is obsessed with the idea that it is an organization that delivers on its promises no matter what the costs to the party in terms of immediate political returns. Over the years, the BJP has convinced itself and has sought to convince others that, in comparison with other parties in India, it carries through policies that it believes to be right for the country. This assertion—that it is the only truly "principled" and "nationalist" party – is one that it works hard to sell both to its own members and the public. The tests were much fitted with that imagery.

Sridharan and Bajpai also link the tests to the role of the leadership in India at that time. Sridharan argues, "[t]he realpolitk factors influencing the decision to test nuclear devices begin with the individual level factors such as the decision-makers' world views and perceptions" (Sridharan, 2006: 83). Bajpai brings in a different dimension of the leadership of Prime Minister Vajpayee. He argues that the "political survival of the Prime Minister had his ability to consolidate power after a narrowly won election" (Bajpai, forthcoming, 2009), and that this was a factor in the decision to go ahead with the nuclear tests. He explains this further and argues that "the Prime Minister's survival and his consolidation of power was dependent on at least three factors:

- to manage the opposition and its allies after coming to power;
- to ward off the hardliners within the Hindutva fold including within his own party;
- to change the PM's image, which was that of a weak, rather ineffectual leader" (Bajpai, forthcoming, 2009).

In this regard Sridharan argues that "a party heading a weak coalition government might have been tempted to use the nuclear card to bolster its survival" (Sridharan, 2006: 82). Mehta too has proposed a similar argument stating that the tests were also aimed at the domestic audience. It was, he says, coalition pressure of a different kind that can be identified as a key reason for the tests. He writes, "Since assuming office, this government has been struggling to find its feet. On the one hand, its concerted attempts to portray itself as a moderate party left it without a clear ideological direction. On the other hand, the political brinkmanship of many of its coalition partners seems to pull the government in many different directions at once. In such circumstances, the nuclear tests have, temporarily at any rate, given the government an aura of credibility and decisiveness" (Mehta, 1998).

Das brings in an altogether different dimension to the domestic variables' camp. She argues that "most of the BJP members identify the cultural history of Indo-Pakistan partition as a factor in India's nuclear concerns about Pakistan" (Das, 2008: 65). Vanaik asserts that the tests were "domestically driven, not externally pressured" (Vanaik, 2002: 323). He considers the tests as part of the 'Hindutva agenda' of the Sangh Parivar, the family of organisations constructed around the Hindu nationalist Rashtriya Swayamsevak Sangh (RSS), and further states that the RSS was openly and actively supportive of them. He also argues that there was a "strong elite consensus" in favour of the nuclear tests (Vanaik, 2002: 325).

Perkovich, in his celebrated account of Indian nuclear history, describes the various domestic political compulsions and calculations behind the 198 tests. While he does take cognizance of the structural factors, he is unambivalent about the importance of the domestic political milieu within which the nuclear decisions were made by various governments including the 1998 tests.

How does this analysis inform a neoclassical understanding of Pokhran II? Are the structural and domestic factors listed above as contributing to the 1998 tests causally independent of each other? More specifically, for our purposes here, should the domestic factors be considered as mere causal variables, as in stemming from within the domestic sphere without any structural influences whatsoever, or should they be understood as intervening variables in the conveyor belt where we have structural forces at one end and nuclear decisions at the other?

I would posit that while domestic factors did contribute significantly to the timing of and rhetoric surrounding the 1998 tests, it must be recognised that many of these factors remained at the ideational and immediate 'trigger' levels. These ideational factors such as 'pre-disposed political culture', 'religious nationalism', and 'national sentiment', were, however, a product not merely of the politico-cultural milieu within India, but were equally a product of the international structure. Arguing that the BJP's ideational orientation towards the bomb was solely domestic in origin is too narrow an analysis to be completely accurate. The BJP's politico-strategic culture was as much a product of the prevailing international situation as the domestic dynamics. This ethos was a product of its cultural nationalist agenda born out of a pre-existing international politico-strategic-religious milieu. Such an agenda is informed by 'memories' such as repeated injuries to the pride of Hindu India by Muslim invaders in the distant past, 'united' India's partition in 1947, continuous attacks on India by Pakistan both directly and indirectly, defeat by the Chinese in 1962, and denial of India's rightful place at the high table of international politics and global security management. Thus Hindu India needs to awaken, rise up and show its might and capacity to the rest of the world: gain by might what is denied as a right. Possessing a nuclear arsenal was a direct response to this ideology.

More so, the national sentiment, elite consensus and popular support for the bomb were influenced by internal debates on the issue in India. These debates were informed by the prevailing global non-proliferation discourse, as well as by the understanding and calculation by India's strategic elite of the structural constraints and incentives of going nuclear under the given circumstances. Therefore, it can be argued, that many of the domestic variables though they might appear as straightforward causal variables, can be, at the ideational level, understood as intervening variables between the structural and policy making levels.

LOOKING FOR NEW VARIABLES: DEVELOPING A RESEARCH AGENDA

These two examples of how domestic politics has influenced foreign policy making in India from a neoclassical realist perspective are just the tip of a new and vital research agenda. This agenda ought to be vigorously pursued to adequately understand the dynamic politics of foreign policy in India, and the way these forces dictate decisions enacted in the policy making realm. Focused research on the domestic aspects of the foreign policy making is scarcely perceptible in the volumes of research output that has been generated on Indian foreign policy. Being as diverse and vibrant as India is, neoclassical analyses of Indian foreign policy will undoubtedly encounter veritable goldmines of research material for such much-needed theoretical inquires. This section, in order to serve as a pioneering attempt in this regard, attempts to identify a few domestic variables that could be taken up for further research within the theoretical parlance of neoclassical realism. It is also pertinent at this juncture to illuminate the political context of India that has made it conducive for domestic politics to act as a source of intervening variables in the country's foreign policy making.

States as the new foreign policy actors

One of the most important aspects to be examined in this regard, and a primary example of an area in need of further critical research, is the emergence of Indian states (federal units) as new actors in the country's foreign policy making process. That the Indian states are increasingly assuming a foreign policy role directly contravenes the traditional understanding of their political capacity and constitutional mandate vis-à-vis the country's foreign policy formation. Yet it is a reality that is increasingly more pronounced. This is also a phenomena capable of positively complicating the traditional approach of foreign policy analysts who have a theoretical bend of mind.

The Constitution of India gives the Union Government virtually exclusive jurisdiction over matters regarding foreign and defence policy. In other words, even if a majority of states oppose a particular foreign policy decision made by New Delhi, the Central Government in New Delhi is not constitutionally bound to recognise this opposition; it can go about its work unhindered (Mattoo and Jacob, chapter in this book). Legislative powers under the Constitution of India are divided into three lists under Article 246 of its Seventh Schedule: the Union List, the State List, and the Concurrent List. As their names reveal: the Union List defines issues that only the central government has the authority to pass legislation regarding; State Governments are given jurisdiction of laws pertaining to items listed under the State List; and the Concurrent List contains items on which both the State and Union Governments can enact legislation. However, in the event of a conflict between a state and the centre on any item under the Concurrent List, the writ of the Central Government prevails. Moreover, it is the Central Government, not the State Governments, that holds the residuary power. (Mattoo and Jacob, chapter in this book). The Central Government is not legally bound to consult the states on matters of foreign policy, nor do the states have any formal place in the foreign policy making fora of the country, and there are no formal structures through which to consult states on foreign policy related issues (Mattoo and Jacob, chapter in this book).

Despite such clearly defined constitutional and institutional restrictions, Mattoo and Jacob argue that states have become more vocal in the recent past, "expressing their foreign and defence policy preferences to the central government" (Mattoo and Jacob, chapter in this book). They outline four interrelated reasons for this:

> There are four interrelated reasons for this growing influence of constituent units on foreign relations. First, the special constitutional status given to some states (as in the case of Jammu and Kashmir) may give the states' political leadership a voice in the country's foreign policymaking. Second, the political weight of a leader of a particular state can also influence foreign policymaking, albeit in an informal manner. Third, coalition governments at the centre have provided space for state governments and leaders to exercise greater say on foreign policy issues because coalition Union governments are formed by regional parties, many of which are based exclusively in one state. Finally, although the Constitution has not undergone change, the forces of globalization have created new practices and possibilities that have already given the states a greater role and will continue to do so in the future. This is especially evident in the case of foreign economic policymaking. Many international financial agencies and institutions, for instance, are negotiating directly with the

state governments in India. (Mattoo and Jacob, chapter in this book).

They have substantiated these arguments by looking "for evidence outside the constitutional framework to see whether the states have been able to influence such decisions through extraconstitutional means and practices" (Mattoo and Jacob, chapter in this book). They also explain two additional developments to argue that states have over time become gradually more important stakeholders in the country's governance: "the movement for local governance (through *panchayati raj*[8] and urban local bodies, namely municipalities) and demands for further reorganization of India's states" (Mattoo and Jacob, chapter in this book). These developments have emboldened the Indian states to assert their role within the Indian Union.

A direct result of recent activism from the states has been their increased participation in the formation of India's foreign economic policy. This has been a direct result of the impact of economic liberalisation and globalisation on the Indian states. The coincidence of financial liberalisation and the rise of the coalition era in India during the early 1990s opened up new vistas for the Indian states. Sridharan, Rudolph and Rudolph, Jenkins, and Mattoo and Jacob[9] have shown how various state governments have been able to (a) influence India's policies towards the World Trade Organisation (WTO) (b) negotiate loans, Foreign Direct Investment (FDI) and other international collaboration with foreign countries and international economic institutions such as the Asian Development Bank (ADB), and (c) managed to emerge as leaders of India's rising

[8]Local self-government institutions.

[9]Lloyd I. Rudolph and Susanne Hoeber Rudolph, "The Iconization of Chandrababu: Sharing Sovereignty in India's Federal Market Economy," Economic and Political Weekly, 5 May 2001, 1542. Rob Jenkins, "How Federalism Influences India's Domestic Politics of WTO Engagement (and is itself affected in the process)," Asian Survey 43, no. 4 (2003): 598-621, at 607. Indian Foreign Policy in the era of Innenpolitik - Amitabh Mattoo and Happymon Jacob, chapter in this book.

economic power in the eyes of the world and participate in multilateral fora such as the World Economic Forum in Davos. While on the one hand the states have been able to benefit themselves with their new-found ability to negotiate with the international system, on the other hand they have also constrained the foreign economic policy of the government of India. Their newly discovered power has made them unwilling to follow New Delhi's line on a variety of foreign economic policy issues and some have even gone so far as to challenge the Central Government through the Supreme Court. The increasing interest of the State Governments in the country's foreign economic policies and their desire to exert influence over them, as well as the power the states have acquired from coalition politics, has led to greater engagement with the state's foreign economic policy making process. As Sridharan points out "[t]he states do not have the power to act as 'Veto players' but they can be obstructive and have learnt to exert pressure on the centre in many ways." (Sridharan, 2003: 481). Sridharan elucidates this hitherto unprecedented pressure exerted by the states on the Central Government: "From an initial position where the centre felt that it was not necessary to ask the states for their input on multilateral trade issues, it has now been made to realise the importance of working with the sub-national units to project the country's position. The centre has been compelled to initiate a series of meetings with the states to devise a consensus on a renegotiation strategy under the WTO to be finalised before 2005" (Sridharan, 2003: 477).

Joseph argues the formation of WTO consistent trade policy by the Indian government clearly demonstrates the importance of actors outside the Union Government in the formation of the country's foreign economic policy. He writes:

> Formulation of WTO consistent trade policy, which has implications on various segments of the society, requires the involvement of various stakeholders and this is in sharp contrast to the pre-WTO scenario where the Ministry of Commerce and

Industry (MoCI) enjoyed a privileged position to make trade policy largely in isolation without consulting the stakeholders. Now, while the consultation process of the Department of Commerce (DoC) helps garnering the views and concerns of stakeholders especially the organized sector like the industry, the consultation of different bodies under the Parliament becomes a channel for airing the concerns of the non-organized stakeholders like civil society groups, farmers groups, health activists, etc. which do not have otherwise direct involvement in the trade policy making. Further, the increased clout of small political parties at the central level, like the left parties in the United Progressive Alliance (UPA) Government, forces the government to take into consideration their concerns and interests as well in the making of WTO consistent trade policy in India (Joseph, article in this book) .

Border States and Foreign Policy Activism

Another underdeveloped area of research is the foreign policy related activities and utterances of Border States. Dossani and Vijayakumar, and Mattoo and Jacob, have demonstrated in their respective chapters in this book how over the years various Border States have tried to capitalise on their unique geographical position to exert foreign and defense policy pressure on the Central Government. In the case of West Bengal, Dossani and Vijayakumar illustrate how the BJP-led Central Government allowed the communist West Bengal government to pursue its own border patrol activities, despite the fact that border patrol is very much under the centre's jurisdiction. The state also influenced India's deportation polices vis-à-vis illegal migrants from Bangladesh. Dossani and Vijayakumar point out that "the state was able to exercise a degree of autonomy and regulate a central policy being undertaken on its territory" (chapter in this book). This example shows that even though the Hindu-rightwing BJP would have liked to react aggressively to a security issue posed by a neighbouring country (Bangladesh) it was unable to do so due to the influence of a federal unit, West Bengal.

Another example in this regard is that of the Jammu and Kashmir government's terrorism related policies, especially under the 2002-2005 Mufti Mohammed Sayeed government which was often accused of being 'soft-separatist'. During the first two years Sayeed was the Chief Minister of J&K, the central government was BJP-led and had in the past displayed an aggressive attitude toward both Kashmir's insurgency problem and dialogue with Pakistan on the Kashmir issue. The BJP quite obviously preferred to use an iron fist to attempt to control the situation in the state. However, much to the dislike of the Central Government Sayeed, whose party was part of the Congress (I)-led opposition coalition (opposed to the BJP-led NDA), took many steps in the state. He disbanded the Special Operations Group which was created to fight militancy in the state, which the central government held dear due to its significance for the country's internal security. Furthermore, the "Mufti government also had adopted a 'healing touch' approach to the Kashmir problem and had decided to release from confinement many persons accused of indulging in acts of militancy despite the central government's displeasure" (Mattoo and Jacob, chapter in this book). Sayeed impacted on India's Pakistan policy since he was "widely regarded as the architect, although indirectly, of several confidence-building measures that were introduced between the two countries," such as the Srinagar-Muzzaffarabad bus service, as well as cooperation between India and Pakistan after the 2005 earthquake.

These examples show that the Indian states—Border States, states having significant stake in the ruling coalition, and economically powerful states—contribute to the country's foreign, defense and economic policies. But do they exert such a significant amount of pressure as to force the Central Government to act against their will? In other words, do pressures of this kind cause the Central

Government to respond ineptly to external systemic constraints and incentives? Additionally, do the states' demands and pressures emanate from domestic dynamics or do they have systemic origins?

Occasionally, such as in case of Tamil Nadu, the demands of State Governments constrain the Central Government from effectively responding to systemic phenomena. On other occasions, as Joseph points out, the intervention of states apart from other domestic actors has helped the Central Government to respond to systemic phenomena in a more cohesive manner. States' demands come from both systemic calculations as well as purely domestic calculations. The responses of the Indian states to the WTO negotiations and other related international economic issues, as well as the Tamil Nadu government's response to the Sri Lanka problem, is due to systemic phenomena (Joseph, chapter in this book); whereas the West Bengal government's interest in border control stems from domestic political calculations.

There is an opening for further research to investigate the impact of the so-called 'Muslim-factor' on Indian foreign policy making, especially vis-à-vis the US and West Asian countries. New Delhi has consistently been forced onto a tightrope walk between its growing relations with the US and Israel on the one hand, and Islamic countries in the West Asian region on the other hand. The foreign policy dilemma arises from the fact that both of these sets of countries are important for India, yet there are obvious tensions over how to manage a concurrent relationship with them both, given US policies toward the Arab-Israeli conflict and the fact that West Asia is home to a large Muslim population.

An equally important question for further research is whether India's underbalancing behaviour vis-à-vis Pakistan and China or for that matter even Bangladesh and its reluctant assertion of itself as a major regional power come from the country's internal ideological, nationalist, 'democratic', and regional vulnerabilities? Despite being a large country with immense natural and human resources, India has not been able to assert itself on the world stage. It has failed so far to become even a regional norm setter. Is this due to the internal dynamics of the country? If so, which factors specifically are responsible for this? Finally, has India's vibrant and poly-centric democracy been a restraining factor in New Delhi's ability to formulate a pro-active (or even aggressive) foreign and defence policy to engage China, Pakistan, the region, and the world as a whole? There are no definitive answers to any of these questions. But surely, there is a dire need for focused and theoretically-inspired empirical research so as to answer these very important questions.

CONCLUSIONS

This chapter argues that neoclassical realism offers a solid theoretical perspective through which to address some of the hitherto unaddressed issues of Indian foreign policy. After laying out the key arguments, themes and explanatory variables of neoclassical realism, it uses them to explain some important aspects of Indian foreign policy, vis-á-vis the influence of Tamil Nadu in the formulation and conduct of India's Sri Lanka policy, as well as the role domestic influences on the nuclear tests in 1998. This chapter also deals with the feasibility of developing a neoclassical realist research agenda for Indian foreign policy.

A careful and thoughtful application of neoclassical realism would, however, confront an important normative puzzle: how much social and elite cohesion occurs in practice and how much is necessary? When deciphering this puzzle a researcher will confront even more disquieting questions, such as: is social and elite cohesion an objective value in multicultural societies? Can elite and social diversity (not necessarily in opposition to 'cohesion') enrich, inform and contribute to dynamic, inclusive and organic foreign policy making? Is it desirable and possible to have elements of 'democratisation' and 'inclusiveness' in foreign policy making in countries where political polycentrism and coalition dynamics are the order of the day? Rigorous research to answer some of these questions will, I believe, also further inform neoclassical realist theorising in future.

In countries such as India where there are multiple dissenting voices and centrifugal forces and where there are those who both operate within the limits accepted by the state as well as those who function outside such limits. In situations (again, as in India) where state cohesion itself is a problematic concept due to the relative absence of state legitimacy, and where a veritable cacophony of voices have had an impact on the ability of the state to posit itself as a 'strong' (i.e. unitary and coherent) force, neoclassical realist understanding gives us the relevant and necessary insights to understand the intimate links between what goes on inside a state and its ability to act. It therefore must be accepted as a vital and pertinent theory of note that deserves increased recognition and investigation. Ultimately, neoclassical realism speaks not just to Indian foreign policy but far beyond, and this chapter seeks to begin just such a conversation.

REFERENCES

"TNA 'reassured' by India's thinking on Sri Lanka," 24 September 2006. Available at http://www.tamilnet.com/art.html?catid =13&artid=19695.

Bajpai, Kanti (2009), "The BJP and the Bomb," in *Inside Nuclear South Asia*, Scott D. Sagan (ed.) Stanford University Press.

Chakma, Bhumitra (2005), "Toward Pokhran II: Explaining India's Nuclearisation Process," *Modern Asian Studies*, 39: 189-236.

Das, Runa (2008), "Explaining India's Nuclearization: Engaging Realism And Social Constructivism," *Asian Perspective*, 32: 1: 33-70.

Dossani, Rafiq and Srinidhi Vijayakumar (2009), "Border States and the new voices in Indian Foreign Policy," in Amitabh Mattoo and Happymon Jacob (eds.), *Domestic Politics and Indian Foreign Policy (Chapter in this book).*

Dueck, Colin (2006), *Reluctant Crusaders: Power, Culture, and Change in American Grand Strategy*, New Jersey: Princeton University Press.

Ganguly, Sumit (1999), "India's Pathway to Pokhran II: The Prospects and Sources of New Delhi's Nuclear Weapons Program," *International Security*, 23 (3): 148-177.

Joseph, Reji K. (2009), "India's Engagement with the World Trade Organization: the Role of non-State Agents" in Amitabh Mattoo and Happymon Jacob (eds.), *Domestic Politics and Indian Foreign Policy (Chapter in this book).*

"Lanka crisis: Envoy called, MPs resign," October 17, http://www.zeenews.com/Nation/2008-10-17/476863news.html.

Mattoo, Amitabh and Happymon Jacob (2009), "Foreign Relations of India: An Increasing State Role," in Amitabh Mattoo and Happymon Jacob (eds.), *Domestic Politics and Indian Foreign Policy (Chapter in this book).*

Mayilvaganan, M. (2007), "The Re-emergence of the Tamil Nadu Factor in India's Sri Lanka Policy," *Strategic Analysis*, 31 (6): 943-964.

Mehta, Pratap Bhanu (1998), "Exploding Myths," *The New Republic*, June 8.

Morgenthau, Hans J. (1968), *Politics Among Nations: The Struggle for Power and Peace*, New York: Knopf.

Ollapally, Deepa (2009), "The Domestic Politics of India's 1998 Nuclear Tests," in Amitabh Mattoo and Happymon Jacob (eds.), *Domestic Politics and Indian Foreign Policy (Chapter in this book).*

Perkovich,George (1999), *India's Nuclear Bomb: The Impact on Global Proliferation*, Berkeley, CA: The University of California Press.

Rathbun, Brian C. (2008), "A Rose by Any Other Name: Neoclassical Realism as the Logical and Necessary Extension of Structural Realism," *Security Studies* 17(2): 294-321.

Reddy, B. Muralidhar "Mahinda Rajapaksa invites Karunanidhi, Jayalalitha," The Hindu, Jan 27, 2009.

Schweller, Randall L. (2006), *Unanswered Threats: Political Constraints on the Balance of Power*, New Jersey: Princeton University Press.

——— (2003), "The progressiveness of Neoclassical Realism," in Colin Elman and Miriam Fendis Elman (eds.), *Progress in International Relations Theory: Appraising the Field*, London: MIT Press, pp. 316-317.

——— (1998), *Deadly Imbalances: Tripolarity and Hitler's Strategy of World Conquest*, New York: Colombia University Press.

Sengupta,, Ramananda "India's Lanka dilemma, May 31, 2006. URL: http://www.rediff.com/cms/print.jsp?docpath=/news/2006/may/31ram.htm.

Shankar, Mahesh and T.V. Paul (2009), "Foreign Policy Making in India: Looking for Theoretical Explanations in IR," in Amitabh Mattoo and Happymon Jacob (eds.), *Domestic Politics and Indian Foreign Policy (Chapter in this book).*

Sridharan, Kripa (2006), "Explaining the phenomenon of change in Indian foreign policy under the National Democratic Alliance Government," *Contemporary South Asia*, 15 (1): 75-91.

——— (2003), "Federalism and Foreign Relations: The Nascent Role of the Indian States," *Asian Studies Review*, 27 (4): 463-489.

Sterling-Folker, Jennifer (1997), "Realist Environment, Liberal Process, and Domestic-Level Variables," *International Studies Quarterly*, 41 (1): 1-25.

Taliaferro, Jeffrey W., Steven E. Lobell and Norrin M. Ripsman (2009), "Introduction," in Steven E. Lobell, Norrin M. Ripsman and Jeffrey W. Taliaferro (eds.), *Neoclassical Realism, The State, And Foreign Policy,* Cambridge: Cambridge University Press.

Taliaferro, Jeffrey W. (2006), "State Building for Future Wars: Neoclassical Realism and the Resource-Extractive State," *Security Studies* 15 (3): 464-495.

Vanaik, Achin (2002), "Making India strong: The BJP-led government's foreign policy perspectives," *South Asia: Journal of South Asian Studies*, 25 (3): 321-341.

Waltz, Kenneth N. (1983), *Theory of International Politics*, New York: McGraw Hill.

Waltz, Kenneth N. (1959), *Man, the State and War: A Theoretical Analysis*, New York: Columbia University Press.

Zakaria, Fareed (1998), *From Wealth to Power: The Unusual Origins of America's World Role,* New Jersey: Princeton University Press.

IV

The Left Parties and the Indo-US Nuclear Deal

Kamal Mitra Chenoy and Anuradha M. Chenoy

The Left in India [both the organized left as represented in Parliament as well as the left outside this formation] as many others see the Indo-US Nuclear Deal more than just an agreement between two states on nuclear trade that has been presented and sold by the ruling United Progressive Alliance [UPA] during the negotiations of the Deal. The Left in India sees this Deal as a strategic embrace of India with the US and thus an attempt to shift the countries foreign policy from its decade's old independent foreign policy represented by non alignment. This shift in India's foreign policy from non-alignment and multipolarity towards the acceptance of US hegemony and the drive for a unipolar world is being shaped by altering the strategic environment by agreements between India and the US where military engagement is being privileged. This shift is manifest with changes in India's foreign policy conceptualizations and relations with traditional allies. The national consensus that existed around non-alignment has broken down as changes in India's strategic thinking are made and articulated by small foreign policy elite in and around the government. The Left pushed for discussions in the Parliament on the Indo-US nuclear deal that clearly revealed the opposition to the deal from all sections of the House outside the UPA and no consensus was forthcoming.

The changes in Indian foreign policy are based on India's aspirations for great power status and coincide with, or at least follow the Indian economic reforms since the 1990's. The background however, was provided when the Bharatiya Janta Party [BJP] with the National Democratic Alliance [NDA] came to power. A major benchmark paradoxically was Pokhran II in May 1998 when India openly went nuclear with a series of tests. After that the BJP-led NDA government far from using its newly displayed nuclear muscle to strengthen its independent foreign policy decided to play second fiddle to the US. The Brajesh Mishra-Jaswant Singh thesis endorsed by the RSS was to work for a trilateral axis of the US-Israel-India, the idea being that in a 'unipolar' world it was strategically necessary to cozy up to the US and its allies. The fact that Israel was considered the most efficient Muslim-basher around, further enthused the Hindutva brigade at the core of the NDA regime. Thus the NDA leadership even went to the extent of giving the US an assurance that Indian troops would be sent to join the 'coalition of the willing' in Iraq. But before it could move to implement this promise it was voted out of power.

Many secularists and the Left had fond hopes that the UPA coalition would break new ground in foreign policy reversing the drift towards US-centric approach. This has not happened. Instead the Manmohan Singh led UPA adopted the Indian version of the Chinese formula, 'walk on two legs.' Under this version, the UPA in its Common Minimum Programme [CMP] has talked of an independent foreign policy striving for a 'multi-polar' world. But in practice, this has meant improvement in relations between India and China as well as with Russia, along with a continued strengthening of a special relationship with the US. Relations with China were upgraded to a strategic 'partnership' and those with Russia reinforced. The Congress however argues that India's rising GDP, its large middle class, its military and nuclear capability makes it a potential power. India's strategic thinkers have argued that non-alignment is 'irrelevant' and not in 'national interest'. They advocate that alignment with the sole superpower is in the interest of making India a great power. The Left has opposed globalization and structural adjustment policies that favor only the rich in this already polarized country, where the vast majority live below the poverty line. It is on such ideological principles that the Left opposed the Indo-US nuclear Deal.

THE RATIONALE FOR THE SHIFT

Several reasons have been presented by Indian strategists for rationalization the shift in Indian foreign policy that make claims that are at best partial. These reasons include the following:

1. The Soviet Union has disintegrated and the bipolar world has ended, one unipolar world has emerged with the US as the sole superpower and so non alignment is irrelevant.

This claim is however partial. After the Soviet Union disintegrated and the ideological counter view that it provided ended, new states and power systems have emerged. The issue of an alternative to capitalism and globalization remains as represented by the growing people's movements on a world wide scale. Further, there was never strictly a bipolar world. The fact that a Non-Aligned Movement [NAM] could exist and thrive is privy to the existence of different poles, even during the severe Cold War. Post Cold War, while there is one superpower, yet there are multiple poles of power. No one power can dominate the world, even after the US' great military superiority. The argument that non-alignment is irrelevant ignores the very basis of the concept, which was not to get aligned with any military bloc. Since only one military bloc exists led by the US, non-alignment now means not aligning with it, but maintaining an independent foreign policy.

2. India is becoming a great power, and the US can help it become a greater power. In conditions of globalization which is led by the US, it would be beneficial for India to attach itself to US interests as this would help Indian interests.

The reality is that India has elements both of great power, middle power and powerlessness. India is a great power because of its territory, economic resources and growth and because of its democratic traditions, stable and cohesive polity, etc. It is a middle power because of its military capability, technology base, scientific personnel, etc. Yet in terms of human development, poverty, incapacity to distribute to the large mass of its people, it remains amongst the poorest countries. Further, no country can become a great power either by leaving large numbers of people behind, by sheer military capability, or by piggy back riding on one super power.

It is in this context that the foreign policy making elite in India has designed a shift of India's foreign policy. Leftist circles have argued that this elite is so globalized that they have 'seceded' from the real India. Others argue that there is an 'India' comprising of the elite and a 'Bharat' comprising of the excluded. The Left claims to represent the excluded. The next question is why is the US interested in aligning with India, when historically it has always been a critic of India's foreign policies?

THE FIRST STEPS OF INDO-US ENGAGEMENTS

In June 2004, Bush and Vajpayee signed the 'Next Step for Strategic Partnership' [NSSP] after a series of talks between the two countries that had been initiated by the NDA government. The Bush Government waived the nuclear related sanctions on India in 2001 and allowed exports to Indian Space Research Organization (ISRO) in 2004 as the basis for the NSSP. This strategy was outlined in their document: 'India as a Global Power: An Action Agenda for the United States,' July 14, 2005, that stated that the US will make India into a 'great power'. This was unveiled in Bush administration strategy paper 'A New Strategy for South Asia', March 2005 where the US invited India to collaborate with it militarily and economically in exchange for this 'great power' status (Background briefing by administration officials on U.S.—South Asia relations 2005, Ashley Tellis 'India as global power' 2005). The paper by Ashley Tellis cited the need to balance China and claimed that India alone in Asia had the potential to do so.

The Indian government under Prime Minister Manmohan Singh welcomed this alliance with the belief that India will now become a great power both at the regional level and internationally. Two agreements between India and the US, the June 28 and July 2005 Indo-US Defence Framework, became the basis laid out the intent "to transform Indo-US relations" stating that: "The leaders of our two countries are building a U.S.-India strategic partnership in pursuit of these principles and interests." (Background briefing by administration officials on U.S.-South Asia relations 2005, Ashley Tellis 'India as global power' 2005). The Left Parties, led especially by Prakash Karat, the new general secretary of the CPI[M] came out strongly against this framework. He clearly placed this as India moving towards the world's leading imperialist power, the US.

MILITARY LINKS: THE INDIA-US DEFENCE FRAMEWORK

The New Framework for India-US Defence Relationship, 28 June 2005, states that [1] the two shall conduct joint exercises and exchanges. [2] Collaborate on multilateral operations. [3] Strengthen capabilities to defeat terrorism. [4] Expand interaction to promote regional and global peace and stability. [5] Enhance capabilities to combat the proliferation of weapons of mass destruction. [6] Expand the two-way defence trade between the two and 'build greater understanding between our defence establishments', conduct peacekeeping operations, etc. (New framework for the U.S.-India Defence Relationship, 2005). This meant that India agreed to join US-led multinational military operations [there was no mention of the UN anywhere in the document], to be part of the controversial Proliferation Security Initiative (PSI) to intercept suspected movements of WMD' related materials even outside areas permitted by international law, collaborate in the US' controversial missile defence, share intelligence, and enhance joint military exercises. According to the Left parties, all this amounted to a major step towards becoming a junior ally of the US. This framework was a clear sign of things to come, they argued.

This Agreement is comprehensive enough to allow India to become a base for US military activities on a wide scale. This sanctions naval exercises in the Straits of Malacca, Alaska, Bay of Bengal and the Indian Ocean as also military exercises in Mizoram and elsewhere. The

Pentagon argues that collaborations or inter-operatability with the Indian military will help US military agenda on counterterrorism, counter proliferation, in peacekeeping, anti-narcotics operations, etc. Suggestions to deepen cooperation in the Indian Ocean are proposed (David Fulghum: 2004). In 2006, India and US agreed to sign a military logistics support and maritime support agreement, 'to ensure secure maritime environment' (US Statement on President Bush visit to India, 2006). The Defence Framework supports the Access and Cross Servicing Agreement [Logistics Support Agreement] that gives US ships access to Indian naval facilities for maintenance and repairs. This essentially means that warships can practically use Indian facilities without a formal base. This form of base is called the 'lily pad' base that US ships and personnel can use from frog hopping to any site. Regular joint naval exercises are part of these agreements. With this clause, India by proxy becomes part of the US, Japan and Australia axis that seeks to dominate the high seas in the region.

The US strategists argue that India's naval capability is superior to that of the ASEAN countries. India can thus provide the US easy access to the entire region and can be used for the US PSI. The Defence Framework make no direct mention of the US sponsored PSI of 2003 or the Container Security Initiative [CSI]. The PSI gives the US and other members the right to apprehend any ship/container that they believe may be carrying weapons of mass destruction [WMDs] or nuclear material. In other words, just like Iraq was attacked on the suspicion of the existence of WMDs, a similar attack could be carried out on any container/ship in the international waters. India's linkage with these initiatives and US military exercises binds India to these operations. But the scope of the Defence Framework and later agreements is so wide that it can be indirectly used for the PSI. The Framework thus allows complete access to US military to Indian military assets and facilities to advance its hegemonic agenda in Asia and Africa. Indian strategists who want a 'Blue Water' navy are willing to be part of US naval adventures in exchange. This is in sharp contrast to India's traditional position of Indian Ocean as a zone of peace safeguarded by India.

As Rashid and Perkovich point out, between 2005-06 there were 21 Indo-US meetings on issues ranging from defence procurement, military service to service, trade and commerce, etc to establish a comprehensive and long-term strategic partnership between the US and India. And further that "the president has approached the new relationship with India with a clear vision of the geopolitical challenges likely to confront the United States in the Twenty First century" (US Statement on President Bush visit to India, 2006). US security strategists believe that by July 2006 Prime Minister Manmohan Singh had already promised that in exchange for nuclear supplies India would separate its military and civilian nuclear facilities, place the latter under IAEA safeguards, maintain a moratorium on testing and work with the US to conclude the Fissile Material Cut off Treaty (Faiza Rashid and George Perkovich: 2005). These issues however were never revealed in the Indian press until much later.

The Left Parties organized several meetings and protests about this Defence Framework. But since the mainstream press and the ruling coalition were so persistent on it, this Agreement was passed without much national debate.

THE LOGISTICS SUPPORTS AGREEMENT

The logistics support agreement is part of the new military-political alliance that India is building with the US. A key element was the 10 year Indo-US military framework of June 2005, which in turn dovetailed with the wide ranging Bush-Manmohan agreement of July 2005. In the furore over the Indo-US civilian nuclear deal some key elements of a military alliance between the two got overlooked. The logistics support agreement would allow US military forces, of the, air, sea and land to get logistics support including repairs, refueling at virtually all Indian naval, air force and army bases. Such key logistical support has in the past been given to no one, for it practically amounts to providing a foreign power bases in India.

Such facilities were never given to our earlier major ally: the Soviet Union. But the shift of arms sales to the US and its close ally Israel, as well as the Hyde Act in which India is bound to follow a "congruent foreign policy" with that of the US, including hostility towards India's old ally Iran; have created the atmosphere for India to go ahead with a logistics policy, to provide US bases. So it is not enough to see the logistics support agreement for what it is, but the agreement must be contextualized in the current, unprecedented friendly relations between the US and India. The logistics agreement is the tip of the iceberg. The US National Security Doctrines of 2002 and 2006 while critical of Russia and China praised India, and the latter Doctrine advocated closer US ties with India.

In the meanwhile the US has put in place its ballistic missile defense threatening Russia, and is obviously wooing India to be part of the containment of China. The emerging alliance would make India part of US military adventures. In this scenario it makes little political or strategic sense to build a close alliance with the US, when the latter refused to back India for a permanent seat in the Security Council or its candidate for UN Secretary General.

These Defence Agreements that have become the basis for the Nuclear Deal, irk the Left more than just the nuclear aspects of the deal. The fact that India gets tied to the US militarily and can in the near future become an ally of US military interventionism worries the Left, even more than the economic re-structuring. This conscious drift away from the Congress' traditional foreign policy of non-alignment was not just a straw in the wind. It was a clear sign of things to come. Expectedly, the Left reacted very strongly to the defence framework and warned against further concessions in the Indian PM's forthcoming trip to the US.

DEMOCRACY AS INTERVENTION?

The Defence Framework was followed by the July 18, 2005 resolve by Manmohan Singh and President Bush to create an Indo-US "Global Partnership" and agreements on the Global Democracy Initiative, where the two would be committed to promoting democracy to third countries on a global scale. Both countries dedicated $10 million a year to promote democracy globally. The question is do both countries have the same vision on democracy? The US believes that Russia and Venezuela are not democracies; they believe that Hamas is a 'terrorist organization' and do not recognize it despite its electoral victory. The US is the mainstay of Israel's policies in Palestine. India has long critiqued the idea of international intervention on the grounds of human rights, democracy or any other social clause. The Left has opposed this Democracy initiative because they do not want India to participate with the US in spreading democracy to Central Asia, to Pakistan, or to Iraq.

The Left has had reservations on the Indo-US Knowledge Initiative on Agriculture which brings the US agricultural multinational companies and products into Indian agriculture that Indian agricultural scientists argue, are based on unequal access for the US. As opposed to this, India's interest in becoming a member of the UN Security Council, a method of becoming a great power, is not mentioned in any Indo-US document (Joint Statement between President George W. Bush and Prime Minister Manmohan Singh, 2005). The Hyde Act and the 123 Agreements have to be placed in this context.

THE HYDE ACT AND THE 123 AGREEMENT

The 123 Agreement is more than just an agreement on nuclear supplies and should be viewed in the broader context of this new alignment. The Hyde Act of the US forms the perpetual framework for this Treaty. It is a US National Act in keeping with the US nuclear non proliferation and their Missile Technology Control Regime [MTCR].[1] The Hyde Act makes special changes to enable the US to supply nuclear fuel and technologies to India as an exception, in return for safeguards and inspections by the International Atomic Energy

[1]The MTCR was used for the Soviet Union to deny it access to even the most basic technology. It continues to be used for Russia and many others.

Agency [IAEA] and also certifications by the US president to the US Congress on India's overall foreign policy positions. The next step for India to operationalize this Agreement would be to sign similar agreements with the IAEA and the Nuclear Suppliers Group.

The Indian foreign minister claims that the Hyde Act is not binding on India. They believe that there can be no attempt to influence India. But the US Congress has different assumptions. The Congressional report that accompanies the Hyde Act states that both houses of the Congress want that this Hyde Act "reflects the widely held view in both the House and the Senate that peaceful nuclear cooperation with India can serve multiple US foreign policy and national security objectives but that this must be secured in a manner that minimizes potential risks to the global nonproliferation regime."[2] There can be no clearer statement of intent.

The Hyde Act states that while exporting nuclear fuel or technology to India the US has to follow principles including that the American president will report and certify annually to the US Congress if India's foreign policy is "congruent to that of the United States" and more specifically India joining US efforts in isolating and even sanctioning Iran (Henry J. Hyde, U.S.-India Peaceful Atomic Energy Cooperation Act of 2006, Public Law 109-401 (2006). The US will cease nuclear cooperation if India conducts a test. And all materials including reprocessed material will be returned (The Hyde Act, section 106 and Section 104 (3) (B)). This Act demands that India participate and ultimately support the PSI that we mentioned above, which enables the US to intercept ships in international seas (The Hyde Act, [Section 104g(2) K]). The advisory in the Act wants to bind India into various US initiated treaties and regimes of which India is not part, including the MTCR, Fissile Material Cut off Treaty, etc. (The Hyde Act [Section 104c E,F,G]). These include that India sign up to the Australia group and the Wassenar Arrangement,

[2]Downloaded from http://www.wmdinsights.com/I12/I12_AF2_SATakes NSGChair.htm

and 'dissuade, isolate, sanction and contain' Iran. President Bush has argued that he would treat these as non-binding. Can he assure India that these are non binding in perpetuity, as the Act remains in perpetuity? The US would pressurize India on all these issues and eventually as India gets more bound, violations on these counts would lead to suspension of the Agreement and a return of the nuclear technology and fuels.

The argument by the Indian foreign minister that India is not bound by the Hyde Act is at best partial because the Hyde Act functions as 'national law' which binds the US. There is no ambiguity in the Agreement on this at all. Article 2 of the 123 Agreement states that the parties to the Agreement: "shall implement this Agreement in accordance with the respective applicable treaties, national laws, regulations, and license requirements concerning the use of nuclear energy for peaceful purposes." This Article 2 can be used by the US at any time to delay, deny or disapprove nuclear supplies and to therefore pressurize India on any foreign policy or domestic policy decision. India's independent decision making gets curtailed in this Agreement in perpetuity. There can be no doubt that the 123 Agreement is bound by the Hyde Act. Further, the US is known to interpret and subscribe to international treaties almost on unilateral basis. For example, while it has walked out of the NPT for the Hyde Act, it also walked out of the Anti Ballistic Missile Treaty unilaterally. It tied countries to its own interpretation of the WTO clauses and has often stated that US laws are superior to international law. Thus, the US will use the Hyde Act when ever it so requires in the future.

The Washington based Stimson Centre has shown that the 123 Agreement was seen as "implementing the Hyde Act" The Act specifically states that US "civil nuclear assistance to India will not directly, or in any other way assist India's nuclear weapons programme." In accordance with the Hyde Act, the Senate foreign relations committee stated: "[It] is necessary to ensure that no sensitive nuclear technologies related to the enrichment of uranium… the reprocessing of spent fuel…. Or the production of heavy water ... are given to India" (The Stimson Centre, Washington). These citations show that the Hyde Act which governs the 123 Agreement is consciously aimed at controlling the Indian nuclear programme and even curbing the transfer of sensitive nuclear technologies. This is contrary to the formulation in the 123 Agreement, which says these facilities "may be transferred ... [by] an amendment to this Agreement" (The Stimson Centre, Washington). Therefore, the 123 Agreement tentatively offers sensitive nuclear technology contrary to the explicit statements of the powerful Senate foreign relations committee. Such a promised amendment would appear virtually impossible given Congressional oversight, especially by the Senate, particularly when President Bush is on his way out and is likely to be succeeded by a Democrat as president.

The text of the 123 Agreement was kept a secret until the Indian Union Cabinet cleared it and it became binding. Public and parliamentary discussion followed only after it became irreversible. The 123 Agreement has been reworked by Indian and US negotiators to make it more palatable since the Indian political class outside the ruling UPA found the Hyde Act highly discriminatory. Thus some of its provisions remain ambiguous and the text is open to divergent interpretations. But this ambiguity will remain only until the 123 Agreement has been operationalized. Once through, the US can interpret this to its convenience.

Members of the ruling UPA went to great lengths to argue that the Hyde Act was purely a US Legislation and had no implications for India.[3] This attempt at dislinking the two was rejected at several occasions by the US administration itself. For example, Secretary of State Condoleeza Rice stated that even any agreement between India and the Nuclear's Suppliers Group, [the final sanction that will allow India to engage in nuclear trade], would be supported by the US only if it is "consistent" with the Hyde Act. Rice stated: "We will support

[3]Kapil Sibal, in a series of articles in a number of papers like Indian Express and during several speeches argued this.

nothing with India in the NSG that is in contradiction to the Hyde act. It will have to be completely consistent with the obligations of the Hyde Act" (*The Hindu*, 2008a).

THE IMPLICATIONS OF THE 123 AGREEMENT

1. The 123 Agreement retains the basic features of the Hyde Act. It gives the US the right to terminate the Cooperation with India at its own will (The 123 Agreement, Article 14.1 and 14.2). This puts India at the mercy of the US. If they do not do what the US wants, the US will stop supplying it with fuel. The billions that India spends on imports related to nuclear equipment will go waste. For example, Howard L. Berman, Chairman of the US House Foreign Affairs panel categorically stated: that the Hyde act "terminates US nuclear cooperation with India if New Delhi resumes nuclear testing" and also "restricts the transfer of sensitive enrichment and reprocessing technologies" (*The Hindu* 2008b). The 123 Agreement incorporates the main "sense" of the Hyde Act.
2. The 123 Agreement unambiguously gives the US the right to return as per Article 14.4. This means that if India conducts a nuclear test, the US has "the right to require the return ... of any nuclear material, equipment, non nuclear material, equipment or component transferred under this agreement and any special fissionable material produced through their use" (123 Agreement, Article 14.4). Though the Agreement provides for some insulation to this right to return, like bilateral consultation, market compensation, etc., the leverage exercised by the US remains clear. Given the latitude provided for the termination of the agreement, uninterrupted nuclear fuel supply is not guaranteed. Thus, if the US finds any Indian foreign policy position going against its national interest, such as India's relations with Iran, India's non-participation in the Proliferation Security Initiative, or FMCT, it can mean that the US can cut off fuel supplies leading to

disruptions. The Agreement specifically states that the US has granted India the right to reprocess in principle, and may involve yet another treaty. Until then, the US has the veto on this. For example Article 14, does not specifically state that any alternate fuel supplies will be given, in case of termination.

3. It reiterates the Hyde Act on prohibiting dual use technologies, as made explicit in Article 5(2) of the 123 Agreement: "Sensitive nuclear technology, heavy water production facilities and major critical components of such facilities may be transferred under this Agreement pursuant to an amendment to this Agreement. Transfers of dual-use items that could be used in enrichment, reprocessing or heavy water production facilities will be subject to the parties' respective applicable laws, regulations and license policies" (123 Agreement, Article 5(2)). This clause thus shows again that national laws such as the Hyde Act will prevail on the US side and that this Agreement itself have to be amended to ensure such transfers. Further, the Agreement ensures that any enrichment, reprocessing or heavy water activity, even when under IAEA safeguards comes under the category of dual use. The foreign minister in the debate in the Lok Sabha on 27 November, 2007, stated that the fast breeder reactors would not come under safeguards.
4. Without saying so specifically, it imposes a test ban, and more [the reasons for terminating the Agreement are deliberately ambiguous] without similar commitments by the US. This is explicit in Article 2 of the 123 Agreement that states that 'national laws' will prevail. Since the Hyde Act states the test ban, the Hyde Act prevails. This is a virtual acceptance of the Comprehensive Test Ban Treaty [CTBT] rejected by the US, without any reference to global and regional disarmament, that makes the deal not only unequal but directed towards capping India's nuclear deterrence. US Under Secretary of State, Nicholas Burns, has categorically stated that India's nuclear reprocessing facilities would in fact come under IAEA safeguards in perpetuity and the Agreement

would have not support the weapons programme. The Indian government denies this, leaving much ambiguity on the issue.

However, for advocates of peace and anti-nuclear weaponization like the authors, a decision for test ban and nuclear disarmament should be India's sovereign decision. In its covert support to the Israeli nuclear programme and to the Apartheid South African regime, no such conditions were laid down. These deals were clandestine but the fact is that nothing in US law stopped them. So, the US argument that the US Atomic Energy Act, 1954 etc. bans any such deal or preferential treatment including vital provisions providing reprocessing technology, is simply not true.

5. The 123 Agreement does not uphold that international law will prevail over national law. Instead does the opposite, it upholds national law over the bilateral agreement that is recognized in international law. The US is known to uphold its own laws over international laws. This, for example, is the reason the US cited for not signing the International Criminal Court and Rome Statute, because the US does not want any of its citizens tried in an international court.
6. India's obligations are permanent. While the US has the right to withdraw and terminate, India has to fulfill its obligations even if the Agreement is terminated at America's insistence. India has to accept permanent international inspections on its civil nuclear plants.

   It has been argued by supporters of the Nuclear Deal that under the 1969 Vienna Convention on the Laws of Treaties, this 123 Agreement would be protected from Congressional interference or even termination. This Agreement is based not on international law but by section 123 of the US Atomic Energy Act, 1954, which gives the US a lot of latitude in putting pressure on India on Iran, or even terminating the Agreement and taking back US origin materials if India tests. This impinges on Indian sovereignty over the Indian nuclear programme, contrary to government assurances.

NUCLEAR ENERGY AND ITS PITFALLS

Nuclear Energy at present is 2.6% of total energy produced. India projects that it will produce 20,000 Megawatts in 2020 that will still be only 7% of the total energy generated. The US has built no nuclear plant since 1979, yet, it will become a major technical supplier because of the strategic partnership. Scientists like Dr. A. Gopalakrishnan, (*The Asian Age* 2007a) have calculated that for importing 30,000 MWe of power reactors, the capital investments will be about Rs.1, 200,000 crores at least. Other scientists, like Dr. P. K. Iyengar, have argued that the "much hyped promise of nuclear technology doesn't translate too much in real terms. Long years of isolation have made us self-sufficient…." (*The Asian Age*, 2007b). It has been shown that the hydrocarbons, coal, wind, solar power are all cheaper sources of energy. One calculation has shown that the cost of nuclear energy will be at least three times as much as that of coal. Experts point out that the claim that nuclear energy is linked to growth is false as India's dependence on hydrocarbons will continue. The Indian Planning Commission Study "Integrated Energy Policy, 2006" shows that even with the most optimistic scenario for nuclear power to be 15,000 MW by 2015 and 30,000 MW by 2021, nuclear energy will add only 7% of the total installed capacity (*The Asian Age*, 2007c).

Questions are thus raised whether India can afford disruptions of fuel supply and more importantly, as former Prime Minister V. P. Singh questioned, can India afford so much for the sake of such a strategic tie up? Besides this, there are other key questions, like the safety and disposal of nuclear waste, alternate sources of energy like thorium of which India has ample supplies, and it's the future of these that remain unanswered. Scientists have shown that contrary to belief, nuclear power is "clean," it is in fact hazardous and accident prone. It can have invisible radiation effects. It leaves poisonous toxic waste which remains active for thousands of years. There is no solution for disposing this waste with complete safety. Before the use of nuclear power the government of any country must make laws of liability and compensation in case of nuclear leaks and radiation. As we saw in Bhopal, India has very few laws or compensation packages for such victims.

It is evident that the deal ties India to the US and makes it dependent on the US for fuel and technology. India's foreign policy decisions will have to be endorsed by the US and coincide with US interests. India will be able to make more untested nuclear weapons that will increase the threat perceptions globally and fuel a nuclear arms race. The exclusions given to India in the nuclear non-proliferation regime will push other countries to do the same, opening the flood gates for the spread of nuclear weapons. India's traditional and historically tested allies like Russia, Central Asian and West Asian countries will feel alienated from India and its new pro-US alignment.

The real benefits will go to US industry and workers, as Condoleeza Rice stated: "It will create thousands of jobs in the US nuclear industry" [April 5, 2006, PBS News Hour].

THE LEFT ARGUMENTS

The Left has been arguing that ever since the US-India Joint Statement of July 18, 2005 all foreign policy moves of the Indian Government confirmed the foreign policy skeptics' worst fears. The Indo-US Statement starts with the common resolve "[t]o create an international environment conducive to promotion of democratic values..." The Left argued that this would be hilarious if the reality was not so tragic. Where is a US-led international environment creating democratic values? In Iraq as in Abu Ghraib and Fallujah? In Afghanistan as in Bagram jail? For illegally categorized 'unlawful combatants' in Guantanamo Bay, who were denied rights under the Geneva Convention being forced to watch the desecration of the Koran? This is most glaring in the section on nuclear energy. Despite the desperate spin doctors on the Indian side and media, it is clear that India has not been recognized as a nuclear weapons state, but only as a 'responsible state with advanced nuclear technology.' Remove the 'responsible' and this could apply to states on the US hit list like Iran and North Korea. All the US has promised is to 'seek agreement from Congress to adjust US laws and policies' and to work 'to adjust international regimes.' There are limits to how much a second term US President can achieve on such issues, and a House committee has already indicated that there will be no exemptions for India.

On the basis of these largely unrealizable promises India has 'reciprocally' agreed to continue its unilateral moratorium on nuclear testing, to identify and separate civilian and military nuclear facilities, place its civilian nuclear facilities under IAEA safeguards including the intrusive Additional Protocol, collaborate with the US to finalize a Fissile Material Cut Off Treaty, adhere to the Missile Technology Control Regime [MCTR] and Nuclear Suppliers Group [NSG] guidelines, and even refrain from transfer of enrichment and reprocessing technologies. In sum, it is an acceptance of the current US' administration's complete non-proliferation package. Of course, though India has 'reciprocally' extended its moratorium on nuclear testing, the US in this bilateral agreement has promised nothing of the sort. India, if it had to accept IAEA safeguards could have done so unilaterally. In addition to accepting the MTCR, NSG guidelines and the proposed Fissile Material Cut Off Treaty, India has reversed its consistent opposition to discriminatory non-proliferation treaties like the NPT. In doing this and agreeing to separate military and civilian nuclear facilities it has further compounded its difficulties. Firstly, as prominent atomic scientists like P. K. Iyengar have pointed out this would be extremely expensive and possible beyond India's means. Secondly, new technologies like fast breeder reactors could be subjected to repeated intrusive checks and delays on grounds of alleged dual use.

Further, and this is why stalwarts of the old regime like Atal Behari Vajpayee and Brajesh Mishra have strenuously protested, this would cumulatively put a cap on India's nuclear arsenal. Of course, a large part of the groundwork for this agreement was laid by the NDA itself. But the UPA is apparently no different. This is also evident from

Defence Minister Pranab Mukherjee's repeated characterization of the world as 'unipolar' after he signed the controversial Indo-US Defence Framework, where the Manmohan Singh-led government also believes that the US must be obeyed, and he obligingly signed on the dotted line.

THE CONTINUING US PRESSURE

Since the Indo-US deal has been held up, while it has gone to the IAEA, there have been a slew of US senators and secretaries of state that have kept up the pressure on India to sign. The Bush administration tried a carrot and stick policy on India. For example, Secretary Rice threatened India at the Senate hearings on the bill in April 2006 that "[a]ll the hostility of the past will be redoubled." Led by the US ambassador to India to Defence Secretary Robert Gates who visited India in the last week of February 2008, with the agenda of pressurizing India on at least three things that include the nuclear deal, signing the Logistics Support Agreement and gaining the tender for the 126 fighter aircrafts that the US has bid for. Gates, like others before him, including democratic senators, including John Kerry, J. Bidden, reminded India that the "clock was ticking," and that the US Congress needed to pass the deal by July 2008 for the president's signature, because after that the US presidential elections would start and the president become engaged in domestic issues and enter the 'lame duck' period. Nicholas Burns, who was to move to the private sector, stayed on for a few more months, with the hope of finalizing the Deal. Senator Boucher even said that the Hyde Act had nothing to do with the 123 Agreement with India. Strobe Talbott, made statements and gave interviews, stating that the BJP had been talking of a similar deal with the Clinton government. He was thus surprised at their resistance to this Deal (*The Indian Express*, 2008). The BJP denied that it was trying to accept a similar nuclear deal. Strobe Talbott was in effect trying to put pressure on the BJP by trying to expose their shifting position, since they were the ones who initiated the dialogue with the US on the nuclear issue and then later opposed the Deal and wanted its re-negotiation when in opposition.

What's in it for the US? First, the US wants a strategic partnership with India, to extend its interests in Asia. Second, the US will gain by becoming a nuclear and arms supplier to India, replacing the traditional suppliers and making millions on the deal as Rice admitted: "It will create thousands of jobs in the US nuclear industry" (PBS News Hour, 2006). Third, it can along with India export small Indian made cheaper nuclear reactors to third countries in the future. Fourth, as Ms. Rice argued the deal "will bring India into the nonproliferation framework and thus strengthen the regime." The Deal binds India to a moratorium on the production of fissile material for nuclear explosive purposes. While this, goes in favor of the international disarmament lobby, it re-enforces the position that India has accepted this not because of commitment to NPT but at US behest.

THE LEFT AND UPA NEGOTIATIONS

The Nuclear Deal talks between the UPA and Left broke down after several stalemated rounds as expected (Left Party Statement, 2008a). The Left had repeatedly asked some questions that remained unanswered:

1. In case the US or NSG countries renege on fuel supply assurances for imported reactors, will India have the ability to withdraw these reactors from IAEA safeguards?
2. Can India withdraw indigenous reactors from IAEA safeguards?
3. If India has to bring nuclear fuel from the non safeguarded part of its nuclear programme, in case nuclear supply assurances are not fulfilled, will India have the ability to take it back?
4. What are the conditions that India will have to fulfill if the corrective steps are to be put into operations? (Left Party Statement, 2008b).

The Congress Party was determined to go ahead with the Deal and the Left was bound to oppose on ideological principles of resistance to

India's alignment with imperialism. On these grounds the Left withdrew support to the UPA in July 2008.

The Left Parties were clear on the reasons for this withdrawal:

1. The Indo-US Nuclear Deal was not part of the Common Minimum Programme between the Left and the Congress and UPA.
2. The Prime Minister gave assurances in Parliament in August 2006 that India's interest would be safeguarded, but the Hyde Act violates these interests.
3. Despite opposition from the Left and many others, the PM went ahead with the negotiations.
4. The PM has disregarded the Parliament and the views of the majority as expressed by the debate in the House in December 2007.
5. The agreements with the IAEA were kept a secret from the country.
6. The Congress has violated its agreements with the Left arrived at in November 2007, where the outcome of the talks with the IAEA would be discussed with the Left.

The Left, thus concluded that this Agreement was no good for the country and decided to withdraw support to the UPA (Left Party Statement, 2008c).

Since it is clear that the Deal was bound to go through sooner or later, why was the hurry shown? This was because the UPA wanted credit for the Deal, and did not want the incoming government to snatch the credit. The real question the Left media asked was: has the Congress got its priorities right? Inflation and poverty of the vast majority is the real big deal in India, not the Nuclear Deal. With inflation rising to 11.42 per cent, it is the main election issue and the UPA's Achilles Heel.

The Nuclear Deal is largely a middle class issue, and even there especially among the lower strata of the middle class, inflation is much more important. The Left felt that this would have a major negative impact on the UPA in the coming elections, with the advantage going to the BJP-led NDA. They felt that the UPA allowed this critical situation to arise largely because of neo-liberal orthodoxy led by the PM, Finance Minister and the Deputy Chairman of the Planning Commission. Instead of slashing the excise duties on petroleum products and keeping the resultant increase in prices minimal as suggested by the Left, the UPA stubbornly passed on the burden on to the consumers.

The Left believes that the Congress has misread the political situation. The Nuclear Deal is no vote catcher. In fact the minority community has been alienated by the US-Israel-India strategic alliance, which the Deal represents. For the poor, who according to the Arjun Sengupta Committee constitute 78 per cent of the population, inflation is the key issue. The Left finally took the Deal to Parliament. After much horse trading, cash for votes scandals and cross voting, the UPA won the vote on the Nuclear Deal by a slim majority.

The PM and a small group of Congress leaders finally had their way on the Indo-US Nuclear Deal. They moved decisively to sign the nuclear deal with the US despite the opposition from the bulk of the political parties. But the confidence motion was preceded by weeks of backroom maneuvering to identify defectors from opposition parties, and to bring around the Socialist Party which earlier scuttled Sonia Gandhi's chances of becoming PM. Obviously the lure of power like the two ministerial posts to the tiny JMM, and undisclosed offers to the SP, which is now talking of the possibility of joining the government, played a major part. Other MPs were reportedly offered cash to vote for the trust vote or to abstain.

The drama of Rs. 1 crore being displayed in the Lok Sabha by 3 BJP MPs offered Rs. 9 crore to abstain is an indication of the levels to which politics has fallen. What is more appalling is the fact that the TV channel that filmed this deal in a sting operation, has refused to telecast it, against the cardinal media principle that important news must be shown. Who has put pressure on CNN-IBM not to telecast? Surely not supporters of the Opposition. So along with the decline of parliamentary ethics, there has been a fall in media standards belying the claims of a free media.

The Deal was debated in Parliament, but hardly any MPs linked the 123 Agreement and the Hyde Act to the Framework of Indo-US Military Relations signed a few weeks before the Bush-Manmohan agreement of July 2005, which laid the ground for the Nuclear Deal. The military agreement commits India to joint operations in a third country, even without the approval of the UN. India is to provide bases to the US for joint exercises and for rest and recuperation of US troops. Even more dangerously, India agreed to be part of the National Missile Defence by which the US aims to degrade the Russian and Chinese nuclear deterrents. This was part of the strategy of the US in its National Security Doctrine 2002, in which the possibility of India being used to contain China was hinted at, apart from numerous statements by US policy makers. This military pact has clearly made India a US strategic ally, forsaking its old ally Russia and its giant booming neighbor China.

A number of scholars and experts pointed out this dangerous linkage, and the fact that to disregard the military pact and concentrate wholly on the Nuclear Deal would be a serious oversight. The Left parties themselves had critiqued the military deal in early July. But its linkages with the Nuclear Deal were not properly brought out. Thus the UPA could get away with legalistic arguments on the irrelevance of the Hyde Act. The simple point that the Hyde Act binds the US which has to ensure the functioning of the 123 Agreement was also not sufficiently stressed. But the UPA leadership knows all this. Therefore, the Left's broad brush critique that these agreements would move India in the direction of being a junior US ally are essentially correct, but it lost a vital opportunity to expose the Treasury benches and educate the country.

The Left parties resolved that in the months following the Parliament vote they would go in for a systematic campaign by patriotic forces to educate the masses about the issues involved. The relatively high costs of nuclear energy, including the provision of an insurance cover by India if there is any mishap, plus the cost of decommissioning an old plant and the storage of highly radioactive spent fuel, has not been stressed enough. Nor have the dangers of nuclear energy. The campaign should also stress on the need of energy conservation measures, apart from the military-nuclear deal aspects.

The Left now believes that the 123 Agreement and the Hyde Act [which later Congress' can amend in US' favor] can be reversed and amended. They plan an informed campaign which also has a peoples' watch on shifts in Indian foreign policy including the Iran-Pakistan-India gas pipeline. They intend to show that their reservations about the military-nuclear deal were correct. But in a sense, the recent commotion in Parliament has thrown up a bigger question: the sanctity of Parliamentary institutions. Legislative and legal measures must be taken so that such wanton horse trading is severely curbed. That's what the nuclear debate also highlighted.

IN CONCLUSION: THE LEFT AND INDIA'S FOREIGN POLICY VISION

India officially continues to adhere to non-alignment. Many of the recent documents on India's foreign policy focus on the concept of the multipolar world as opposed to the US commitment of a unipolar world. The unipolar concept entails US domination to include unilateral decisions on areas of key US interest, placing US law above international law, forced globalizations, 'balance of power' between states, containment of states, regime change, unilateral attacks on 'rogue' states, imposition of US style democracy, non proliferation enforced by the US, etc. The multipolar world concept on the other hand is based on the existence of multiple power centres, multilateral institutions and laws, plural methods of development, democracy and markets, co-existence of multiple cultures among other things. It is supported by Russia, China-France and many others. India has seen it as an extension of the non-alignment idea. The deeper relations envisaged between India-Russia-China in organizations like the Shanghai Cooperation Organization (SCO), have already received a set back when the Indian Prime Minister did not attend its 2007 meetings. India ignored the SCO's invitation to participate in its military exercises and decided instead to participate instead in the US sponsored US-Australia, Japan–India naval exercise of Malabar 07 in the Bay of Bengal, showing its new tilt.

US policy makers reject the idea of both non-alignment and the multipolar concept and have launched a campaign to convince India about these. For example: Secretary of State, Condoleeza Rice, who announced in March 2005, that it was US policy to "help" India become a world power, said in June 2005 that New Delhi would have to abandon "old ways of thinking and old ways of acting" (*The Financial Express*, London, 2007a). Speaking to the US-India Business Council, she said: "I know there are some that still talk about non-alignment in foreign policy.... It has lost its meaning" (*The Financial Express*, London, 2007b). She has repeated this in different words, asking India to drop non-alignment and join instead 'the coalition of democracies' led by the US. Strobe Talbott, former deputy national security advisor to the Clinton government called the multipolar concept "as a pretty stupid proposition" (Strobe Talbot: 2006). In India sections of the press and strategic thinkers have since been echoing these words and sentiments.

The Left parties believe that US pressure is working on India. In September 2005 India went against the rest of the NAM Countries and voted with the US on Iran sanctions. India, that from 1995-2005 had opposed the US in the UN on 80% of all its votes, now has voted with them on sanctions against Iran, and has opposition to a Small Arms and Light Weapons Treaty, etc. Its not surprising therefore, that India has stopped talking of democratization of the United Nations and its goal of joining the Security Council.

The US draft to the Nuclear Supplier Group incorporates elements of the Hyde Act, as predicted by the Left. The Left made a statement that the draft placed by the US to the NSG itself has several implicit conditions on India, like the extension of voluntary moratorium on nuclear tests to a multilateral undertaking, acceptance of any future changes in NSG guidelines without any say in the NSG, and agreeing to the additional protocols in IAEA embedded in the 123 and other Agreements on issues of enriching and reprocessing as well as other dual use technologies (CPIM Statement on 'NSG Waiver', 2008).

Thus NSG positions conform to the Hyde Act, closing India's options, not promising a continuous supply of fuel or reprocessing facilities and use of dual technologies. As the Left had warned, the Hyde Act would be the binding principle in the Indo-US nuclear agreement, despite repeated and vehement denials by the Congress Party and its spokesmen, including the Prime Minister of India.

The Left's Position on India's foreign policy is similar to what the Congress position itself was in the late 1950s and 1960s under Jawaharlal Nehru when he spoke against military alliances and against the militarization of India's foreign policy. India's policy at that time clearly came out against military blocs, racism and colonialism of all kinds. The Left in India believes that the US which was the epitome of imperialism in those days has not changed its colors. Evidence from the illegal occupation of Iraq point to this. So, the party that has changed its colors is the Congress. The Left believes that in opposing the Nuclear Deal they were representing the true interest of India's people. They withdrew support to the government even though it decreased their own power. Were they correct in doing so? Only history can tell.

REFERENCES

http://cpim.org/

Background Briefing by Administration Officials on U.S.-South Asia Relations, March 25, 2005, at [http://www.state.gov/r/pa/prs/ps/2005/43853.htm]. Ashley Tellis, former senior advisor to the U.S. Ambassador in New Delhi, *India as a New Global Power*, Carnegie Endowment for International Peace, July 2005, at www.carnegieendowment.org/files/ceip_india_startegy_2006.final.pdf

New Framework for the U.S.-India Defense Relationship, June 28, 2005, at http://www.indianembassy.org/press_release/2005/June/31.htm.

David Fulghum, *Indian 'scare', Aviation Week & Space Technology,* Oct. 4, 2004, cited in: CRS Report for the Congress, US-India Bilateral Agreements in 2005, September 2005, [Available at http://www.au.af.mil/au/awc/awcgate/crs/rl33072.pdf]

US Statement on President Bush visit to India February 22, 2006, at: http://www.whitehouse.gov/news/releases/2006/03/20060302-13.html

Faiza Rashid and George Perkovich, *A survey of the Progress in US-India Relations,*(2005) Carnegie Endowment for International Peace, July, at www.carnegieendowment.org /files/ceip_india_startegy_2006.final.pdf

"Joint Statement Between President George W. Bush and Prime Minister Manmohan Singh," *(2005)* July 18, at [http://www.state.gov/p/sa/rls/pr/2005/49763.htm].

New Framework for the US-India Defense Relationship, *(2005)* June 28, at [http://www.indianembassy.org/press_release/2005/June/31.htm]. See also Congressional Record Service, Issue Brief IB93097, and India-U.S.

Henry J. Hyde US-India Peaceful Atomic Energy Cooperation Act of 2006, Public Law 109-401 (2006).

The Hyde Act, [Section 104g(2) E(i)], available at: http://frwebgate.access.gpo.gov/cgi-bin/getdoc.cgi?dbname=109_cong_reports&docid=f:hr721.109.pdf

The Hyde Act, section 106 and Section 104 (3) (B)

The Hyde Act, [Section 104g (2) K]

The Hyde Act [Section 104c E, F, G]

The Stimson Centre, Washington, available at: www.stimsoncentre.org

Rice insists on Hyde Act for Accord with the NSG, the Hindu, February 15, 2008.

The 123 Agreement, Article 14.1 and 14.2.

123 Agreement, Article 5(2)

"Assured Fuel Supply a Miracle?" *Asian Age*, August 5, 2007.

"123 Agreement is a Gilded Cage," *Asian Age*, August 17, 2007

Seema Mustafa (2007) "Real Cost of Nuclear Energy," *Asian Age,* August 23.

Strobe Talbott in conversation with Shekhar Gupta, *Indian Express*, March 3, 2008.

PBS News Hour, April 5, 2006.

Left Party Statement, June 18, 2008, http://cpim.org/ [accessed on August 24, 2008.]

Left Parties Statement, July 8, 2008, http://cpim.org/ [accessed on August 24, 2008.]

Left Parties Statement on *'Withdrawal of Support to the UPA Government'*, July 9, 2008, http://cpim.org/ [accessed on August 24, 2008.]

Condoleezza Rice quoted in *Financial Express*, (London) August 3, 2007.

Strobe Talbot, in Padma Desai, *Conversations on Russia: Reform from Yeltsin to Putin,* (2006) Oxford University Press, New Delhi, p.180.

CPIM Statement on *'NSG Waiver'* August 23, 2008, http://cpim.org/ [accessed on August 24, 2008.]

V

Provincial Interests and Foreign Policy: Indian Provinces' Responses to the Malaysian and Kenyan Ethnic Crises

*Jabin T Jacob and Vibhanshu Shekhar**

It is now widely accepted that coalition politics in India is here to stay. While national parties, such as the Congress (I) and the Bharatiya Janata Party (BJP), will continue to be at the centre of any coalition for a while, yet other parties, such as the Bahujan Samaj Party (BSP), are beginning to advertise national ambitions by reaching out beyond their traditional provincial bastions; regional parties—parties that are primarily located and have their power bases in particular Indian provinces—will remain agenda-drivers in national governments at the centre. In addition, economic globalization and the processes it has set in motion, have led to growing linkages between provincial and global entities that have provided actors at the subnational level opportunities to involve themselves in global affairs. It is perhaps, natural therefore,

*Jabin T Jacob is a Research Fellow at the Institute of Peace and Conflict Studies (IPCS), New Delhi. He holds a PhD in Chinese Studies from the School of International Studies, Jawaharlal Nehru University and his areas of interest include centre-province and inter-province relations in China and the role and influence of Chinese and Indian provinces in national foreign policymaking. Jabin can be contacted at jabinjacob@gmail.com. Vibhanshu Shekhar is a Research Associate at the School of International Studies, Jawaharlal Nehru University. He completed his PhD in Southeast Asian Studies from the same school and focuses on issues of Indian diaspora in Southeast Asia, maritime security, pluralism in Indonesia and India's Look East policy. Vibhanshu can be contacted at vibesjnu@gmail.com. The authors would like to thank N Manoharan for his help in gathering the reactions from Tamil Nadu and his insights on the issue.

to argue that regional parties will also increasingly, seek a say in the nation's foreign policy.

There are several issues where the Indian provinces and regional parties have had foreign policy concerns. Matters of foreign economic policy certainly have a great impact on provincial governments and regional parties, but foreign policy involving political issues has hitherto, largely been of negative impact and consequence. With regard to China, these have included the Chinese support for northeast India's insurgencies until the 1970s, and in recent years, accusations by the provincial government in Arunachal Pradesh of continuing Chinese incursions along the Line of Actual Control (LAC). With respect to Pakistan, these have included support to the so-called liberation struggles in Punjab and Kashmir, while Bangladesh has been accused by successive Assamese governments of failing to stop illegal immigration into India. In the south, the links of several Tamil parties with and their support for the Tamil struggle against Sinhala domination in Sri Lanka are well known.

This chapter aims to demonstrate the continuing potential of India's subnational units to play a significant role in influencing the courses of the nation's foreign policy. Two recent events in India's neighbourhood are used as case studies in this regard. The first is that of the ethnic Indian agitation in Malaysia that began in November 2007 and the second is that of the violence in Kenya following its presidential elections a month later in December, affected the economically-strong Indian community there as well. In the first instance, the unrest was largely dominated by the Tamil community and has particular resonance in the province of Tamil Nadu, while in the second, the Indians affected were largely traders of Gujarati-origin. Both instances saw calls by the respective provincial governments for the central government in New Delhi to take more proactive action. Both the events are profiled in greater detail below and the reactions to them in India—specifically from Tamil Nadu and Gujarat—are examined.

An attempt is made to examine the nature of the provinces' responses to these crises and the extent to which the provincial governments were able to force the central government to take particular initiatives or modify its course of action. With the exception of the Sri Lankan Tamil problem such ethnic crises across Indian borders rarely created a ripple either nationally or in the concerned province. While the conditions of the Tamil diaspora in Malaysia and of the Gujarati diaspora in Kenya are substantially different, the economic advantages to be accrued to the respective province are also different and may in fact, be of little practical significance. We argue that provincial interests in both Tamil Nadu and Gujarat could not keep silent while their ethnic brethren were in distress, owing not just to the increasing contacts with the diaspora, but also because it was either politically necessary (for the Tamil Nadu government) or expedient (for the Gujarat government) to raise the matter before New Delhi. Thus, we argue that provincial governments can view foreign policy choices differently from the central government. However, far from this always leading to a conflict of interest with the centre, we point out that provincial governments, understand that they do not operate in a zero-sum environment vis-à-vis the central government or the target host country of the ethnic disapora. This means that provincial governments can be expected to temper their views and actions. This latter fact is in evidence especially in the case of the Tamil Nadu government's response to the Malaysian crisis. These issues of provincial government interventions in foreign policy matters that essentially fall within the ken of the central government and the implications thereof are examined in greater detail below.

ETHNIC INDIAN PROTESTS IN MALAYSIA

Native Malays constitute just over half of Malaysia's population of 25 million at about 54 per cent with ethnic Chinese forming the second largest group at 31 per cent and ethnic Indians coming in next at some 7 per cent (Karim, 2008). The Chinese dominate the economy while the Malays under the government's affirmative action Bumiputra or "sons of the soil" policy have slowly increased their economic resources in addition to entrenching themselves as undisputed political class of the country. Ethnic Indians, meanwhile, who arrived in the Malay Peninsula under British colonial rule as indentured labour for the rubber plantations, have suffered the consequences of their history, being backward in both economic and other social indicators such as education or health. In addition, since Malaysian independence, they have also suffered from the national government's discriminatory policies, something that they were not as well placed to deal with as the Chinese community.[1] In recent years, the increasing Islamic turn in government policy[2] has also resulted in the demolition of Hindu temples in the name of development, contributing further to the sense of grievance of ethnic Indians who are largely Tamils and Hindu.

Things finally came to a head on 25 November 2007, when the Hindu Rights Action Force (HINDRAF), a group of over 50 Hindu NGOs, led a demonstration of some 10,000 ethnic Indians in Kuala Lumpur demanding the same rights and opportunities as ethnic Malays.[3] The protest and the reactions of the Malaysian government highlighted spectacularly both for India and the rest of the world, the nature of the problems besetting ethnic minorities in Malaysia and in the country's 50th year of independence, no less. However, because of its Tamil-Hindu orientation and the manner in which it chose to go

[1]The better off among Malaysian Indians are second and third-generation Tamils who benefited from local public and private higher education while the crème de la crème of foreign graduates are middle-class Tamils, Tamil Muslims, Jaffna Tamils, Sindhis, Punjabis and Sheiks whose forefathers came voluntarily through community networks, seeking a better life in Malaya (see Karim, 2008).

[2]For example, in July 2007, Malaysian Deputy Prime Minister, Nazib Tun Razak, declared that "Islam is the official religion and Malaysia is an Islamic state" (see Fernandez, 2007).

[3]The protestors had gathered in front of the British High Commission and sought to hand over a petition to the High Commission seeking the support of the British monarch for a US$4 trillion class action suit filed in London in August by HINDRAF for the exploitation of Indians who were brought to Malaysia as indentured labour.

about trying to garner international support from India and by references to the Sri Lanka's separatist Liberation Tigers of Tamil Eelam (LTTE), the HINDRAF won no friends within the Malay-dominated government, inviting strong and forceful action from the Malaysian state.[4]

However, within India, both Tamil regional parties as well as branches of the national parties in the province were quick to express their concern for the events in Malaysia. Tamil Nadu Chief Minister, M. Karunanidhi, of the Dravida Munnetra Kazhagam (DMK), wrote to Prime Minister, Manmohan Singh, to take the necessary measures to end the "sufferings and bad treatment" of Tamils in Malaysia, saying that the people of Tamil Nadu were concerned at the goings on in Kuala Lumpur (Hindu, 2007a). However, matters were complicated when Malaysia's Justice Minister, Nazri Aziz, told the Tamil Nadu Chief Minister to "lay off" saying that the protests in Malaysia "ha[d] got nothing to do with him" (Indian Express, 2007a). This prickled sensitivities in Tamil Nadu further. Karunanidhi was quick to join issue with the Malaysian minister, saying, "It is my duty to defend Tamils" and "if there is any punishment for doing the duty, I am prepared to accept it." Nevertheless, he also made clear that it was not his intention to criticize the Malaysian government (Hindustan Times, 2007).

In the Indian Parliament, proceedings were disrupted in the Lok Sabha with members of Parliament (MPs) from Tamil Nadu, cutting across party lines, asking the central government to take up the matter of the mistreatment of ethnic Indians and of the statement against Karunanidhi with Kuala Lumpur (Indian Express, 2007b). Rajya

[4]The Malaysian government accused the HINDRAF of having links with the LTTE, arresting several of its activists and charging many with sedition. HINDRAF's agitation was also denounced by Malaysia's Work Minister, S Samy Vellu, president of the Malaya Indian Congress (MIC), the main political party representing ethnic Indians and a member of the ruling Barisan Nasional (BN) coalition running the Malaysian government (Singh, 2007). Samy Velu, who was invited by New Delhi to the following year's Pravasi Bharatiya Divas – where he was blamed by expatriate Indians in Malaysia who were present – would later go on to lose his seat in the general elections. Indeed, the BN's heavy loss in the elections could in part be attributed to the HINDRAF agitation and the subsequent roiling of ethnic tensions (Singh, 2008; Sinha, 2008).

Sabha MP from the DMK, R Shunmugasundaram questioned the Malaysian minister's right to comment on a letter sent by a Chief Minister to the Prime Minister, "we cannot lose our self-respect to continue to have friendly relations with another country" (Hindu, 2007b). Tiruchi Siva, another DMK member in the Rajya Sabha pointed out that Malaysia's ethnic Indians' had been engaged in a peaceful demonstration with portraits of Mahatma Gandhi, but the police had used tear gas and water canons to crush them (Merinews, 2007). Some MPs even raised slogans against Malaysia, demanding a statement from the Indian External Affairs Minister (EAM) and forcing the Lok Sabha to be adjourned briefly (Telegraph, 2007). Meanwhile, the Hindu nationalist BJP, the main national opposition party, was also quick to point out the religious angle to ethnic Indian grievances in Malaysia, highlighting the destruction of temples there (Indian Express, 2007b).

The EAM, Pranab Mukherjee, in *suo motu* statements made in both houses of Parliament, noted that the Indian government "remains deeply solicitous for the welfare of people of Indian origin living abroad," noting however, that India had "friendly relations" with Malaysia. He also noted that "[c]ertain observations" had been made against the Tamil Nadu Chief Minister and that the matter was being taken up (Ministry of External Affairs, 2007a, 2007b).

Other Reactions from Tamil Nadu

The All India Anna Dravida Munnetra Kazhagam (AIADMK) and the Congress (I) in Tamil Nadu were also quick to urge the centre to intervene in the issue (Hindu, 2007c; Tamil Eelam News Services, 2007). Former Tamil Nadu Chief Minister, J Jayalalithaa of the AIADMK calling for the release of those arrested declared, "it was saddening to know that the plight of several Malaysian Tamils remained what it was in respect of their ancestors" (Hindu, 2007c). "Tamils in Malaysia had been treated like third class citizens despite their help in boosting the Malaysian economy," she said (Sri Lanka Guardian, 2007). Rajya Sabha MP, V Narayanasamy of the Congress

(I), lamented that ethnic Indians who were demanding rights equal to those enjoyed by Malays were "jailed for no fault of theirs when they were agitating peacefully." This he said, when Malaysia had given such rights to ethnic Chinese (Merinews, 2007). Another Tamil Nadu politician and popular actor Vijayakant, alleged that Malaysia was "becoming a Sri Lanka" where the government "sidelined Tamils from all government departments" (quoted in Malaysiakini, 2007).

The Dravidar Kazhagam—the original Dravidian party—too, criticized the Malaysian Justice Minister for criticizing Karunanidhi, saying that the latter had only expressed his anguish over the attack on the Tamils in Malaysia, and that his views were shared by other parties in Parliament. It too wanted the Prime Minister to take steps to ensure the right to livelihood of the Tamils in Malaysia (Hindu, 2007d).

Marumalarchi Dravida Munnetra Kazhagam (MDMK) general secretary, V Gopalasamy (Vaiko), was among the first to react to the Tamil protests in Malaysia, writing to the Prime Minister, to take urgent steps through diplomatic channels to protect ethnic Indians in Malaysia. He noted, "More than 90 per cent of ethnic Indians in Malaysia are Tamils. They have contributed to bring economic prosperity in Malaysia, shedding their sweat of labour all these years. But they have been discriminated in education, jobs and business opportunities by Malaysian authorities." He also said that the Malaysian action against the peaceful rally was "disturbing and causes apprehension" about the future safety and welfare of the community of ethnic Indians in Malaysia (Times of India, 2007a). MDMK Lok Sabha member, C Krishnan, urged the Indian government "to take immediate steps" saying the ethnic Tamils in Malaysia were "treated as underprivileged and slaves" and that "Hindu temples have been destroyed" (Lok Sabha, 2007).

The Pattali Makkal Katchi (PMK) in a resolution condemned the "brutal" attack on Malaysian Tamils. It refused to accept the Malaysian government's position that no one should interfere in its internal affairs, calling upon the central government to press the Malaysian government to stop attacks on ethnic Tamils and to ensure equality for them in education and job opportunities. The party noted that the Tamil diaspora were denied fundamental rights and treated as secondary citizens across the world. The discrimination and oppression of Tamils in Malaysia was the result of New Delhi's and the global community's silence over the continuing human rights violations in Sri Lanka (OneIndia, 2007).

Rajya Sabha MP from the Communist Party of India (CPI), D Raja, expressed his party's "concern over the condition of Indian-origin Tamils in Malaysia," who he said were "subjected to repression and discrimination" and who were "fighting for equality with other sections of Malaysian people" (Telegraph, 2007). He pointed out that "They have become Malaysian citizens but do not enjoy equal rights and their human rights have been violated. The government should take it up in an appropriate manner" (Merinews, 2007).

KENYA'S GUJARATIS IN DISTRESS

According to the report of the High Level Committee on Indian Diaspora, the total number of ethnic Indians living in Kenya—also known simply as 'Asians'—is roughly 100,000, out of which, Persons of Indian Origin (PIOs) account for 85,000 and non-resident Indians (NRIs) number approximately 15,000 (Ministry of External Affairs, 2001). In the late 1960s, it has to be remembered, hundreds of Kenyans of Indian origin fled the country to the UK, from laws which targeted Indians with British passports, preventing them from holding gainful employment (High Commission of India, Nairobi, 2008). Many have been there for four generations, but remained politically powerless, and there is still pressure in some quarters to expel them from the country altogether (BBC News, 2008). The 50,000-strong Gujarati community makes up the largest segment of the Indian diaspora in Kenya dominating economic activities in a country where more than 60 per cent of native population live on less than a dollar per day.[5]

[5]The majority of Indians of Gujarati-origin are to be found in Nairobi and Kisumu. Ethnic Indians are also settled in the cities of Mombasa, Nakuru and Eldoret.

Other ethnic Indian communities living in Kenya include the Sikhs, Marathis, Bengalis, and Malayalees.

During the first week of January 2008, Kenya saw more than 1,000 people killed and some 250,000 people displaced (UN News Centre, 2008) in the violence that occurred in the aftermath of the presidential election results, which re-elected the incumbent President and the leader of the Party of National Unity (PNU), Mwai Kibaki. The opposition leader of the Orange Democratic Movement (ODM), Raila Odinga, refused to accept the poll verdict and accused the winning candidate of resorting to large-scale rigging during the counting phase of the presidential election. Immediately after the results were announced, the supporters of Odinga, belonging to Luo community, came onto the streets in Kisumu, the third largest city in Kenya and having a sizeable Gujarati population, and started torching and looting shops and houses.[6] The violence soon acquired an ethnic dimension, in which ethnic groups supporting the candidature of Odinga, began targeting people and businesses belonging to the ethnic groups supporting the incumbent President Kibaki.[7] The inter-ethnic violence was much more pronounced in the areas of the Rift Valley, Eldoret, Kisumu and Nairobi, where mainly the Kikuyus were targeted. The conflict also had an economic dimension and became widespread in these areas where the members of poorer Luo community were present in large numbers. The Kikuyus are the landowners and are considered

[6]The Kikuyus are the largest ethnic group in Kenya constituting approximately 22 per cent of Kenya's population and the Luos are the third largest ethnic group in Kenya representing some 13 per cent. While the Luos are dominant in the central highlands, such as the Rift Valley, Kisumu, and Eldereto, the Kikuyus are a much more widespread community. The Kikuyus are an economically well-off and landowning community, while the Luos are largely poor and landless peasants and workers. The incumbent President, Kibaki belongs to the Kikuyu community, while the opposition leader, Raila Odinga is a Luo.

[7]The popular support to the Party of National Unity comes from the Kikuyu, Embu, and Meru communities. The key ethnic groups supporting the Orange Democratic Movement are the Luo, Luyha and Kalenjin.

as outsiders.[8] In other words, the political violence was based on a larger social and economic platform—the landless and poor Luo natives versus the rich, landowning Kikuyu migrants. The violence continued at different levels till both the sides agreed to a compromise formula, mediated by the former UN Secretary General, Kofi Annan. Raila Odinga became the Prime Minister with several party members acquiring ministerial posts.

Ethnic Indians do not seem to have been direct targets of the Luo rampage, as evident from no reported killings or injuries inflicted upon any of them. The Indian Ministry of External Affairs released an official briefing in January 2008, based on the report of the Indian High Commission in Kenya, that "this violence (in Kenya) is not targeting the Asian community broadly speaking or persons of Indian origin specifically speaking." The briefing further emphasized that "no person of Indian origin was being subjected to any violence or being physically harmed" (Ministry of External Affairs, 2008a). However, the Gujarati community in particular, suffered severe economic losses as their properties, businesses and houses were torched and looted. Ethnic Indians living in the city of Kisumu, where the violence first erupted, became the first targets of the Luo rampage, which soon embroiled Indians living in other cities and provinces, such as Nairobi. Indians had to flee to safer areas and take shelter in places like temples. The Deputy High Commissioner of Indian in Kenya reportedly admitted that the majority of Indians living in Kisumu had fled either to Nairobi or Uganda (Times of India, 2008a). According to one estimate, the total loss incurred by ethnic Indians during the violence is more than Rs. 5 billion or one billion Kenyan Shillings and more than three-fourths of Indian businesses suffered some kind of damage (Times of India, 2008b).

[8]A majority of the landholding in the Rift Valley belong to the Kikuyus, who bought these in the 1960s and 1970s, whereas, the native population of the Valley, the Kalenjins remained deprived of their land rights (For details, see Vasudevan, 2008: 25).

Two factors can be identified, which seem to have triggered attacks on the Indian properties, houses and businesses. First, the pro-establishment approach of ethnic Indians and recent financial scandals involving two ethnic Indians in particular. Moreover, there have been strong economic links between the Gujaratis and the Kikuyus, who form the main Kenyan business community (Oonk , 2006: 260; Lal, 2008). This economic nature of the relationship prompted Odinga supporters to attack Indian properties as well. Moreover, an ethnic Indian reportedly connived with the former President Daniel Arap Moi and members of the Kibaki government to export fake gold jewellery (Rediff News, 2008). Ethnic Indians, especially Gujaratis, reportedly also offered financial help to the KNU to manage their electoral expenses (NDTV News, 2008a). A second reason relates to the dominant role that ethnic Indians play in the Kenyan economy, even though they constitute a very miniscule proportion of the national population. Ethnic Indians, representing just 0.25 per cent of population, control 30-35 per cent of national economy, a situation resented by large number of native Kenyans (High Commission of India, Nairobi, 2008). The post-electoral chaos thus provided an opportunity to the economically marginalized communities to launch attacks against the economically dominant Indian community.

Responses of the Gujarat Government to the Kenyan Crisis

It has to be remembered that Gujarati diaspora settled in different parts of the world are known to have played a key role in the development of Gujarat and supporting the provincial government led by the BJP's Narendra Modi. The provincial governments of Gujarat, at regular intervals, have enacted different laws in order to ensure the sustained participation of the Gujarati diaspora in the development of the province. One such example is the creation of Non-Resident Gujarati Foundation (NRG) in 1998. In the World Gujarat meeting held in January 1999, Gujaratis living in the Eastern African countries also took part in the meeting (Sahoo, 2006: 93-96). Moreover, one of the important sources of funding for the BJP and its radical affiliates, such as Vishwa Hindu Parishad (VHP) has come from the Indian-Americans (Biswas, 2005: 56). The BJP received large-scale private donations through various 'charities,' organized in the US, which "have been highly significant in the funding of the recent state-supported massacre of Muslims in Gujarat."[9]

It was perhaps, not surprising that immediately after the outbreak of the violence in Kenya and the damage inflicted upon the Indian community, the provincial government of Gujarat called upon the central government to "ensure the safety and security of ethnic Indians" in Kenya. The Gujarat government used different mechanisms and platforms to express its concern for Gujaratis in Kenya. The provincial government communicated not only with the Indian Prime Minister, but also with the Gujarati Diaspora and with other Indians while interacting at the Pravasi Bharatiya Divas—the Indian central government-organized annual gathering for PIOs and NRIs—held in January 2008 in New Delhi. In his first letter to the Prime Minister, released on 31 December 2007, the Chief Minister of Gujarat, Narendra Modi, wrote,

> I request the Indian Government to immediately beef up security for our Indian brothers in Kenya. Indian youth in Kenya who want to return should be brought back, and if required through the sea route or they should be taken to Nairobi and arrangements made for their stay there. Since their houses have been burnt, missing documents must be overlooked and they should be allowed to move to safer areas without any hitch, keeping in mind their Indian blood (Times of India, 2008c).

[9]One such organization is the US-based India Development and Relief Fund, which has reportedly been funding the Hindutva movement in India and in Gujarat, in particular. See the report titled "The Foreign Exchange of Hate: IDRF and the American Funding of Hindutva" (Sabrang Communications Private Limited, Mumbai and the South Asia Citizens Web, France, 2002). See also Nussbaum, 2003: 21.

Further he claimed that, "The state government has information that people of Gujarati origin have suffered heavy losses to their property due to the violence" and that the central government ought to "issue emergency visas to people who want to temporarily return to India and make all arrangements for their safe home coming" (Indian Express, 2008a) Modi also criticized New Delhi for not providing information about the safety of Gujaratis living in Kenya to their relatives in India, saying, "Gujaratis are the main target of attack in the post-poll rioting and violence in Kenya. Their relatives in Gujarat are obviously concerned about their wellbeing. Yet, it is unfortunate that they are unable to know how things are in Kenya" (Times of India, 2008d).

Addressing the concerns of the Gujarat government, two concerned ministries immediately released press statements declaring that "all ethnic Indians are safe," and "ethnic Indians have not been targeted specifically during the riots." These statements were issued by the Minister of Overseas Indian Affairs, Vayalar Ravi and the Minister of State for External Affairs, Anand Sharma (Ministry of External Affairs, 2008a; Times of India, 2008e). Responding to the Gujarat government's letter, the Prime Minister assured that "the Government of India is closely monitoring the situation in Kenya, and is also in touch with the Kenyan authorities to ensure that the people of Indian origin are provided adequate safety" (Hindu, 2008).

In contrast to the proactive, even confrontational, response of the Gujarat government, the provincial leadership of the Congress (I) remained somewhat quiet on the issue and seemed to have followed the position of the central government. The only statement released by the Congress party came from the central leadership, when Jayanti Natarajan raised the issue of safety and security of ethnic Indians in Kenya. She said that the party viewed the situation in Kenya "with great concern" but that "it is purely an internal matter of Kenya. We call upon the government to take steps to protect the lives of the people of Indian origin in Kenya" (NDTV News, 2008b). The issue was also raised in the Lok Sabha, by MPs, representing different political parties and different parts of the country (Lok Sabha, 2008).

PROVINCES, THE CENTRE AND FOREIGN POLICY

During the 2008 Pravasi Bharatiya Divas, the EAM, Pranab Mukherjee, commended Indian provinces that organized meets with their respective diasporas noting that this would ensure "significant engagement in the States' development." He also pointed out to the diaspora that it was "critical ... to engage with States as State Governments directly interact with the people and influence policies at the grassroots" (Ministry of External Affairs, 2008b). In a sense, Mukherjee is trying to overturn the history of negative impact that shared ethnicity has usually resulted in, whether in the case of Tamil Nadu and Sri Lanka or cross-border ties between several of India's northeastern provinces and parts of Myanmar. However, there is a flipside to such efforts in the form of increased pressure on the central government from provincial governments concerned about the fate of ethnic Indians in foreign lands. Still the fact that the Minister chose to stress the continuing importance of the role of provincial governments in India's reaching out to the outside world indicates that New Delhi believes the advantages of this process outweigh the disadvantages.

The implications of such a policy are far-reaching as showcased by the cases of Malaysia and Kenya. With a global economic output estimated at some US$400 billion, the 30-million strong Indian diaspora has emerged not only as a powerful economic community globally, but also as a potential source of resource-generation for development back in the mother country (Sify News, 2007). The diaspora is an important economic player in India in three important sectors – investments, foreign remittances and philanthropic activities. While hitherto, it is the central government that has been chiefly involved in repositioning the Indian diaspora as a "strategic resource of the Indian state," (Mani and Varadarajan, 2005: 53) and in taking various policy initiatives, such as providing fiscal concessions and tax exemptions, to the diaspora to invest in India, New Delhi can be politically constrained by the need not to overreach in order to respect the sensibilities of host foreign governments. Indian provinces are therefore, increasingly stepping into this space to engage with the Indian diaspora using ethnic and cultural linkages, and providing their own economic incentives. Several provincial governments have been especially active in soliciting funds and investments from their respective ethnic diasporas, particularly in the United States and, in the case of Kerala, also from NRIs in the Gulf Cooperation Council (GCC) countries in West Asia.

As a result, there is a new emerging dynamic involving the provincial governments, the central government and the Indian diaspora. Though the central government remains the principal actor in formulating policies towards the Indian diaspora and countries hosting them, its actions and decisions could increasingly be informed by the demands and interests of provincial actors. This is only one side of the picture. The other, as the case of the Malaysian reaction against Karunanidhi's statement shows, is that foreign governments can take offense even if it is a provincial Indian government that is involved. New Delhi, therefore, seems to be entering uncharted territory as provincial governments go global, they will simultaneously need to be informed about the rules of political interaction with foreign governments. However, will the provinces play ball if they are not given a commensurate say in foreign policymaking at the centre? And why in an era of coalition politics, where even the smallest constituent can bring a government down, would they have the incentive to 'behave responsibly' or impose costs on themselves? Things are further complicated when the governing dispensations at the centre and the province are in opposing political camps as in the case of the Gujarat government.[10]

[10]In the case of the Tamil protests in Malaysia, it must be noted that the BJP also emphasized the destruction of temples in Malaysia while Janata Party president, Subramaniam Swamy, pointed out that, "It's not a Tamil issue. The Tamil Muslims are not participating in the agitation." The latter went on to accuse Karunanidhi of being imprudent in making such a huge issue out of the subject (Merinews, 2007). These statements invited adverse reactions from *The Milli Gazette*, a prominent English-language fortnightly that addresses itself specifically to Indian Muslims in an article titled, "Let's not export saffron mischief to Malaysia!" (Iyangar, 2008).

First, are provincial governments interested in foreign policy? It is still too early to reach a definitive answer to this question, but in general, the statements by the Tamil Nadu and Gujarat provincial governments show that Chennai and Gandhinagar—the capitals of the two states respectively—were not hesitant to take up issues that were essentially the domain of the central government. Both provincial governments called upon New Delhi to take up matters with the Malaysian and Kenyan governments respectively, and to ensure the security of ethnic, Indians in those countries, making no distinction between PIOs and NRIs.[11] The Gujarat Chief Minister went so far as to tell the Indian High Commission on Nairobi that it be more lenient, while verifying legal documents of ethnic Indians on the ground that most of their documents might have been destroyed along with their houses (Indian Express, 2008b).[12] At the Pravasi Bharatiya Divas, Modi was bold enough to suggest that the central government ought to develop a specific policy framework, which could address the basic problems of ethnic Indians living in different parts of the world.

Differences might be perceived in the reactions of the Tamil Nadu and Gujarat provincial governments to the respective ethnic crises. A major part of the reason why the ruling DMK in Tamil Nadu could not adopt a more strident tone is perhaps because it was also part of the ruling United Progressive Alliance (UPA) coalition at the centre and could not go out of its way to embarrass New Delhi. It is also possible that the DMK, quickly realizing that there was very little it could or wanted to do under the circumstances, was ready to take the centre at its word that something was being done about the situation. In this context, it is likely that the Malaysian minister's rather harsh remarks against Karunanidhi also allowed the Tamil parties to concentrate on

[11] The High Level Committee on Indian Diaspora, in its report defines the Persons of Indian Origin (PIOs) as "foreign citizens of Indian origin or descent," and the Non-Resident Indians (NRIs) as "Indian citizens, holding Indian passport and residing abroad for an indefinite period, whether for employment, or for carrying on any business or vocation, or for any other purpose" (Ministry of External Affairs, 2001).

[12] Modi also asked that the Yellow Fever vaccine certification procedure be done away with while processing the visa applications of Gujaratis returning to India.

the 'insult' closer home and feel that the regional patriarch had stood up to a foreign government.

The diaspora, meanwhile, is a "strategic resource" not just in economic terms but also politically. As the Indian diaspora in the United States has shown in recent years, the diaspora can lobby to influence and mould policies in their host countries to serve Indian national interests, as well. Hitherto, this lobbying has worked only in a few countries of the West and it is usually the case that these diaspora groups function as 'national' (read 'Indian') groups rather than as ethnic groups. Two important reasons can be put forth. First, while coming from diverse cultural, linguistic and spatial backgrounds within India (Gujaratis, Punjabis, Sindhis, Tamils), ethnocentric majority discourse in the host country stereotype them as a homogenous minority group, meeting out similar treatment of exclusion, whether initial or sustained. This process of stereotyping constantly reminds the immigrant community of their common nationality and binds them together. In other words, the national representation of the minority immigrant 'Indian' community is essentially a response to the majority stereotyping. Second, while responding to majority stereotyping, minority Indian immigrants have found 'Indian' as the largest and most-comprehensive rallying point, which can enhance their numerical representation, and which is least likely to be subjected to divisive parochial loyalties based on language, region, or religion (Baumann, 2001: 59; Mani and Varadarajan, 2005: 45-74; Sahoo, 2006: 89-90; Biswas, 2005: 43-67). However, there is also a 'provincialism' among diasporas, that can be 'anti-national' in character as in the case of the Sri Lankan Tamils whose diaspora in Western Europe forms the major resource base for the separatist LTTE and the Sikh communities in the United States and Canada who still support the cause of Khalistan.

Back home, as the Tamil Nadu and Gujarat governments showed, instances of diaspora distress in foreign countries can be used to score political points among domestic audiences. Provincial governments and interests could use ethnic linkages across borders to pressurize the central government to make concessions or to adopt certain policies that favour provincial interests. This was most notably what happened in the case of the Tamil problem in Sri Lanka where the central government was also under pressure by the provincial government in Chennai to intervene on the side of the Sri Lankan Tamils.[13]

Many might argue here, that to prevent things from getting out of hand, the central government should continue to maintain sole control over foreign policy and prevent slippage and provincial ingress in such a vital area. We therefore, ask a second question—what incentives do provincial governments have to play by the rules and behave responsibly in such situations? The incentive, we argue, lies in the nature and scale of economic interactions between the provincial government in question and the host country of the particular ethnic diaspora. In the case of Tamil Nadu, for example, the AIADMK, the other major Tamil regional party, which had none of the political compulsions of the DMK vis-à-vis the centre, was also seen to be largely measured in its reactions and not as critical of the central government as it might have been. That this has been so suggests other factors at work here that have forced the two main Tamil parties to restrain themselves and not adopt the policies and tactics they did with respect to the Tamil issue in Sri Lanka. Apart from the fact that the scale of the two ethnic Tamil problems and the level of violence employed are different, there seems to be an economic component to the whole issue that needs to be considered.

[13]For more on the nature of India's Sri Lanka policy and the influence of Tamil Nadu on this policy, see Mayilvaganan, 2007: 943-64. Mayilvaganan points out that while following the Rajiv Gandhi assassination, Tamil Nadu's main political formations have distanced themselves from the Sri Lankan issue and the LTTE, depending on the goings-on in Sri Lanka, sympathy for the Tamils there has often resurfaced and major political leaders in the province have continued to make pronouncements on their plight. He also suggests that New Delhi has in recent years, approached the issue of Sri Lankan Tamils in a "cautious" manner, adopting a policy of consulting and sharing its concerns with the provincial government. Indeed, according to Mayilvagnan, the ruling DMK has wielded a strong influence on the coalition government at the centre, of which it is a part, where foreign policy decisions on Sri Lanka are involved.

Both the DMK and AIADMK have at various times pushed the necessity of developing closer economic linkages with Malaysia as a way to ensure Tamil Nadu's economic growth and development. For example, in 2003, then Chief Minister, Jayalalithaa, called for strengthening of trade and investment ties between Tamil Nadu and Malaysia, pointing out specifically that Tamil Nadu's software industry could complement Malaysia's hardware manufacturing sector and how her province sought Malaysia's expertise in infrastructure development and in the tourism sector (Hindu, 2003). Similarly, in a meeting organized in Chennai on 30 November 2007—*after* the protests in Kuala Lumpur had broken out—by the Confederation of Indian Industries, the Malaysian government solicited investment in its economy highlighting areas such as the automotive sector, machinery and equipment, construction, information technology and biotechnology. In Chennai itself, Malaysian companies are currently involved in the development of infrastructure and property projects such as the US$34 million IT Expressway, the US$67.6 million Chennai Water Supply Augmentation Project, and the 18.8km Chennai bypass, valued at US$19.9 million besides the US$72.7 million Ulundurpet-Padalur BOT Road Project in the province, (Ministry of International Trade and Industry, Government of Malaysia, 2007) reflecting the progress made on Jayalalithaa's call. These factors could conceivably have tempered the reactions of the major Tamil political parties. In sharp contrast to the case of Tamil Nadu-Sri Lanka relations, where there was and remains little economic interaction of substance, the Tamil Nadu-Malaysia relationship is one that is based on substantive and growing economic and people-to-people contacts.

Subsequent incidents have also shown Tamil Nadu that there are real costs associated with overplaying the ethnic card. For example, in January, the Indian press reported that the Malaysian government had suspended the recruitment of Indian workers, following the agitation by ethnic Tamils. This was however, soon denied by the Malaysian Public Works Minister Samy Velu, during his visit to India, claiming that Indians would be recruited, "when needed," and that they were "welcome" (Chaudhury and Patranobis, 2008)[14] India and Malaysia also soon finalized a draft labour agreement on the recruitment and welfare of each other's workers (Suryanarayana, 2008a) and the Malaysian Home Minister, Mohd Radzi Sheikh Ahmad, too denied that there was any move to freeze the recruitment of Indian workers (Hindu, 2008b; Suryanarayana, 2008b). However, in late May, there was fresh concern in India when it was reported that the Malaysian government had withdrawn the visa on arrival (VoA) facility for Indians. The new Malaysian Home Minister, Syed Hamid Albar, declared that Indians would require a two-week social pass and a return ticket if they wished to visit Malaysia, a move that Kuala Lumpur said was aimed at curbing illegal immigration (Times of India, 2008f). However, even this move was reversed within the week as Malaysia's Human Resources Minister, S Subramaniam, declared that his government would continue with the VoA facility for Indians (Economic Times, 2008).[15] With its heavy reliance on workers from India and a large tourist influx from India, it has been argued that these moves by the Malaysian government might have been self-defeating (See for example, Hindustan Times, 2008) but it goes on to prove how sensitive foreign governments—particularly those where race relations remain fraught as is the case in Malaysia[16]—can be to real or perceived

[14]Malaysia hosts about 2.1 million workers from 11 "source countries," including India, and Indians comprise about 8 per cent of the two million foreign workers in the country, constituting the third largest foreign work force. While most Indians work in low-paying jobs, some hold top professional posts in banks and information technology industries and most foreign-qualified Malaysian doctors happen to be ethnic Indians. Similarly, the richest Malaysian, Ananda Krishnan, is an ethnic Tamil. See also Hindustan Times, 2008; Iyangar, 2008.

[15]The Minister also denied media reports that Tamil programmes from India would not be aired by the local RTM channel, saying that the Malaysian Broadcasting Department never had plans to discontinue airing local and foreign Tamil dramas.

[16]It is interesting to note that during the controversy over Karunanidhi's remarks, the Malaysian Parliamentary Secretary in the Foreign Ministry, Ahmad Shabery Cheek, pointed out that Indians in Malaysia were better off than those in India, if the United

threats, especially from a growing economic and political power like India. While this is a larger issue for New Delhi to consider, the Tamil Nadu provincial government could not have been oblivious to the fact that the immediate impact of the Malaysian moves, had they not been eventually reversed, would have been on its own citizens who form a major component of Indian workers in Malaysia. There are for example, some 5,000 temple priests from the Indian province who work in Malaysia (Suryanarayana, 2008a) and who would have been affected by the new labour and visa regulations.[17] Thus, it might be argued that encouraging closer links between Tamil Nadu and Malaysia and giving the provincial government greater freedom in interactions and dealings with the foreign government can also guarantee responsible behaviour besides providing another string to India's foreign policy bow.

In the case of Kenya, two issues seem to have factored prominently in the quick response of the Modi government. First, the Gujaratis in Kenya actually represented a segment of the entire overseas Gujaratis, who have developed greater transnational linkages due to the process of globalization. As has been mentioned earlier that the overseas Gujaratis have played an important role not only in the development of the provincial economy but also been an important source for the funding

Nations' Millennium Development Goals were used as the benchmark. In his reply in Parliament to opposition leader, Lim Kit Siang, who raised the issue of Karunanidhi's concerns, he stated, "We have many Indian workers here, and their presence is a testimony that the situation in Malaysia is far better than [that] in India." (Hindu, 2007d). Indeed, Malaysian Indians are not unaware of the often despicable conditions of their ethnic brethren in Tamil Nadu, while Malaysian Tamils of Sri Lankan origin are keenly conscious of the plight of people in the so-called Tamil Eelam. Also it is important to note, as was stated earlier, that the HINDRAF protestors were appealing not to India but to the British monarch to take their side. Further, following the protests, many Malaysian Indians were considering migration to Australia rather than India (Times of India, 2007b).

[17]While the former Malaysian Home Minister said there was no intention to reduce the renewal period of work visas for temple priests from India, he indicated the government's preference for Malaysian Hindus in any recruitment of temple priests. Further, work visas for temple priests are treated differently from those for other categories of workers (Hindu, 2008b).

of the BJP, the provincial government's inaction would have given an impression that it has not been able to protect/represent the interests of the overseas Gujaratis. Second, the Gujaratis living in Kenya formed a part of the bigger kin-based network, which has been very influential in the Western world. Many of the Gujaratis living in the developed world of the North America and Western Europe are, what is known as 'twice banished' or 'double displaced' people, who had migrated from countries like Fiji, the Caribbeans, Eastern Africa to the developed world. A large number of the Kenyan Gujaratis had migrated to the United Kingdom in the aftermath of repressive policies in Uganda and Kenya during 1960s. Moreover, some of the Gujaratis living in Kenya have also been acting as frequent returnees in the case of any possible ethnic tensions or political instability in the host country. As a result, there has developed a strong kin-based network connecting the Kenyan Gujaratis, British Gujaratis and Gujaratis living in India (Khadria, 2007: 104-06). The inaction on the part of the Modi government can distance the overseas community from the party and curtail the foreign funding for the functioning of the party, a possibility which the BJP can not afford to choose. Therefore, it seems a rather natural choice on part of the Modi government to raise the issue of the Kenyan crisis at every possible forum, such as with the central government, and the Pravasi Bharatiya Diwas meetings.

A third question can be asked at this stage: is there a case for the Indian central and provincial governments taking a political route to dealing with the diaspora? HINDRAF leader P Waythamoorthy's statement that the ethnic Tamil problem in Malaysia could potentially result in another Sri Lanka-like situation (Menon, 2007) and his meeting with Tamil political leaders no doubt reflected hopes for specific support from Tamil Nadu. However, it is unlikely that any political dispensation in Chennai can today pursue a policy akin to the one followed with respect to the Lankan Tamils until the Rajiv Gandhi assassination. Then, it was a case of the Indian central government seeking to address sentiments in Tamil Nadu over the treatment of Sri Lankan Tamils (Mayilvaganan, 2007: 946) or perhaps of riding piggyback on ethnic Tamil feelings to intervene in Sri Lanka's affairs. Today, the times have changed and while the motivations continue to exist, the machinations of the past have been discredited and proven to be of no lasting good to anyone involved. However, this and other risks still exist and may be exemplified by the case of the Gujaratis in Kenya. Given perceptions in Kenya that the Indian community was taking sides in Kenya's political competition, there could have been negative consequences for India-Kenya relations had, for example, the Luo candidate come to power. That this situation could still come to pass, should be a matter of concern for both Gandhinagar and New Delhi. It is therefore, imperative that the centre and the provinces work together to formulate a policy of interaction and engagement with ethnic Indian diasporas the world over, in a manner that potential political flashpoints are identified and dealt with preemptively. At the very least, New Delhi will need to watch closely the activities of PIOs and NRIs in foreign lands and as well as those of its provincial governments in their international dealings for consequences to India's overall national interests.

A final question that arises is of what New Delhi and the provincial governments could offer host countries to encourage them to treat the Indian diaspora with respect, consideration and equality. The issue becomes all the more sensitive when the ethnic Indians are actually citizens of the countries involved rather than Indian citizens. A *Hindustan Times* editorial offered one possible answer in the case of Malaysia, "The West has always been wary of Malaysia on several counts, ranging from its growing Islamisation to its lack of democratic rights. In this context, it makes sense to strengthen ties with its Asian counterparts, the biggest of which is India"(Hindustan Times, 2008). Indeed, New Delhi can offer such cooperation, and Tamil Nadu and the Indian diaspora could well function as useful intermediaries. While India has been burned once in its attempt to mediate between the two sides of the conflict in Sri Lanka and to establish the peace there, one must ask if India should not now renew its efforts to this end, this time taking a different tack and involving the provincial government of

Tamil Nadu, in developing closer economic linkages with Sri Lanka under the already very successful India-Sri Lanka FTA.[18]

Meanwhile, as the African continent enters a new phase in its history of being courted by both the United States and China, India could enter the contest not just to promote its own national interests but also to provide Africa an alternative policy of engagement different from either the American or the Chinese, one that would more people- rather than elite-oriented and be based on sustainable economic engagement rather than mercantilist or focused solely on the exploitation of the continent's energy resources. In this context, rather than only draw up plans to welcome back those affected by the violence in Kenya, India must also be making plans to ensure how it might use the leverage produced by generations of PIOs in Kenya and elsewhere in the African continent to ensure both its own interests and as well as those of the African nations themselves.

CONCLUSION

A combination of the success of economic reforms in certain provinces and of coalition politics at the national level underwritten by strong regional parties is beginning to translate into a 'decentralization' of foreign policymaking in various instances. Indian provinces and their leaders are increasingly vocal in their opinions on foreign policy and international affairs and their views are beginning to have an impact on how the centre makes its foreign policy calculations.

The fact that ethnic ties can impact foreign policy is not a new discovery but that these might increasingly be driven not just by central governments but by actors down the line such as provincial

[18]Tamil political parties such as the PMK, a member of the UPA coalition at the centre have while continuing to draw attention to "genocide against Tamils" in Sri Lanka, also called for New Delhi to play an "active and constructive" role in helping end Sri Lanka's ethnic conflict (Nerve News, 2008). It is also interesting to note that in the wake of the failure of the Ceasefire Agreement (CFA) in Sri Lanka, one blogger suggested that Malaysia ought to play a role in getting the Sri Lankan government and the LTTE to talk to each other again (Kula.blogsome.com, 2008).

governments owing to not just political calculations but the latter's growing economic clout is a trend that needs to be acknowledged and examined in greater detail. In the two crises examined in this chapter, can it be said that Chennai or Gandhinagar managed to influence New Delhi in its foreign policy behaviour in any significant way? We argue that the answer is in the affirmative. Whereas in the past, India would often limit its reactions the distress of ethnic Indians to saying that they were citizens of another country, and that it could not interfere in the internal affairs of another country, it was evident in the latest instances that the central government was responding to provincial concerns in a way and for reasons it had not hitherto responded. While the degree of influence exercised by the respective provinces on New Delhi's foreign policy actions, remains a matter of subjective opinion, there is no denying the fact that such influence is on the rise. As regional parties on the one hand, and globalization on the other, gain in strength, the way future international issues involving Indian provinces will pan out is difficult to predict. What is clear is that Indian provinces will have an increasing role to play in the country's foreign policy. It seems quite possible that there will be occasions where provincial interests can make it difficult for New Delhi to conduct foreign policy. However, it is important to remember that not just problems, but solutions too, can be subnational in origin. National governments will, therefore, need to be open to such possibilities to give additional options to their foreign policies. Thus, we argue that India cannot project its power through its foreign policy without taking into consideration the dynamics of domestic politics in the country. Indian foreign policy behavior will be constrained and determined not just by systemic factors but also by domestic determinants.

As the two case studies in this chapter, show, Indian provinces are increasingly laying claim to the "strategic resource" of the Indian diaspora, cognizant of its value and proactive in tapping them, whether for economic or political gains. There is a need to leverage diaspora links to function as a positive factor not just in India's external relations but also to domestic benefit. Unlike in the past, the Indian central government today has more opportunities to channel diaspora and provincial government activity to more positive ends. While continuing to exercise overall supervision of foreign policy, the Indian central government needs to be more open to giving leeway and freedom of action to the provincial governments to engage with foreign national or subnational governments. Moving in the opposite direction by recentralizing powers from the provinces would in the current milieu, be a regressive step. It is necessary for the centre and the provinces to act as partners in the spirit of the Indian federal system not just to achieve provincial and national economic development but also to sustain India's rise on the global stage.

REFERENCES

Adigal, Natteri (2007), "Should TN politicos protest Tamils mistreatment in Malaysia without knowing facts?" Merinews, 2 December, http://www.merinews.com/catFull.jsp?articleID=128216.

Baumann, Martin (2001), "The Hindu Diaspora in Europe and an Analysis of Key Diasporic Patterns," in TS Rukmani (ed.), *Hindu Diaspora: Global Perspective*, New Delhi: Munshiram Manoharlal. pp. 59-79.

BBC News, (2008) "On This Day, 4 February 1968: More Kenyan Asians flee to Britain," 4 February, http://news.bbc.co.uk/onthisday/hi/dates/stories/february/4/newsid_2738000/2738629.stm.

Biswas, Shampa (2005), "Globalization and the Nation Beyond: The Indian-American Diaspora and the Rethinking of Territory, Citizenship and Democracy," *New Political Science*, 27 (1), March: 43-67.

Chaudhury Nilova Roy and Sutirtho Patranobis (2008), "Malaysia denies ban on India, Bangladesh workers," Hindustan Times, 8 January, http://www.hindustantimes.com/StoryPage/StoryPage.aspx?id=5b503ffc-d889-41ad-b485-2ec5f59d19b8&&Headline=Malaysia+denies+ban+on+Indian+ workers.

Economic Times (2008), "Visa-on-arrival for Indian tourists not revoked: Malaysia," 4 June, http://economictimes.indiatimes.com/News/News_By_Industry/Services/Travel/Visa_Power/Visa-on-arrival_for_Indian_tourists_not_revoked_Malaysia_/articleshow/3099976.cms.

Fernandez, Clarence (2007), "Islamic State Label Sparks Controversy in Malaysia," Reuters, 25 July, http://www.reuters.com/article/email/idUSKLR232935.

High Commission of India, Nairobi, Kenya (2008), "Fact Sheet: Kenya,," April, http://www.meaindia.nic.in/foreignrelation/24fr01.pdf.

Hindu (2003), "Chief Minister invites Malaysian investment in infrastructure," 5

December, http://www.tn.gov.in/pressclippings/archives/pc2003/hindu05122003/hindu051203.htm.

Hindu (2007a), "Karunanidhi writes to Manmohan," 28 November, http://www.hindu.com/2007/11/28/stories/2007112858870100.htm.

Hindu (2007b), "Manmohan voices concern over unrest in Malaysia," 1 December, http://www.hinduonnet.com/2007/12/01/stories/2007120155721400.htm.

Hindu (2007c), "Plea to Centre on Malaysian Tamils issue," 29 November, http://www.hindu.com/2007/11/29/stories/2007112963650700.htm.

Hindu (2007d), "'I did not criticise Malaysian Government'," 30 November, http://www.hindu.com/2007/11/30/stories/2007113060460100.htm.

Hindu (2007d), "DK criticises Malaysian Minister," 2 December, http://www.hindu.com/2007/12/02/stories/2007120260090500.htm.

Hindu (2008a), "Centre is monitoring Kenya situation: PM," 5 January, http://www.thehindu.com/2008/01/05/stories/2008010551870300.htm.

Hindu (2008b), "India-Malaysia ties in perspective," 12 January, http://www.hindu.com/2008/01/12/stories/2008011256361000.htm.

Hindustan Times (2007), "Karuna joins issue with Malaysia's 'lay off' remarks," 29 November, http://www.hindustantimes.com/storypage/storypage.aspx?id=0e0859d4-737c-4827-8a55-7ec14d7cc965&MatchID1=4617&TeamID1=3&TeamID2=4&MatchType1=1&SeriesID1=1163&PrimaryID=4617&Headline=Karuna+joins+issue+with+Malaysian+minister

Hindustan Times (2008), "Malaise in Malaysia," 9 January, http://www.hindustantimes.com/StoryPage/Print.aspx?Id=87161253-993d-4ee5-9635-6afd2259c43d Iyangar, Sampathkumar (2008), "Let's not export saffron mischief to Malaysia!" Milli Gazette, 1-15 January, http://www.twocircles.net/2008jan08/let_s_not_export_saffron_mischief_malaysia.html.

Indian Express (2007a), "Lay off, Malaysia tells Karunanidhi," 29 November, http://www.expressindia.com/latest-news/Lay-off-Malaysia-tells-Karunanidhi/244820/.

Indian Express (2007b), "LS adjourned over treatment of ethnic Indians in Malaysia," 30 November, http://www.indianexpress.com/story/244968.html.

Indian Express (2008a), "Kenya Crisis: Ensure safety of Gujaratis, Modi to PM," 2 January, http://www.expressindia.com/latest-news/Kenya-Crisis-Ensure-safety-of-Gujaratis-Modi-to-PM/256858/.

Indian Express (2008b), "Indians not Targeted in Kenya: MEA," 2 January, http://www.indianexpress.com/story/257069.html.

Karim, Wazir Jahan (2008), "Indian community in post-colonial Malaysia," *New Straits Times,* 7 January, http://www.nst.com.my/Current_News/NST/Sunday/Columns/20080106093447/Article/index_html.

Khadria, Binod (2007), "Diasporas in Development: from 'Social Parasites' to 'Economic Boon'?" *Asian Population Studies*, 3 (2), July: pp. 103-114.

Kula.blogsome.com (2008), "Malaysia must play a leading role to get Sri Lanka and the

Tamil Tigers to the negotiation table for a permanent peace," 5 January, http://kula.blogsome.com/2008/01/05/malaysia-must-play-a-leading-role-to-get-sri-lanka-and-the-tamil-tigers-to-the-negotiation-table-for-a-permanent-peace/.

Lal, Rashi (2008), "Kenya: People Affected by Violence Indians first, Gujaratis next," Merinews, 6 January, http://www.merinews.com/catFull.jsp?articleID=129090.

Lok Sabha (2007), "Problems being faced by Tamilians in Malaysia," Part II Proceedings other than Questions and Answers, XIV Lok Sabha, http://164.100.24.208/debate14/debtext.asp?slno=9072&ser=Malaysia&smode=t

Lok Sabha (2008), "Attacks on Indians in Kenya," Questions for Oral Answers, Parliament of India, 5 March, http://164.100.24.207/questionslist/MyFolder/05032008.pdf.

Malaysiakini (2007), "Protect Tamils in M'sia, Indian PM told," 28 November, http://www.malaysiakini.com/news/75382.

Mani, Bakirathi, and Latha Varadarajan (2005), "'The Largest Gathering of the Global Indian Family': Neoliberalism, Nationalism and Diaspora at Pravasi Bharatiya Divas," *Diaspora*, 14 (1), 2005: pp. 45-74.

Mayilvaganan, M (2007), "The Re-emergence of the Tamil Nadu Factor in India's Sri Lanka Policy," *Strategic Analysis*, 31 (6): 943-64.

Menon, Jaya (2007), "Malaysia could be another Lanka: Hindraf leader," Indian Express, 1 December, http://www.indianexpress.com/story/245265.html.

Ministry of External Affairs, Government of India (2001), *Report of the High Level Committee on Indian Diaspora*, 19 December, Non Resident Indians & Persons of Indian Origin Division, http://indiandiaspora.nic.in/contents.htm.

Ministry of External Affairs, Government of India (2007a), "Suo Motu Statement by the Minister of External Affairs, Shri Pranab Mukherjee in Rajya Sabha regarding 'HINDRAF Demonstration in Malaysia'," 30 November 2007, http://www.mea.gov.in/pressrelease/2007/11/30pr02.htm.

Ministry of External Affairs, Government of India (2007b), "Suo Motu Statement by the Minister of External Affairs, Shri Pranab Mukherjee in Lok Sabha regarding 'HINDRAF Demonstration in Malaysia'," 30 November 2007, Ministry of External Affairs, Government of India, http://www.mea.gov.in/pressrelease/2007/11/30pr01.htm.

Ministry of External Affairs, Government of India (2008a), "Briefing by Official Spokesperson on the situation in Kenya," Press Briefing, 2 January, http://meaindia.nic.in/pressbriefing/2008/01/02pb01.htm

Ministry of External Affairs, Government of India (2008b), "Address of Shri Pranab Mukherjee, Minister for External Affairs as Chief Guest at the Plenary Session on "Developmental Challenges of the States: Partnership Opportunities" (Plenary IV of Pravasi Bharatiya Divas 2008)," 9 January, http://meaindia.nic.in/speech/2008/01/09ss01.htm.

Ministry of International Trade and Industry, Government of Malaysia (2007), "Seminar on Business Opportunities in Malaysia," 30 November, http://portal.miti.gov.my/cms/genArticlePdf?id=com.tms.cms.article.Article_9c0243b8-c0a81573-aba0aba0-b54a0db6.

NDTV News (2008a), "Kenya Violence: Indians in trouble," 5 January, http://www.ndtv.com/convergence/ndtv/story.aspx?id=NEWEN20080037806.

NDTV News (2008b), "Quote-Unquote," 2 January, http://www.ndtv.com/convergence/ndtv/gentemplate_generic.aspx?template=Indiansabroad.

Nerve News (2008), "PMK wants India to play 'active' role in Sri Lanka," 19 April, http://www.nerve.in/news:253500141570.

Nussbaum, Martha (2003), "Genocide in Gujarat: The International Community Looks Away," *Dissent*, Summer: pp. 15-23.

OneIndia (2007), "PMK seeks Central intervention in Malaysian Tamils issue," 4 December, http://news.oneindia.mobi/2007/12/03/498856.html.

Oonk, Gijsbert (2006), "East Africa," in Brij V. Lal (ed.) *The Encyclopedia of the Indian Diaspora*, Singapore: Didier Millet and National University of Singapore. pp. 254-262.

Rediff News (2008), "We have Lost Money, We will Earn it Back," 3 January, http://www.rediff.com/cms/print.jsp?docpath=/news/2008/jan/03sheela.

Sabrang Communications Private Limited, Mumbai and the South Asia Citizens Web, France (2002), "The Foreign Exchange of Hate: IDRF and the American Funding of Hindutva," November, http://stopfundinghate.org/sacw/downloads/sabrang_sacw.pdf.

Sahoo, Ajay Kumar, (2006), "Issues of Identity in the Indian Diaspora: A Transnational Perspective," *Perspectives on Global Development and Technology*, 5 (1-2): 81-98.

Sify News (2007), "Indian Americans can invest more in India: Vayalar Ravi," 24 September 2007, http://sify.com/finance/fullstory.php?id=14532301.

Singh, Yogendra (2007), "Malaysia's Ethnic Indians Demand 'Politics of Recognition'," IPCS Article No. 2443, 12 December, http://www.ipcs.org/southeastasia_publications2.jsp?action=showView&kValue=2459&country=1016&status=article&mod=a.

Singh, Yogendra (2008), "Malaysian General Elections 2008: A Move Towards Pluralistic Politics," IPCS Article No. 2530, 30 March, http://www.ipcs.org/southeastasia_publications2.jsp?action=showView&kValue=2546&country=1016&status=article&mod=a.

Sinha, Ashish (2008) "Expats blame Indian-origin minister for Malaysia row," *The Economic Times*, 10 January, http://economictimes.indiatimes.com/News/PoliticsNation/Expats_blame_Indian-origin_minister_for_Malaysia_row/articleshow/2688375.cms.

Sri Lanka Guardian (2007), "Former CM Jayalalitha slams attacks on Malay Tamils," 30 November, http://www.srilankaguardian.org/2007/11/former-cm-jayalalitha-slams-attacks-on.html.

Suryanarayana, P S (2008a), "India, Malaysia finalise draft labour pact," 11 January, http://www.hindu.com/2008/01/11/stories/2008011159971200.htm.

Suryanarayana, P S (2008b), "Religion and the politics of Hindraf," 18 January, http://www.hindu.com/2008/01/18/stories/2008011853371100.htm.

Tamil Eelam News Services (2007), "TN urges Action on 'sufferings and bad treatment' of Malaysian Tamils," 30 November, http://www.tamileelamnews.com/news/publish/tns_9031.shtml.

Telegraph (2007), "Malaysian courtesy: Lay off - Karunanidhi's plea on Tamil rights sparks war of words," 30 November, http://www.telegraphindia.com/archives/archive.html.

Times of India (2007a), "Protect ethnic Indians in Malaysia: Vaiko," 27 November, http://timesofindia.indiatimes.com/Protect_ethnic_Indians_in_Malaysia_Vaiko/articleshow/2575764.cms.

Times of India (2007b), "Malaysian Indians ponder migration to Oz after protest," 1 December, http://timesofindia.indiatimes.com/articleshow/2586587.cms.

Times of India (2008a), "Gujaratis Lose Rs 500 Crore in Kenya violence," 6 January, http://timesofindia.indiatimes.com/Gujaratis_lose_Rs_500_crore_in_Kenya_violence/articleshow/2677957.cms.

Times of India (2008b), "Kenya Violence Targets Gujaratis," 2 January, http://timesofindia.indiatimes.com/India/Kenya_violence_targets_Gujaratis/articleshow/2667204.cms.

Times of India (2008c), "Help violence-hit expats in Kenya, Modi urges PM," 2 January, http://timesofindia.indiatimes.com/India/Help_violence-hit_expats_in_Kenya_Modi_urges_PM/articleshow/2669687.cms.

Times of India (2008d), "Modi to PM: Help Indians return," 3 January, http://timesofindia.indiatimes.com/articleshow/2670345.cms.

Times of India (2008e), "Indians in Kenya are safe: Vayalar Ravi," 1 January, http://timesofindia.indiatimes.com/Indians_in_Kenya_are_safe_Vayalar_Ravi/articleshow/2667065.cms.

Times of India (2008f), "Malaysia issues new visa rule for Indians, Bangladeshis," 30 May, http://timesofindia.indiatimes.com/Indians_Abroad/Malaysia_issues_new_visa_rule_for_Indians_Bangladeshis/articleshow/3086358.cms.

UN News Centre (2008), "250,000 Kenyans displaced by post-electoral violence, UN estimates," 4 January, http://www.un.org/apps/news/story.asp?NewsID=25209&Cr=kenya&Cr1.

Vasudevan, Parvathi (2008), "Kenya; How Much More of Troubled Times," *Economic and Political Weekly*, XLIII (9), 1-7 March: pp. 24-26.

VI

Indian Federalism and the Conduct of Foreign Policy in Border States: State Participation and Central Accommodation since 1990

Rafiq Dossani and Srinidhi Vijaykumar

Section 1: Introduction

The role of subnational units (states, provinces, cantons, lander) in international affairs is a growing subject in the literature on federalist affairs (see, for example, Hocking, 1993; Michelmann and Soldatos, 1990). Scholars of political science have traditionally seen the conduct of foreign policy as the exclusive domain of the national government. This would seem an especially apt observation about India's federalist system. The Indian constitution has given the center particularly strong powers—so strong, in fact, that some have described it as 'quasi federal' because of the lack of autonomy it affords to the states (Hardgrave, Jr. and Kochanek, 1986:44; Jain and Nair, 2000). Yet, there is an increasing consensus that the states have not been shy of foreign policy advocacy. Some have argued that the era of coalition government has increased such advocacy and, potentially, influence, especially in the context of globalization and economic reform and liberalization (Sridharan, 2003; Mehta, 1997).

This paper considers the role of India's border states in the conduct of foreign policy toward their transnational neighbors and asks whether coalition governance results in more power generally or to some state actors more than others. In particular, we explore whether the effectiveness of a state's foreign policy advocacy depends on that state's position in the coalition. Effectiveness may also be influenced by the type of advocacy—on ethnic or security issues, for example, as opposed to economic ones—and by constitutional limits.

That India's constitution grants greater power to the center than to the states has been well documented in scholarly literature (Hardgrave, Jr. and Kochanek, 1986:115-18; Jain and Nair, 2000: 47-55). A few key points highlight this center-oriented position. The constitution clearly delineates powers to the states, the center, and those over which the states and center have concurrent adjudication. However, whenever there is any conflict over the laws on the Concurrent List, the national parliament laws prevail over those of the state legislative assemblies (Jain and Nair, 2000:48). In addition, according to article 248 of the constitution, all residuary powers are given to the Union, unlike in the United States, where residuary powers go to the states. In practice, this has meant that the central government controls most of the powers of taxation (an important exception is agricultural income tax, which is a state subject).[1] This has led the states to negotiate revenue sharing and other financial allocations among themselves and with the center through centrally supervised bodies, such as the planning commission and the finance commission. Finally, the center appoints the governor of each state, a conventionally powerless position that nonetheless can and has been used on occasion to influence state policy and politics, such as the dismissal of state governments.

Despite the immense powers granted to the center, states are extremely important actors in the Indian political system. States retain sole or primary constitutional authority over education, agriculture, law and order, health, welfare, and local government. Central leaders

[1]Agriculture is a state subject, hence agricultural income tax is also a state subject. States have usually chosen not to levy a tax, so that agricultural income is generally tax-exempt. Even in this area, the center has acted to reduce state power. For instance, income from plantations has been exempted from the definition of agricultural income and been subjected to non-agricultural income tax levied by the center.

may make policy on these and other concurrent subjects, but they may find that the states do not always implement the center's recommendations. In particular, finance and planning commissions have met with resistance from powerful state leaders (Jain and Nair, 2000:209-10).

In a discussion of state advocacy in foreign affairs, 'involvement in foreign policy' can involve different degrees of influence. For example, the central government may informally consult a border state government to understand the impact that placing troops in the area prior to offensive action would have on local opinion. The outcome of such consultations may influence the central decision about timing, location, and the like, but the state government would not be considered to have played a strongly influential role. On the other hand, if the state government advocated against war and was found to have changed the central government's position on the subject, then such a role would be considered strongly influential. Jenkins (2003) argues against overstating the states' level of influence, and makes important qualifications about various scholars' works. He points out that Indian states' increasing exposure to and involvement in international affairs does not necessarily translate into autonomy in conducting foreign policy. He also argues that although states interact increasingly with multilateral institutions (such as the WTO), the result has been 'to take domestic policy to an arena—the intergovernmental negotiations within the WTO—where India's subnational authorities have difficulty gaining access' (Jenkins, 2003: 69). In other words, Jenkins suggests that states influence foreign economic policy, but only within a limited framework and amid a complicated network of state politicians, national politicians, and bureaucrats. This paper's argument, as discussed above, counters this thesis as it explores the ways that states have successfully influenced foreign policy.

SECTION 2: POWER SHARING IN INDIA: A FRAMEWORK

Kincaid (1990) coined the phrase 'constituent diplomacy' to define the international activities of subnational groups. He asserts that constituent diplomacy is on the rise, and that there has always been some state activity in international affairs. Indeed, he says that 'there is an ambiguity in federal polities about the status of constituent governments in world affairs and about the authority of the general government to act unilaterally in foreign affairs' (*op.cit.*: 64). Kincaid delineates a number of actions which would traditionally be thought of as belonging exclusively to the national government, but some of which, he argues, had at times involved the participation of subnational units. His list (*op.cit.*: 67) includes the authority to:

1. Declare war
2. Build and maintain armed forces
3. Conduct relations with foreign nations and international organizations
4. Appoint and receive diplomatic and consular officials
5. Conclude, ratify, and implement treaties
6. Assure that treaty law is supreme over any federal or constituent laws that conflict with it
7. Control entry and exit across national borders
8. Acquire or cede territory

Indian states are constitutionally prohibited from engaging in the first through sixth items on the list, as well as the eighth. And yet, there are uncertainties—areas where the center would prefer state participation, and areas where the state is pushing to participate despite center unwillingness. The authority to 'conduct relations with foreign nations and international organizations' (item three), for one, has become increasingly ambiguous in recent years. For example, the center encourages the states to negotiate energy agreements with foreign companies. A recent and oft-cited example of this is Maharashtra's power purchase agreement with Enron Corporation of the United States. Even more interesting is item seven, which concerns border security. The Indian constitution does not specify who has the authority to control entry to and exit from the nation, beyond empowering the center with authority over all foreign relations matters. As state parties have increased their voice in government, they have demanded an increased role in controlling migration into their states. Nowhere is the ambiguity of federal jurisdiction more apparent than in the case of border patrol. In West Bengal, the state police and Border Security Forces (a centrally-controlled paramilitary group) often work together to control the movement of migrants and goods from Bangladesh. The final authority over controlling the border is extremely unclear: the states have the authority to maintain law and order and to provide ration cards (a key form of identity) to each 'citizen,' but the central government has the (far stronger) authority to conduct relations with Bangladesh and protect national security.

Sridharan (2003) argues that states have gained influence in foreign affairs advocacy because of two trends which have devolved more power to the state: the increasing regionalization of Indian politics, and economic liberalization. Through economic liberalization, there is an environment in which states can play a key role in foreign economic policy, by seeking foreign direct investments and promoting foreign trade. For example, states participate in negotiations with foreign investors and attempt to influence those with the WTO. Indian economic reform, Sridharan posits, has aligned politics more closely with economic welfare. Combined with globalization, this gives state-level politicians an interest in accessing global economic opportunities. Key examples of state interaction with external agencies are in energy reform and agriculture negotiations (*op.cit.*: 468-71).

In addition, Sridharan argues that coalition governance gives regional parties the opportunity to influence the formulation of foreign policy, and to advance policies of specific interest to their states. The trend toward regionalization was marked by the debacle of the Congress party in the 1996 election.[2] What has emerged is a multiple party system, in which regional and local parties play a large role. The

[2]Several major political corruption scandals during the Rao-led Congress Party government from 1991 to 1996 contributed to the party's worst ever electoral defeat in the 1996 elections.

age of coalitions at the center,[3] which began with the formation of the BJP-led National Democratic Alliance (NDA) in 1998, has allowed state-focused rather than nation-focused parties to access a share of national power, which they can then use to further foreign policies that help their own states. In the May 2004 elections, voters elected the Congress Party to power, showing that coalitions were not a preserve of non-Congress parties. The Congress formed a coalition called the United Progressive Alliance, which consisted of parties such as the Dravida Munnetra Kazhagam (DMK), the People's Democratic Party (Kashmir), Rashtriya Janata Dal (Bihar), and was supported from the outside by the left parties. Sridharan says that the increase in state advocacy 'has occurred at a time when no single national party is able to win a majority without traversing the high road to a state capital in order to forge an electoral alliance. The space for the regional parties to assert themselves at the national level opened up as the one-party dominant system came to an end in Indian politics' (*op.cit.*: 469).

Sridharan's argument suggests that increased state participation in foreign policy ought to be a general practice across states. This paper addresses the question of whether coalition governance truly opens a space for the participation of all regional parties, or if it only gives certain sets of states the scope to engage in extra-constitutional activities (ECAs). It may be true that all states undertake ECAs because coalition governance reflects a weakness on the part of the center, or, as Sridharan puts it, because the center cannot assume state cooperation as a given. Alternatively, it may be that all states do not engage in more ECAs when there is a coalition government because states whose ruling factions are part of the national coalition prefer not to destabilize the center through such actions. States outside the coalition would be subject to harsh repercussions (for example, President's Rule) if they undertook the same activities. Another possibility is that only states within the coalition actually engage in ECAs because they are not afraid of central backlash, given their ability to threaten the stability of the

[3]Coalitions at the state level have been common for many decades.

government. And yet another possibility is that states outside of the coalition actually undertake more ECAs because they have no voice in the coalition government and are therefore are less likely to get what they want in any case.

The possible outcomes are summarized as the following four hypotheses:

H1a. State parties undertake more ECAs when part of the central coalition.

H2a. States parties undertake more ECAs when they are not part of the central coalition.

H1b. States parties undertake fewer ECAs when part of the national coalition.

H2b. State parties undertake fewer ECAs when not part of the national coalition.

Sridharan's work suggests that H1a and H2a ought to hold true and, therefore, that H1b and H2b do not hold true. As argued below, it is also possible for H2a and H1b to hold true while H1a and H2b do not hold true.

Table 1 presents a framework of Indian states' new foreign policy activities since 1990, the year that marked the start of the decade of economic reform and globalization in India. We separate activities by constitutionality, and by two types that exemplify Kincaid's items three and seven above, viz., cross-border economic activities and cross-border control of co-ethnic populations, respectively. In most cases, control of co-ethnic populations has had implications for India's national security. India shares a border with Pakistan in Kashmir, Punjab, Rajasthan and Gujarat in the north and west; with China and Nepal in the north-central states of Uttar Pradesh and Bihar; with Bangladesh in the eastern state of West Bengal and the small northeastern states to the east of Bangladesh; and with Sri Lanka in Tamil Nadu in the south (a littoral border). Due to commonalities in ethnicity, religion, and stages of economic development, only some border states have an incentive to undertake foreign policy activity, notably Kashmir, West Bengal, Tamil Nadu, and the northeastern states.

Table 1: States' border-related foreign policy activities since 1990

	Constitutional, economic	**Constitutional, co-ethnic**	**ECA, economic**	**ECA, co-ethnic**
States's ruling party is part of central coalition			- Water treaties, West Bengal 1996 (Sridharan, 2003) - Cross-border trade policy, West Bengal, 1999-2003; North-eastern States and Sikkim, 2000[4]	- Intervention in Sri Lanka, Tamil Nadu, 2006 (Sridharan, 2003)
State's ruling party is outside central coalition	- Cross-border bridges, roads in NE states, 2003, West Bengal, 2002-04[5]			- Joint border patrol, West Bengal, 2004 (see below). - Release of suspected militants in Kashmir, 2002 (see below). - Interference with border security forces, Kashmir 2002-3, West Bengal 2004 (see below). - Issuance of identity cards to those crossing the border, West Bengal up to 2003, (see below). - Influence on deportation policy, West Bengal 1998 (see below).

As Table 1 shows, given constitutional limits, there are few economic or co-ethnic focused cross-border activities that states can engage in that are actually constitutional. However, this has not stopped state parties from involving themselves in these policies. The

[4]Times of India articles 'W. Bengal Wants Border Trade with Sikkim,' 17 September 2003; 'N-E CMS Wants Border Trade Restored,' 21 June 2000; 'NE States To Press for Sub-Regional Ties,' 13 June 2000. See also 'Basu for Bangla Trade Corridor,' The Statesman, 20 December 1999.

[5]'ADB Seeks Remake of N-S Board' The Economic Times, 12 May 2002; and 'W. Bengal Wants Border Trade with Sikkim,' The Times of India. 17 September 2003.

table shows that the majority of states' increased advocacy in foreign policy has occurred in co-ethnic matters by states whose ruling party is outside the central coalition. State parties within the coalition, although they have engaged in extra-constitutional economic policy, are reluctant to undertake ECAs that influence co-ethnic affairs. For example, the ruling parties in Tamil Nadu and Kashmir between 1998 and 2002 belonged to the ruling coalition at the center during a time of considerable turmoil in Sri Lanka and Kashmir, but these did not undertake ECAs to regulate co-ethnic matters.

We use case studies of West Bengal and Kashmir during the reign of the National Democratic Alliance at the center (1998–2004) to analyze the hypotheses regarding the relationship between a state party's position in the coalition and its ECA. During this time, the ruling party in West Bengal, the Communist Party of India (Marxist) CPI(M), was in opposition at the center and ruled in the state. In Kashmir, the National Conference was in power at the state level until 2002 and was a party in the ruling coalition at the center. From 2002 and until the national elections in 2004, the People's Democratic Party (PDP)-Congress coalition ruled in Kashmir and was in opposition at the center.

Border Policy on the East: The Bengali Connection

The policies of West Bengal have been shaped by the state's unique geography, sandwiched between the rest of India and Bangladesh. Bangladesh was formed in 1971 after it fought a war of partition with Pakistan. Although initially friendly, relations between India and Bangladesh worsened in the mid-1970s because of domestic opposition to Bangladeshi policy, which was perceived as being over-dependent on India (Saha, 2000: 55-67). Bangladesh then went through a series of coups and military governments, which increased anti-Indian sentiment.

The two countries' concerns reflect their different geopolitical aspirations. As Kathryn Jaques (2000: 17-18) puts it, India and

Bangladesh have a 'fundamental difference in the foci of their foreign policies. Indian concerns are typified by the broader fear of Bangladesh's potential to produce destabilizing conditions in the subcontinent which, in the long term, could invite external meddling and perhaps, ultimately, the disintegration of the Indian Union.... By contrast, Bangladeshi foreign policy has been moulded by the fear of India's regional hegemonistic designs.' In describing India's security interests in Bangladesh, Padmaja Murthy (2000: 8) has argued that the four principal Indian concerns are:

1. The porous Indo-Bangladeshi border, which allows insurgents in Northeastern Indian states to take refuge in Bangladesh.
2. The massive illegal immigration that occurs through the border, which has implications for the politics of West Bengal—that is, new immigrants have tended to support the ruling state party, the CPI(M).
3. The pro-Pakistani elements holding influential positions in the Bangladeshi government, a concern given India's volatile relations with Pakistan.
4. The strong political and defense links that Bangladesh has with China and Pakistan.

It is worth noting that two of these issues specifically concern border policy, and by extension, regional and internal Indian stability.

West Bengal has a complex position in the India-Bangladesh equation. West Bengal is the only state to have been ruled by the Communist Parties for over three decades (Kerala is the other state with significant communist influence). It shares nearly a 2,200 km border with Bangladesh.

Some believe that West Bengal's government has no role whatsoever in border issues such as immigration and deportation, and that its responsibilities begin only after migrants cross over the border.[6]

[6]'Illegal immigration: Need for good policy and timely action,' The Statesman, 11 May 2004. For opinions from state actors on the need for center action, see 'Cong no to refugee status for intruders,' Times of India, 6 November 2001; and Saha, 2000: 174.

Others think that increasing joint operations between state and center are essential for security, and that the state government should bear a large part of the burden of dealing with cross border issues.[7] This next section of this paper examines the ways the state has attempted to influence policy, and argues that, even in areas where the center disapproves of a state's actions, the state has still successfully pursued its own policy – an indication of the beginning stages of autonomy. These trends were visible when the CPI(M) was in opposition to the central coalition during the NDA years, and shows that coalition governance affords opportunities to opposition states parties to pursue more autonomous policies.

Illegal Immigration

The population density and poverty of Bangladesh, combined with its poor treatment of Hindus since the rise of the Bangladesh Nationalist Party in 1978, have created immigration problems of epic proportions. Since the formation of Bangladesh in 1972, approximately 15 million illegal immigrants have entered India from Bangladesh, both Muslim and Hindu. Of those, over five million reside in West Bengal (Pathania, 2003). According to one Indian politician, 'The six border districts of West Bengal, viz. South 24 Parganas, North 24 Parganas, Nadia, Murshidabad, Malda, and West Disnajpur; four districts of Bihar...; and ten districts in Assam... have become "extensions of Bangladesh."'[8] The massive influx of immigrants brings with it the danger of separatist tendencies. The Bangladesh Liberation Organization has already called for a separate homeland for the non-Muslim minority in Bangladesh and those forced to migrate to India (Saha, 2000: 174). To date, there has been no significant record of violent action in support of this idea in West Bengal. Under the NDA, allegations of increasing Pakistani-inspired terrorist infiltration into West Bengal from Bangladesh have

[7]See L.K. Advani's comments in 'Heat on illegal immigrants,' The Statesman, 8 January 2003.

[8]See 'Neighbour or Invader' in dinanathmishra.com, February 23, 2003:1.

been common. India's past problems in managing insurgency in the northeast are also alleged to have increased, due to easy sanctuary that insurgents have found in Bangladesh, via the West Bengal border.

According to the Foreigners Act of 1947, the center has the right to control the movements of foreigners, to 'make provision, either generally or with respect to all foreigners ... for prohibiting, regulating, and restricting the entry of foreigners into India, or their departure therefrom or their presence or continued presence therein.' Although the Foreigners Act requires the cooperation of state officials and police, the power of regulation clearly lies with the center. And yet, on numerous occasions, the center has wanted to hand the matter off entirely to the states. Thus, in 2003 then-deputy Prime Minister (and Home Minister) L.K. Advani, in a reference to immigration via Bangladesh, noted that 'Over 11,500 Pakistanis have entered the country with regular papers and passports but have overstayed. There is no reason why our states should be soft on them. Immediate steps should be taken to identify them, locate them, and throw them out. They [the states] should launch drives to detect and deport these foreigners.' Advani further noted that the center's powers to detect and deport illegally residing foreign nationals had been delegated to states and Union Territories.[9] The center has obviously encouraged states to play a larger role in immigration policy despite its own strong mandate to do so. In many of the principal efforts taken to control illegal immigration—border patrol, fencing, deportation, and the issuance of national identity cards—the state has only an uncertain constitutional mandate to play a role. With respect to border patrol, according to Item 1 on the State List of the Indian Constitution, states are responsible for all matters of public order and policing. But according to Item 10 on the Union List, the center is responsible for all matters relating to foreign affairs. The Foreigners Act clearly gives the center authority over deportation, and there is little constitutional basis for the state to be at all involved in the multi-purpose national ID card system. And yet, the center has encouraged states to participate in all these issues.

[9]'Heat on illegal immigrants,' The Statesman, 8 January 2003.

Such central encouragement for state participation in immigration policy came at a time when the center was led by the NDA. Historically, under the Congress party—but even more so under the NDA—tension has arisen between the center and West Bengal over whether the state government allows illegal immigration to increase its voter bank. Critics of the CPI(M) say that officials turn a blind eye to illegal immigration because those who enter tend to vote communist. According to critics of the BJP, such statements often have fascist overtones, and they further observe that the NDA makes these claims in order to stir communal tension—the implication being that most of those who enter illegally are Muslim, whereas in fact, the larger number are Hindus. Given this background, it is all the more surprising, (and likewise indicative of a weakening at the center) that the national government has allowed the state government scope to pursue its own border policies.

Border Patrol

The Border Security Forces (BSF), a central paramilitary organization, plays a large role in border patrol, principally in West Bengal, Kashmir, and the Northeastern states. Founded in 1965, it is responsible for protecting India's land border during peacetime and for preventing transborder crimes, and it has an extensive intelligence network.[10] The BSF is called a paramilitary force because it occupies a hazy area between being part of a police force and being a professional military organization. Since the 1990s, when insurgency levels increased, the BSF has also been involved in anti-insurgency and counterterrorism activities. The state government has very little control over the BSF, even though the BSF strictly monitors villages along the border and has been accused of unprovoked firings and human rights violations. After an incident on Uttam Saha in the Raiganj district—in which the BSF took over a ten-kilometer belt along the Indo-Bangladeshi border, and

[10]Government of India, Ministry of Home Affairs, *Border Security Force,* [accessed August 20, 2004], <*http://mha.nic.in/bsf.htm#bose*>.

allegedly engaged in highhanded and violent behavior toward the villagers—the West Bengal government asked the center to review the organization's role.

There are signs, however, that the state has successfully controlled the BSF through other avenues. A West Bengal high court recently forced the BSF to hand over five of its members in a criminal proceeding, saying that if the BSF wanted to take charge of the accused for trial, they could take 'appropriate legal steps before an appropriate forum.'[11] The center protested, saying that the BSF Act—written in 1968 to clarify the basic duties of the force—had empowered the BSF to handle all investigations within its own organization. Despite these sentiments being well known, the High Court granted jurisdiction to the state government. The state government asserted its autonomy through its judicial process in early 2004, and experienced no backlash from the center.

Deportation

West Bengal has been remarkably successful at influencing deportation policy. The state has always been careful about this issue because of the ethnic background shared between the peoples of West Bengal and Bangladesh. It is easy, the state argues, for an Indian Bengali to be wrongfully accused and mistakenly deported. The strategies employed by the Union and state regarding illegal immigration have increasingly coincided, but even when there was discord, the state showed signs of autonomy. In 1998, when the Maharashtra government attempted to deport around eighty Bengalis from New Delhi through West Bengal into Bangladesh, the West Bengal government protested, having long demanded that Maharashtra inform it in advance about any deportations. In this instance, the West Bengal government asserted that some of the immigrants were bona-fide Indians, and again demanded that it be given advance notice because the deportations would be happening on its soil. Despite protests from the center that

[11]'State to probe BSF rape case,' Times of India, 12 March 2004.

the Maharashtra government had followed the law and acted in accordance with the Foreigner's Act, the West Bengal government prevailed when the Union home ministry accepted three of its major demands. Those were first, that Maharashtra consult the West Bengal government before deciding to push back any immigrants; second, that the state government be given thirty days to check if any potential deportee was actually from West Bengal; and third, that the deportation be carried out only after the mode of pushback was discussed.[12] In this case, the state was able to exercise a degree of autonomy and regulate a central policy being undertaken on its territory.

KASHMIR: STATE INVOLVEMENT, LEGITIMACY, AND PEACE?

Now we turn to another border state, but one with altogether a different place in Indian political thought and culture. In this section, we see that the state coalition government of Mohammad Sayeed Mufti has undertaken a remarkable number of ECAs even though, from 2002 to 2004, his government was not a part of the central coalition.

The issue of Kashmiri autonomy has long been a central concern of both Indian and Pakistani foreign policy. The two countries have fought three wars over the region in the past half century since independence. The people of Kashmir began to play an increasingly important role in the conflict in the 1980s. Before this point, the conflict in Kashmir was generally associated with cross-border infiltration from Pakistan and denial of democratic processes by India—both external factors. Since the mid 1980s, however, the Kashmiri conflict has assumed an *internal* dimension, as insurgents within the state have waged guerrilla war, and various factions have called for independence. In the past decade, separatists' groups demanding independence from the Indian Union have been on the

[12]See 'State gets its way on deportations,' The Statesman, 25 September 1998.; and 'Illegal migrants—Maharashtra has the right to deport,' The Statesman, 15 September 1998.

rise, along with others who demand a return to pre-1953 levels of autonomy.

Kashmir has only recently, in 2002, had what most cite as its first fair and free elections since 1987. These have facilitated a more 'federal' relationship, instead of one in which the center exercises direct rule or rule by proxy. James Manor (1998), in his article about the viability of the Indian federalist system, argues that one of the principal reasons that relations between New Delhi and the states have tended to remain manageable is the existence of political institutions that 'can still make the politics of bargaining work'. He points out that 'Political competition has a number of different outlets. Not only are there elections for national and state legislative assemblies; there are also positions of influence available in three tiers of decentralized, elected councils, and in numerous quasi-official boards, cooperatives.... The existence of so many opportunities to capture at least some power persuades parties and politicians to remain engaged with elections and logrolling, even when they are defeated in some arenas' (*op.cit.*: 23). This lack of political competition characterized elections in Jammu and Kashmir between 1987 and 2002. Previously, there had been no viable alternative to the National Conference (NC), which was backed by the center. In the 2002 elections, the People's Democratic Party (PDP) performed well and, in alliance with the Congress party, formed the government, taking over from the NC.[13] Despite the boycott of the elections by the independence-seeking Hurriyat and other parties, it finally seemed that democracy was at work.

The legitimacy of this government means that it has the potential to exercise more real autonomy from the center, even though the Congress rules both in coalition with the PDP in Jammu and Kashmir and at the center. Indeed, the slogan of the PDP-Congress government has been to apply the 'healing touch' locally—in other words, to work for the best interests of the Kashmiris and to counter negative influences from the Indian center. With policies such as the release of

[13]The NC still won the largest number of seats of any one party in the state legislature.

militants and the disbanding of the Special Operation Group, the Chief Minister has taken steps in this direction. These trends are similar to those in West Bengal, with the state beginning to participate in ECAs even when the state party is not in a coalition at the center.

In order to understand the constitutionality of state actions, a brief review of the critical constitutional agreements pertaining to Kashmir is necessary. The most important ones include Article 370, the Constitutional Order (1950), the Delhi Agreement (1952), the Jammu and Kashmir Constitution (1957), and the Kashmir Accords (1975).

In October 1947, Article 370 was introduced and adopted by the Constituent Assembly. Article 370 shields the state from certain national legislation and also gives the state powers to legislate on matters of land settlements, rights to property, immigration, and political titles—powers denied to other states (Hewitt, 2001: 142-43). It gave the national parliament substantive rights in three areas only: defense, foreign affairs, and communications. These same issues were covered in the Instrument of Accession.

The Constitutional Order of 1950 was issued by President Rajendra Prasad, and affirmed the relationship outlined in Article 370. In July 1952, Nehru and Sheikh Abdullah signed the Delhi Agreement, in which they discussed Kashmir's position in greater detail. They did not, however, come to a consensus on several important issues, including a separate chapter on Fundamental Rights of State, the eventual jurisdiction of the Supreme Court, and the Emergency Powers. The Constitutional Order of 1954 extended jurisdictional power to the Parliament on almost all the issues in the Union List, and applied the Fundamental Rights of the state constitution. Between 1953 and 1986, forty-two constitutional amendments were passed which increased the power of the center.

In 1975, Sheikh Abdullah, emerging from a twenty-year imprisonment, signed the Kashmir Accords with Indira Gandhi, which essentially confirmed all the constitutional changes that had occurred over the past two decades.[14] In the past decade, Kashmiris and others have increasingly clamored that puppet national assemblies unduly gave away their constitutional rights, and that there should be a return to pre-1953 constitutional status. Others have advocated for complete independence and still others for joining Pakistan.

This constitutional altercation is part of a much larger dispute about Kashmir's place in the Indian Union, and the amount of autonomy the state will have. As a state party, the PDP has acted on three specific issues that affect border policy. Most notably, they have demanded that the separatist Hurriyat group be included in dialogue with the center, that the militants be released, and that the Special Operation Group be disbanded. The NC, which was part of the NDA coalition until 2002, was less effective in this regard.

Dialogue with the Hurriyat

Part of the PDP-Congress Common Minimum Programme, written in 2002, is 'to request the Government of India to initiate and hold, sincerely and seriously, wide-ranging consultations and dialogue, without conditions, with the members of the legislature and other segments of public opinion in all three regions of the state.'[15] Although this objective mentions no names, it was a clear indication that the government wanted to include the Hurriyat in negotiations. The Hurriyat, founded in 1992 and then factionalized into the All India Hurriyat Conference (AIHC) in the late 1990s, demands a referendum in which Kashmiris could be given the opportunity to leave India without necessarily joining Pakistan. In other words, Kashmiris would vote for an independent state. It is certainly within constitutional boundaries for the state to make such a request, but by no means was it necessary for the center, eventually, to agree to it.

[14]'The Autonomy Demand', *Frontline*, 17(14), July 8–21, 2000, [accessed August 29, 2004], <http://www.flonnet.com/fl1714/17140040.htm>.

[15]Government of Jammu & Kashmir, '*Elements of a Common Minimum Programme for a Congress-PDP Coalitions Government in Jammu and Kashmir,*' [accessed August 10, 2004], *<http://jammukashmir.nic.in/govt/welcome.htm>*.

The NC repeatedly made this request, but to little avail. The center did offer to include the AIHC in dialogue in 2000, around the time that Farooq Abdullah, then chief minister of Jammu and Kashmir, introduced an Autonomy Bill that essentially demanded a return to the pre-1953 situation. It is believed that the center then offered to enter negotiations with the Hurriyat as a way of marginalizing the NC.[16] Although Farooq Abdullah and the NC were important partners in the coalition, they were also constrained by their dependence on the center. The PDP-Congress coalition has a legitimacy that the NC lacked, and is therefore freer to pursue its own agenda. Even though it is outside the central coalition, it has been far more successful in opening a broad dialogue. At the end of 2002, Advani promised talks with the Hurriyat, which began and were continued by the Manmohan Singh government until they stalled in August 2004.[17] In this way, the state government exercised greater autonomy about who it wanted included in negotiations over the state's future and the future of Indo-Pak relations.

Release of Militants

One of the areas in which the state has exercised extensive autonomy is in the release of militants, both local insurgents and cross-border infiltrators. As part of its common minimum programme, the state government pledged to 'release all detainees held on non-specific charges, those not charged with serious crimes and those who have been held on charges that are such that the period they have spent in jail exceeds their possible sentence.'[18] Directed mostly toward militants of

[16]See 'Jammu leaders cool to center's talk offer,' Times of India, 9 April 2000; and 'India: Separatism or Autonomy: NC,' The Hindu, 23 June 2000; and 'Government to consult NC before talks with J&K Ultras,' The Economic Times, 26 December 2000; and 'Hurriyat has no role in Indo-Pak talks: BJP,' The Hindu, 26 May 2001.

[17]See 'Keep the peace: New govt has its job cut on the internal security front,' The Economic Times, 14 May 2004.

[18]'Elements of a Common Minimum Programme for a Congress-PDP Coalitions Government in Jammu and Kashmir', *op.cit.*, (part 3).

the Hurriyat and Hizb-ul-Mujahideen (an organization dedicated to the integration of J&K with Pakistan), this statement clearly signaled the administration's disapproval of the now-discarded Prevention of Terrorism Act (POTA) and the wide-reaching detention powers it granted. Although the state is responsible for law and order,[19] the center is responsible for 'Preventive detention for reasons connected with Defense, Foreign Affairs, or the security of India.'[20] Therefore, neither the state nor the center has clear-cut constitutional authority on this issue.

When the PDP came to power, and began releasing militants, the center specifically complained that the state government had been 'acting unilaterally despite being sent a letter by the Union home secretary suggesting that decisions with a bearing on the country's battle against terrorism be taken after consulting the Center.'[21] The center, however, did allow the state to continue in this process, because (according to many) it wanted to allow the state time to stabilize and did not want to be seen as de-legitimizing a newly elected government. After fiery debates and exchanges in October and November 2002, in December, the state agreed to put the cases before a screening committee, before it released the militants. According to one article, 'Under pressure from coalition partner Congress and the Center, the PDP-led Jammu and Kashmir government has agreed to release militants only after a screening committee examines the cases first. The five-member committee—including a Central nominee—will reportedly be headed by Mr D.S. Singh, finance commissioner, home [Jammu and Kashmir].... Though the screening committee will be constituted, it will not be an impediment in the release of a number of detainees whose prison terms under the Public Safety Act are to expire shortly.'[22] Although the center interfered and disapproved, the state still accomplished its primary objective.

[19]According to Items 1 and 2, Seventh Schedule, State List, Indian Constitution.

[20]See Item 10, Union List, Seventh Schedule, Indian Constitution.

[21]'Center, Congress in war of words,' Times of India, 27 November 2002.

[22]'Ultras to be freed after screening,' The Statesman, 6 December 2002.

Disbanding the Special Operations Group

Another bone of contention between the state and center has been the disbanding of the Special Operations Group (SOG). The SOG was founded in 1995 as a counter-insurgency wing of the Jammu and Kashmir police (unlike the BSF or Central Reserve Police Force, which are paramilitary groups). It consisted of non-Muslim, non-Kashmiri recruits, as well as some former militants, and was apparently formed to 'create the impression that the counterinsurgency effort had local support.'[23] Over time, it had become increasingly unpopular, with reports of human rights abuses, torture, and humiliation of civilians. The army and police force, on the other hand, believed that the intelligence and manpower that SOG provides had proven essential in the fight against terrorism and militancy.

To understand the constitutionality of the state's decision to disband the SOG, it is important to recall that the SOG was a state creation under the NC. Because the SOG was a state-run organization and because it dealt with law and order, it may be argued that it was under the state's jurisdiction according to Items 1 and 2 on the State List of the Indian Constitution. However, because it was engaged with anti-terrorist actions, the center would have had grounds to protest its disbandment. The center did indeed request a 'revival of the SOG in some form or the other' by arguing that 'normal policing' was not adequate to deal with the extraordinary terror threat faced in the state.[24] Despite these pressures, the state government did not back down. It disbanded the SOG in early 2003 and subsequently refused to re-establish it. Here again is an example in which the center was justified in intervening, but instead allowed the state to have autonomy.

[23]'Behind the Kashmir Conflict – Abuses by Indian Security Forces and Militant Groups Continue,' Human Rights Watch Report, July 1999, [accessed September 3, 2004], <http://www.hrw.org/reports/1999/kashmir/back.htm>.

[24]'Mufti rules out SOG by another name,' The Economic Times, 2 June 2003.

SECTION 3. CONCLUDING DISCUSSION

In this paper, we have shown that state-level ruling parties (the CPM and the PDP-Congress) that undertook foreign policy-related actions —when they were not part of the central ruling coalition—have been successful. By contrast, we have also shown that a state-level party (the NC) that was part of the ruling coalition was unsuccessful at foreign policy. These findings support hypotheses H2a and H1b, that coalition governance creates a space for opposition parties at the center to play a role in national politics through their activities at the state level, but not for ruling state parties that are also part of the national coalition. Although we have not presented it in detail, the case studies are further supported by evidence against hypotheses H1a and H2b (see Table 1) about the passive roles of the ruling state parties in Tamil Nadu and Kashmir in Sri Lanka's and Pakistan's affairs, respectively, at a time when these parties belonged to the national ruling coalition (1998–2004). Further, during the tenure of the subsequent national government (the Congress-led UPA), the ruling party in Tamil Nadu since 2006, the DMK, has been passive on co-ethnic foreign policy issues. So has the ruling PDP-Congress coalition in Kashmir. All these parties are part of the UPA, as of 2008.

As noted above, our case studies focused on foreign policy advocacy with neighbors (Kincaid's #7). However, they have not dealt with the full range of possible challenges to federal authority. We have pointed out that Indian states have also conducted negotiations with international organizations (Kincaid's #3). In this respect, Sridharan validates her analysis with the example of energy negotiations by the Andhra Pradesh government. Note that these negotiations occurred while the ruling party in Andhra Pradesh supported the central government. Yet several states—such as Karnataka, whose ruling party at the time, the Congress Party, was not part of the central coalition between 1998-2004—also entered into such international agreements on energy which support Sridharan's hypotheses (H1a and H2b), and its BJP Chief Minister Yedyurappa, elected in 2008 during the tenure of the Congress-led UPA coalition government in New Delhi, actively sought foreign investments in his state subsequent to his election.

A resolution to the puzzle of why co-ethnic activities, but not economic activities, are the focus of states' ECAs clearly needs further work. A possible explanation is that the constraints of economic activity are well codified, and as a result, that checks and balances exist. For example, if a state signed a water-sharing treaty with a neighboring country without central approval, it would have no mechanism to enforce the treaty in the absence of a convertible currency and without the participation of centrally regulated banks that would transmit funds. On the other hand, co-ethnic activities, such as the release of militants, are non-codified in the sense that they do not involve bodies that the center regulates or controls.

If, as many believe, India is to have coalition governments at the center for many years, our findings have significant implications for the trajectory of states' autonomy. A change of guard at the center, which would moderate the central government's policies over time, could result in a change in ECAs at the state level, but might not bring about similar moderation in state-level policies.

REFERENCE

Dua, B.D. and M.P.Singh (eds) (2003) *Indian Federalism in the New Millenium.* New Delhi: Manohar.

Hardgrave, Jr., R.L. and Kochanek, Stanley A. (1986) *India—Government and Politics in a Developing Nation,* 4th ed. San Diego: Harcourt Brace Jovanovich.

Hewitt, Vernon. (2001) *Towards the Future? Jammu and Kashmir in the 21st Century,* Cambridge: Granta Editions.

Hocking, Brian, ed. (1993) *Foreign Relations and Federal States.* London: Leicester University Press.

Jaffrelot, Christophe (2002) *India's Silent Revolution.* New Delhi: Permanent Black.

Jain, U.C. and Nair, Jeevan. (2000) *Encyclopedia of Indian Government and Politics, vol. 7, Centre-State Relations.* Jaipur: Pointer Publishers

Jaques, Katherine. (2000) *Bangladesh, India, and Pakistan.* New York: St. Martin's Press.

Jenkins, Rob. (2003) 'India's States and the Making of Foreign Economic Policy: The Limits of the Constituent Diplomacy Paradigm,' *Publius,* 33(4): 63-82.

Kincaid, John. (1990) 'Constituent Diplomacy in Federal Polities and the Nation-state: Conflict and Co-operation' in Jans J. Michelmann and Panyotis Soldatos (eds) *Federalism and International Relations—The Role of Subnational Units.* Oxford: Clarendon Press.

Linz, Juan J., Alfred Stepan and Yogendra Yadav (2007) ' "Nation State" or "State Nation"? India in Comparative Perspective' in Shankar Bajpai (ed.), *Democracies and Diversity: India and the American Experience.* New Delhi: Oxford University Press.

Mahajan, Gurpreet. (2007) 'Federal accommodation of ethnocultural identities in India' in Baogang He, Brian Galligan, and Takashi Inoguchi (eds), *Federalism in Asia.* Northampton, MA: Edward Elgar Publishing, pp. 82-100.

Manor, James. (1998) 'Making Federalism Work,' *Journal of Democracy* 9(3): 21-35

Michelmann, Jans J. and Panyotis Soldatos (eds) *Federalism and International Relations—The Role of Subnational Units.* Oxford: Clarendon Press.

Mehta, Pratap B. (1997) 'India: Fragmentation amid Consensus', *Journal of Democracy*, 8(1): 58–59.

Murthy, Padmaja. (2000) *Managing Suspicions: Understanding India's Relations with Bangladesh, Bhutan, Nepal, and Sri Lanka.* New Delhi: The Institute for Defence Studies and Analyses.

Pathania, Jyoti M. (2003) *India & Bangladesh – Migration Matrix.* South Asia Analysis Group http://www.southasiaanalysis.org/papers7/paper632.html. [accessed October 1, 2008].

Saha, Rekha. (2000) *India-Bangladesh Relations.* Calcutta: Minerva Associates.

Sridharan, Kripa. (2003) 'Federalism and Foreign Relations: The Nascent Role of the Indian States', *Asian Studies Review,* 27(4): 463-89.

VII

Federalism, Intergovernmental Mechanisms and Coalition Governments: Continuity and Change

Rekha Saxena

Federal theory, both in its classical preoccupation with dual or shared sovereignty versions and subsequent cooperative and/or collaborative versions, has been essentially an inward-looking theory that goes well with classical realist theory in international relations that tended to treat the aggregate State as billiard balls. Even though the federal and international relations theories deal with two separate levels of analysis, reference here is to the fact that both these perspectives treat inter-state relations at the supranational level as one in which two independent states deal with each other as sovereign entities. In other words, sovereign states as actors claim supremacy over any other authority within the nation or federation. They prefer not to accept any other superior authority within the boundary nor external to it. Within this dual theoretical heritage, the federal government arrogated to give itself exclusive control over foreign policy making.

Within the subset of federal states, one can delineate two broad models of treaty making power, i. e., the presidential federal one, an archetype of which was first put forward by the Constitution of the United States of America (1787), and the British Commonwealth parliamentary federation of Canada founded in 1867. India belongs to the second typology.

The treaty making power in terms of the Constituent Assembly as well as the text of the Constitution is an exclusive jurisdiction of the union government and the approval of the Parliament is neither required prior nor subsequent to the signing of the treaty. Only in cases of those treaties that entail a parliamentary legislation, does the role of the Parliament come in. That also, it is important to point out, comes *post facto*, i.e. when the executive presents the Parliament with a *fait accompli*. This view is also buttressed by case laws engendered thus far by the Supreme Court (Saxena, 2006).

This interpretation has become subject to a rethinking at least since two new factors have entered into the altered scenario since the early 1990s.These factors are: a) the increasing federalization of the previously predominantly parliamentary (in reality one- party executive-driven political system) of India in the preceding decades, and b) the liberalization and globalization of the Indian economy. These two significant factors have been reinforced by other intervening factors such as differentiation of the national and state party systems, the advent of multi-party system and federal coalition governments with strong representation of regional parties producing the phenomenon of divided governments. All these factors together have also contributed to the more frequent recourse to national and international tribunals and commissions, judicial interpretation, review and activism on account of jurisdictional questions that came into play relating to relationships between the federal and provincial states and those between the national state and global multilateral agencies and organizations. The issues range over inter-state river water disputes within India, and with its neighbours, to mention just one question. If the 'constitutionalization of the third tier' of the federal system by 73rd and 74th amendments goes beyond legislation and acquires the momentum of some sort of movement, then the rural and urban governments may also become a more effective factor in federal governance. This is because, governance in mega cities is becoming an important issue involving the satellite towns that often falling in more than one state, e.g. the National Capital Region of

Delhi straddling the status of Delhi, U.P., Haryana and Rajasthan. Question of migration into metropolises from almost all over the country is increasingly causing tension in Mumbai and elsewhere. In some states, new social movements relating issues of use of water and forest resources, social audit of development programmes at the grassroots' level etc., are hitting national headlines and drawing social scientists to those locations for closer studies, e.g., Right to Information initiatives at the local level taken by social activist Aruna Roy in Rajasthan, social audit of National Rural Employment Guarantee (NREGA) schemes in rural Andhra Pradesh and grassroots *bhrastachar virodhi andolan* in Maharashtra.

Similarly, there are two additional developments that may have some impact on the emerging federal equations in times to come. First, the tribal self governments under the Fifth and Sixth Schedule of the Constitution add a somewhat unique sub federal governance, in as much as that these autonomous institutions are the responsibility of the union government even though they are located in some specific states. The Governor of the State looks after the tribal affairs as the representative of the President of India and acts in his own discretion in these matters rather than on the advice of the State Council of Ministers. Secondly, the peace process initiated in the recent years in Jammu and Kashmir (J&K) involving the governments of India and Pakistan as well as the governments in J&K and Pakistan Occupied Kashmir (POK) may lead to new institutional innovations under constitutional law as well as international law in due course. Such processes are likely to be replicated on India's borders with its other immediate neighbours in the central and eastern Himalayan and Bay of Bengal borders and in the deep south (Singh, 2008:74-5).

This paper seeks to take a detailed look at mechanisms of intergovernmental interactions in the Indian federation especially in the changing scenario of coalitional governments, as also federal and corporate governance, required by the emerging new partnership between the state, civil society and the market. The chapter argues that the importance of intergovernmental mechanisms to facilitate these relations are increasing in the emerging scenario outlined above (Dhavan ,1996, Dhavan and Saxena , 2006)[1].

Intergovernmental interactions in India have been by and large an affair of 'executive federalism' (Smiley, 1980: chapter 4)[2] rather than 'legislative federalism' which could have been expressed through Rajya Sabha, but never got off the ground.[3] This was for three reasons. Firstly, by constitutional design, the Rajya Sabha appears to be intended to be more of a parliamentary than a federal second chamber because it represents states proportional to their population rather than states qua states, unlike the American Senate which represents the states, large or small, equally with two directly elected Senators each. Rajya Sabha is indirectly elected by the elected members of the state legislatures which give it a federal constituency though not the legitimacy of being a directly elected House. Secondly, although Rajya Sabha shares equal legislative powers with the Lok Sabha, except for money bills, but in a joint sitting with Lok Sabha, where legislative disputes between the two chambers are resolved by vote, Rajya Sabha suffers from smaller numbers(233) as compared to the Lok Sabha (545). Thirdly, state delegations in Rajya Sabha cannot claim to represent the state governments per se, as the members of the German *Bundesrat,* for example, can who are either provincial chancellors or ministers themselves or their nominees. Moreover, the National Democratic Alliance (NDA) government in 2003 by a constitutional amendment in the Representation of People Act, 1951, also tried to rob the symbolic federal significance of the Rajya Sabha by abolishing the residence or domicile requirement for members representing their respective states. This means that a citizen of India, non-resident in the state whose seat he/she represents can come from any state or union territory of the federation. A case filed by a former Rajya Sabha member Kuldip Nayar challenging this amendment on the ground that it destroyed the federal character of the Rajya Sabha, was not sustained by the Supreme Court, which maintained that the amendment was not unfederal. The Court underlined the 'parliamentary ' tilt of Rajya Sabha (Nayar, 2006).

In the opinion of some observers, the federal role and relevance of Rajya Sabha has increased with the diversification of the party system with different parties ruling in New Delhi and states (Singh,2003: 197). Yet, this change has not really contributed to the raising of this house to the level of what may be called 'legislative federalism'. It is thus safe to conclude that intergovernmental relations still continue almost entirely at the level of executive federalism supplemented by the federal coalitional council of ministers giving representation to strong regional parties, and by the Supreme Court of India as the forum of federal arbitration.

The mechanisms of intergovernmental interactions cannot simply be a matter of formal constitutional provisions in any country. Relations of such magnitude and complexity are not amenable to managing and regulating through a rigid legalistic process. The nature of the problem demands flexibility and adaptability to changing conditions and to the views of the two orders of the government. This is amply demonstrated by the Indian experience. The governments of India have displayed different approaches at different points in time with regard to article 263 of the Constitution which provides for the establishment of an Inter-State Council (ISC). From 1950 to 1990, the first five Prime Ministers did not form the Inter-State Council despite this constitutional mandate and preferred to have non-constitutional—but not unconstitutional—bodies like the National Development Council (NDC) or ad hoc intergovernmental conferences like Chief Ministers'/Ministers'/Secretaries' conferences. It was in 1990 that the Inter-State Council was finally set up by the first coalition government in New Delhi formed by a group of non-Congress parties who called themselves the National Front (NF) under the Prime Ministership of Janata Dal's V.P.Singh.[4]

Some observers (Saez 2002, Saxena 2007) of the Indian federal scene have come to the conclusion that intergovernmental relations, especially through formal channels, have not been salient in Indian policy-making, either during the phase of one-party dominance under the Indian National Congress or in the phase of multi-party coalition governments since 1989. These conclusions are both correct and incorrect in the sense that absence of intergovernmental forums conducted through formal channels does not mean the absence of such relations at all, for example, the Inter State Council was not set up until 1990 but there were functional substitutes for it in the National Development Council, and chief ministerial and secretarial conferences.

Further with the advent of federal coalition governments since 1989, the earlier expectation that the importance of IGIs would increase has not always been fulfilled. This is due to the reason, as also discussed below, that the coalition governments typically include a large number of parties, including regional parties powerful in states which get direct representation in federal cabinet as partners. The formal intergovernmental forums are therefore sidelined or overshadowed. Partners in the federal coalitions have often been successful in getting powers and fiscal packages through their direct equation with the prime minister. For instance, during the National Front government led by H.D. Deve Gowda, the union Finance Ministry relaxed procedures to allow state governments to initiate negotiations with the world bank or foreign direct investors without the prior formal permission of the union government. Moreover, Punjab got special financial package from I.K. Gujral, and Assam and the North-East got a similar treatment from Prime Minister Manmohan Singh.

MAJOR INTERGOVERNMENTAL INTERACTIONS (IGI) FORUMS

There are numerous bodies and processes that are both formal and informal through which IGIs have been conducted. Several such bodies have emerged over the years, some by cabinet resolution (without a formal presidential order), some under Acts of Parliament, and some on the initiatives of the union or/and state governments.[5] Thus, it can be said that apart from the first degree of constitutional formality under which ISC was established under article 263, there is a second degree of institutional formality, namely, parliamentary enactments by which such bodies are set up, e.g. Zonal Councils. The third degree of institutional formality characterizing such bodies are set up by a cabinet resolution e.g. the National Development Council (NDC) set up in 1952 by Prime minister Jawaharlal Nehru for approval of five-year plans by the two orders of governments. It would appear that going by the norms of the federal executive as designed by the constitution, the proper way of setting up such a body would be either a presidential order on the advice of the cabinet in consultation with the state governments or a parliamentary enactment in consultation with state governments assented to by the President. A cabinet resolution in the matter would appear to be a fait accompli which may pass off under the pretext of conventions of the constitution which are not strictly codified. Informal inter-governmental mechanisms on the initiatives of the union or state governments are not strictly unconstitutional, but they are certainly extra-constitutional. They may however be justified under the exigencies of an emergent situation as ad hoc steps with mutual consent between the two orders of the government. Examples of such mechanisms are the Chief Ministers' Conferences, Ministers' Conferences and Secretaries'[6] conferences. Besides, there is another category of informal conferences representing parliamentary and executive functionaries not necessarily and all that formally representing their governments like Speakers'/ Governors'/ Presidents' conferences.

It may be added that a forum larger than intergovernmental scope with the inclusion of representation from civil society was introduced by Prime Minister Nehru, in the wake of the Chinese aggression in 1962, in the form of the National Integration Council. In addition to the executive heads of union and state governments and some other ministers, it included top journalists, educationists, professionals, literateurs and artists. The Council met occasionally in the Nehru and Indira Gandhi eras but fell in disuse thereafter until Prime Minister Narasimha Rao revived it in the first half of the 1990s. It was not convened by the successive governments. In October 2008, the Congress-led United Progressive Alliance Prime Minister Manmohan Singh, called a meeting of the NIC in the backdrop of escalating communal and terrorist violence in the country to devise ways and means and a concerted strategy of dealing with these menaces (The Hindu, 2008).

MEMBERSHIP, AUTONOMY, REPRESENTATION OF INTERESTS AND DECISION-MAKING IN INTERGOVERNMENTAL FORUMS

The ISC and the NDC have overlapping membership as they include the Prime Minister and some key Union Ministers, Chief Ministers of States and executive heads of the Union Territories. In case of the NDC, the Deputy Chairman of the Planning Commission is also a member. The NDC was set up to review and finalize the National Plans made by the Planning Commission and to look into socio-economic policies affecting national development. The Prime Minister/Chief Ministers' Conferences, Ministerial conferences, Secretaries' conferences are self- defining in as much as they respectively include the First Ministers, Ministers and officials from the two orders of the union and state governments. They are chaired by the Prime Minister or respective union ministers or union officials to coordinate policies of two levels of the government. The five Zonal Councils set up under the States' Reorganization Act (SRA), 1956, are high level advisory bodies comprising chief ministers of states in that zone, development ministers and chief secretaries of these states, and a member of the Planning Commission. Each Zonal Council is headed by the union home minister. Its purpose is to provide a common meeting ground in each zone for ensuring resolution of inter-state problems, fostering balanced regional development and building harmonious union-state relations. The Zonal Councils are the sole formal IGR mechanism for regional or territorial development. It was hoped that these bodies would serve as a mechanism of decentralization at the intermediate level below the Centre and above the States. However, their performance is marred by irregular meetings and negligible achievements, mainly due to apathy of an overburdened union government and fractious states in a region. The only exception is the North-Eastern Council that has notable record of activities and performance.

The above bodies adequately represent the union and state governments in the areas of their respective concerns. It is somewhat more difficult to assess the question of autonomy and interests of federating entities, particularly in case of less formal and informal organizations, as their meetings are normally convened by the union government. In case of the ISC, there is greater constitutional standing in as much as its rules of business require the union to convene a meeting. Previously, agendas and issues for discussion were also fully under the discretion of the Prime Minister but now the rule has been amended to allow Chief Ministers to raise certain issues (*Inter State Council Secretariat*, 1990). An insistent state government can now build up pressure on the union government to convene a meeting or raise a matter at a meeting. But since the Prime Minister chairs it, he/she may exclude a demand or a matter that a state attempts to raise under the ISC rules. The decision is not by majority, but by consensus as sensed by the Prime Minister. Yet it is clear that it would be difficult for a Prime Minister to totally ignore an insistent and sizeable section of opinion on the floor of the ISC.

An insider's view (Singh, 2003) confirms that such alignment and realignment of interests and strategies among the participating governments do take place in ISC meetings. If the union's proposal affects certain states badly, they come more prepared to put forward their points of view and oppose it. If the policy affects a group of states, they may unite against the Centre. For example, in a discussion on Article 356 providing for central intervention in a State government in crisis situation, some States, which are politically more vulnerable to such pressures since they are ruled by a party other than that in power in New Delhi, are more likely to mobilize in opposition to the center. The Sarkaria Commission Report ,Volume II includes memorandums of some regional parties and state governments demanding repeal of Article 356 from the constitution and abolition of the office of the Governor. Moreover in several meetings of the Standing committee of the ISC and its larger Council itself, sharp demands were made for deletion of Article 356 from the constitution or at least bringing the power of the center to take over state administration in Emergencies under strict constitutional control. Similarly, if there is a proposal from the Union government to change a taxation law, the States that stand to lose from it are likely to join together to oppose it. For instance, during the introduction of VAT regime a few years back, the BJP-ruled state governments delayed its implementation until the last due to the pressure of the traders lobbies. However, at the end of the day, all points of views are taken into account in creating a consensus. "A lowest common denominator is aimed at which protects the interests of the state governments and also promotes the objectives of the Union government." Yet evidently consensus does not always mean unanimity. For instance, the meeting of the ISC in Srinagar in August 2003 was reported to have 'unanimously' decided to amend article 356 to incorporate safeguards for protecting the autonomy of the States as suggested by the Sarkaria Commission (Commission on Centre—State Relations, Report, 1987-8) and supported by the Supreme Court in S.R. Bommai vs. Union of India 1994 (Bommai, 1994).[7] But the press also reported that at least two chief ministers—those of Punjab and Tamil Nadu speaking from Chandigarh and Chennai—suggested that it would be more desirable to delete article 356 from the constitution. While this demand has been persistent almost right from the beginning, it has never led to either a serious movement on part of the aggrieved states or a constitutional amendment by the aggregate legislatures.

NDC meetings are not very different from those of the ISC. The NDC has been mainly used to facilitate the process of planning involving the two orders of government and for the approval of the plan documents by the executive heads of the Union and State governments. The State governments submit their five-year plans and annual plans to the Planning Commission which prepares a National Plan after discussion with delegations from State governments consisting of Chief Ministers and relevant Ministers and Secretaries (Nanda, 2003).[8]

The Planning Commission draft is then discussed and approved by the Union government. It is then presented to a meeting of the NDC for intergovernmental approval. "The NDC is a policy making body and its recommendations are not just advisory suggestions but policy decisions and policy directives. It is a national forum for planning which gives informal sanction to the underlying concept of cooperation between the Centre and the States. It brings states into an organic relationship with the organization of national planning" (Majeed, 2002: 10).

An official participant's view of the process suggests that typically, the Prime Minister inaugurates the NDC meeting, followed by the speeches of Deputy Chairman of the Planning Commission, the Finance Minister and the Chief Ministers. All participants come with prepared speeches which are circulated in the meeting so there is little interactive discussion. Finally, the Planning Commission (which works as the Secretariat of the NDC) puts forward the final document for approval (Nanda, 2003). However, behind this seemingly consensual approach, there are active prior negotiations between Planning Commission officers with the state governments.

In case of the NDC, there has been occasional dissatisfaction and criticism. For instance, the Andhra Pradesh Telugu Desam Chief Minister N.T. Rama Rao walked out of an NDC meeting being chaired by the Congress Prime Minister Rajiv Gandhi in the mid-1980s complaining about the lack of time granted for presenting the point of view of his government (*Indian Express*, 1988). However, more often than not, non-Congress governments including the Left Front governments of West Bengal, despite their occasional differences with the Plan documents, have generally gone along rather than dissociating themselves from the whole process. The State governments have also at times complained that the agenda papers are sent to them late, preventing effective preparatory work (Nanda, 2003).

It would appear that both in the case of ISC and NDC the opportunity for open-ended negotiations or discussion is somewhat limited because of the constitutional restraints and the inbuilt technicalities of the planning documents (Singh and Nanda, 2003). It is probably for this reason that lower level ministerial and secretaries' meetings involving the two orders of the government are more open and interactive. These ad hoc conferences are called to discuss emergent political and administrative problems on which the representatives from the two levels are able to have a less constrained discussions and deeper negotiations with more open minds. Many feel that the real nitty-gritty of intergovernmental relations are conducted in these forums.

These meetings are usually convened by the union ministry concerned. They set the agenda but if the concerned ministry from a State government wants some specific item to be included in the agenda, they can do so. The meeting is chaired by the concerned Union Minister/Secretary. All ministers/Secretaries from big or small States are given adequate time to express their views. If needed, the meeting is extended to more than a day. The decision is not by voting, but by consensus. The delegates negotiate and bargain, and try to convince each other. The proceedings are recorded. The final decision is based on a draft that reflects a consensus on which all delegates can agree. If the state governments and the Centre have different views, then there is an attempt to talk further and find out how to accommodate them (Nanda, 2003). Other formal and informal bodies like various national councils in different policy areas also work under these conventions or rules.

IMPLEMENTATION AND FOLLOW-UP ACTION

The performance of ISC in following up and implementing intergovernmental agreements has been abysmal. There has hardly been any constitutional amendment or parliamentary enactment in pursuance of the recommendations made by the ISC so far as the political institutional dimension is concerned. For example, the Sarkaria Commission Report had recommended the constitutional entrenchment of the NDC and Planning Commission, and for making the Finance Commission a permanent body. None of these recommendations have been carried out. However, some of the recommendations of this Commission relating to taxation and fiscal matters have resulted in constitutional amendments.[8] But even in this context, the Sarkaria panel's suggestion for a constitutional commission to review the whole taxation system has not been done. Some limited tax reform administrative committees have been set up from time to time, such as the Raja Chelliah Taxation Reform Committee and the Vijay Kelkar draft proposal for tinkering with some union taxes in the mid-1990s.

As far as the NDC is concerned, there is hardly any follow up at the political level until the next NDC, although the Planning Commission goes through the motions of periodic reviews of the Plan in relation to both the Union and State governments. In case of Ministerial and Secretaries conferences, once the decision is taken, it is left to the parties concerned to implement the decisions. By the time of the next meeting, everyone becomes more alert and takes stock of the progress made in the implementation. However, there is no centralized monitoring.[9]

EFFECTIVENESS

It is not very easy to measure and evaluate the effectiveness of these bodies in clear-cut terms. The ISC did not meet for six years after it was set up in 1990. This is in contravention to the ISC notification that said that it should meet three times a year. Its first meeting was held in 1996, and in the one and a half decades since, it has met ten times.[10] This appears to be rather surprising in view of the fact that this period has been one of the paradigm shifts in union-state relations in

India. In the same period, however, its standing committee has met ten times and a sub-committee has had six meetings to prepare the groundwork for the full council meetings.[11] This failure of the ISC to emerge as an active intergovernmental mechanism in the Indian federal system needs explanation. The reasons may be discussed in terms of two phases: (1) The first four decades of Indian federalism before the ISC was not formally set up, and (2) the period since its inception in 1990s. During the first phase of Congress Party dominance at the Centre as well as in most States, intergovernmental issues were generally resolved across the party table at Congress Party forums like the Congress Working Committee (CWC) and that Congress Parliamentary Board (CPB) comprising powerful Union Ministers and State Chief Ministers. This not only overshadowed the NDC but also atrophied the necessity for setting up the ISC. Moreover, economic planning, which was a more complex issue, necessitated creation of the NDC by executive action presumably to make it easier for the union to manage intergovernmental affairs in its own way without the constraints of a formal body. The successive governments continued this practice. The delayed arrival on the scene of an Inter-State Council under the Constitution can at least partly be explained by the preference of the Congress governments at the centre in the past to deal with intergovernmental matters at a forum less comprehensive than the Inter-State Council or ad hoc bodies outside the framework of the constitutional provision. For example, the Government of India set up under article 263 of the Constitution the Central Council of Health in 1952, the Central Council for Local Government and Urban Development in 1954, and the Council for Sales Tax and State Excise Duties in 1968. All these bodies are partially intergovernmental in scope.

Further, though the Sarkaria Commission recommended the setting up of the ISC under article 263, it reduced its importance by suggesting that the NDC continue as a separate body. The continued existence of two separate bodies has meant an active NDC in the more salient area of economic federalism and the eclipse of ISC in the political domain, at least thus far. Its importance has further been reduced with the formation of minority/coalition governments in the post 1989 phase where different sets of parties including the regional ones, ruling in some States have become partners in the ruling federal coalitions. This has allowed the regional parties direct access in the Union cabinet. Therefore, they have not been very keen to activate the ISC/NDC.

As a result, the frequency of the NDC meetings has also declined. It has met 52 times (till December 2007).[12] During approximately 39 years of Congress dominance/Janata Party/Congresss restoration under Indira and Rajiv Gandhi phase from 1952 until 1989, the NDC had 40 meetings with an average of 1.1 per year. In 17 years of multi-party coalition/minority governments since Nov-Dec 1989, it had thirteen meetings, an average of 0.75 meetings per year. Further, neo-liberal economic reforms in India accelerated since 1991 have not resulted in the abolition of the Planning Commission but its role is considerably reduced as public investment in the economy has declined. There has also been some decentralization of the planning process due to a greater extent of federalization of the political system since 1990s.

Despite its lack of constitutional status, the NDC is not as idle and inconsequential as the ISC appears to be. It deserves major credit for initiation of development policies and for the dynamism of union-state relations. Its agenda have often rather crowded with crucial issues of intergovernmental significance. Planning related issues have naturally been its most important preoccupation. Other important issues discussed are as follows: food, agriculture, power, irrigation, rural development, social sector (including health, education and employment), centrally sponsored schemes etc.

The issues discussed in ISC meetings are fairly common: recommendations of Sarkaria Commission report covering entire gamut of union-state relations, Article 356, inter-state river water disputes, greater autonomy of states, centrally sponsored schemes, devolution of financial powers to states and panchayati raj, governors' role, consideration of state legislation reserved by governors for presidential assent, resource mobilization etc. However, there has hardly been any constitutional amendment or parliamentary enactment in pursuance of the recommendations made by the ISC except in case of fiscal transfers. There are other issues which could have figured there but on account of conventional patterns of union, state relations, they could not figure there. These matters have even gone to the Court, like the WTO treaty.

It is not easy to measure and evaluate the effectiveness of these bodies in clear-cut terms. Models of organizational effectiveness cannot be uncritically appllied to this task, as these agencies are neither a close bureaucratic system, nor a highly institutionalized and a regular political organization like a Parliament with well established structures and procedures. They are more of an informal gathering with minimal rules of business. Given this fact, only open-system approaches to organizational study can be used here. To this end, Theodore Caplow's multivariate model of organizational effectiveness may be employed here. In his estimation, four factors impinge on organizational effectiveness in an open system: stability of structure, integration of interactional intercourse, voluntarism or non-coercive decision, and achievement of goals. The first three factors in different ways contribute to the fourth factor i.e. "net result of the organization's activity." Using this model in a generalized way, it is possible to argue that both the NDC and ISC reasonable satisfy the first three indicators of stability, integration and voluntarism. For their organizations are defined by executive orders, they can increase the frequency of their meetings and consciously try to promote internal harmony and reduce conflict, and they decide by consensus as sensed by the Prime Minister. So far as the factor of goal achievement is concerned, these bodies especially the NDC can be said to be fairly successful in keeping the union-state negotiations and decisions going in the realm of intergovernmental relations.

The most important factor affecting the working of the ISC and NDC is the party system. The most important intergovernmental accommodations occur within the party system, whether through bargaining among regional factions in the earlier period of one-party dominance of the Congress party, or, more recently, through a more regionalized party system. The degree of discussion and debate in an intergovernmental forum is likely to be more intense in a fragmented party system than in a one-party dominant system. The second factor that influences the effectiveness of these mechanisms concerns the issues and identities in question. For instance, developmental and other non-controversial issues are more likely to be resolved at an intergovernmental forum than issues dealing with major constitutional matters. Moreover, intergovernmental consensus can sometimes be possible under the pressure and urgency of the moment and the ideological climate. Union governments have generally been more accommodative in arriving at a workable understanding on development plans and fiscal federalism than on constitutional amendments and the division of powers between the union and the states. So, urgency of an issue at an intergovernmental forum is most likely to promote political expediency in favour of consensus resolution. Further, the shift to the consensus on neo-liberal economic policy paradigm explains why the agreement has been feasible on economic reforms, just as the earlier consensus on 'state socialism'—Marxists, especially Trotskites, say 'state capitalism'—in the Nehru era—facilitated agreement in that period. Yet another important factor is the personality of the Prime Ministers and the Chief Ministers concerned. The stronger the personalities involved on both sides at an intergovernmental forum, the less likely are the chances of a consensual outcome. The rift between Rajiv Gandhi and NTR Rama Rao in an NDC meeting in the later part of the 1980s is a case in point. Furthermore, demographic and geographical factors also influence the differential in the political weight of the larger States in comparison to that of the smaller States. For example, most Prime Ministers of India have come from U.P, demographically the largest state of the union. Finally, since the rules of business and proceedings are informal in these forums, flexibility also contributes to their success. The more the political actors at an intergovernmental forum are prepared and well briefed on the agenda in advance, the more likely they are to bring dispassionate and rational discussion to the table (Saxena, 2002).

REFORMS

As far as suggestions for reform are concerned, the Sarkaria Commission Report (1988) had given more attention to these mechanisms and had recommended their constitutionalization and federalization. The National Commission to Review the Working of the Constitution (NCRWC) chaired by Justice Venkatachaliah (and its report 2002) has also underlined the importance of ISC and recommended utilization of its full potential for evoking more equitable Union- State relations. This Commission, while endorsing the recommendations of the Sarkaria panel on Centre-State Relations, recommended that "in resolving problems and coordinating policy and action, the Union as well as the States should more effectively utilize the forum of Inter-State Council. This will be in tune with the spirit of cooperative federalism requiring proper understanding and mutual confidence and resolution of problems of common interest expeditiously" *(Report of the NCRWC),* 2002: 164). Similarly, the Common Minimum Programme (CMP) of the United Progressive Alliance (UPA) government also stressed the need for strengthening union-state relations through activation of intergovernmental agencies like the ISC (*CMP of the UPA*, 2004).

In the recent regional roundtables on Indian federalism culminating into the Fourth International conference on Federalism sponsored by the Forum of Federations, Ottawa and hosted by the Inter State Council Secretariat of India, the following two points were discussed in the context of making the ISC more consequential as well as more autonomous from the union Home Ministry, Government of India. Firstly, the Presidential order of 28 May 1990 that established the ISC, omitted clause A of Article 263 of the constitution which reads as follows: "inquiry into and advising upon disputes which have arisen between the states." This omission, it was felt, has taken out of the purview of the ISC, a very important power of formally instituting an inquiry into an inter state dispute. In the long run, political settlement of disputes is not only long lasting but it also reduces the burden on the judiciary whose cutting edge may be blunted by over use.

Secondly, the location of the ISC secretariat in the union Home Ministry tends to make it into an organ of central government rather than an autonomous federal agency. Two alternative sites for its location were considered, namely the Cabinet Secretariat and the Rajya Sabha Secretariat. It was felt that the latter would be a more appropriately autonomous ground as the Rajya Sabha is the representative chamber of the states of India.

Apart from a few procedural reforms like holding regular and preferably in-camera meetings with an advance agenda, preparatory groundwork, and flexible and consensual rules of business, the most important structural reform that can be suggested is the merger of the NDC and the ISC as the key apex intergovernmental mechanism. This will have two desirable effects (Saxena , 2001).

First of all, it would avoid unnecessary bifurcation at the apex intergovernmental body with the same membership in the NDC and ISC. The division of work between the two in terms of economic and political policy making is apparently made on the reasoning that it would prevent politicization of the planning process. In any case, politics cannot really be divorced from economic decision making. In fact, a certain degree of political contestation is necessary to inject a dose of democratic bargaining and to remove the distortions of an imposed consensus that may really conceal an unjust political order.

Secondly, this artificial separation also results in narrow construction of policy areas not only along economic and political issues but also in the proliferation of a large number of national councils for a variety of policy areas that now lack the political status to lend weight to their recommendations. These national councils may still be continued as bodies of technocrats whose recommendations must be considered by a top-level intergovernmental agency representing the executive heads of the two orders of government. Moreover, there is no constitutional obstacle to the merger of the NDC and ISC as article 263 of the constitution does not really restrict the functions of the ISC to any specific policy domain.

Thirdly, keeping the two bodies apart, with two separate secretariats, is also an avoidable profligacy. If the two are merged, the secretariat of the NDC, i.e., the Planning Commission, itself could be expanded to include an economic wing and a political wing. This makes enormous sense today when the governments of India, for almost two decades now, have been promising to reduce deficit but have largely failed to deliver. The reform suggested will cut costs substantially without hampering the deliberative capability and the efficiency of the merged new body which may aptly be called the Intergovernmental Council or Federal Council of India.

In a wider context, Douglas V. Verney has talked about the need of promoting the idea of 'responsible federalism', comparable to the notion of 'responsible government' already reasonably established in the domain of parliamentary government (Verney, 1990). To this end, he has proposed that in order to further federalize the Inter-Governmental Council, its general body may be chaired by the President (thus making it the President-in-Council), while its steering committee may continue to be chaired by the Prime minister. He has suggested that the steering committee of the Council may also be used for recommending promulgation of President's rule in a state under article 356. This will make President's rule less controversial and will acquire greater federal legitimacy.

Even if the NDC and the ISC are not merged as suggested above, it may well be that the time has come when the ISC may be made more effective with additional responsibility. This process will constitutionally reinforce the reform brought about by the Supreme Court in S.R. Bommai which has reduced the political misuse of article 356.

However in early 2005, during the UPA regime, governors of three states, Goa, Jharkhand and Bihar dismissed state governments under Article 356 under questionable circumstances that was against the spirit of the Bommai judgement. These governors with Congress background obviously were trying to be more royalist than the King himself. Both Congress President Sonia Gandhi and Prime Minister Manmohan Singh were upset at these events, as was the President of the Republic, APJ Abdul Kalam. The latter was reported "to have insisted on an explanation from the governor [of Jharkhand] during the meeting he had with the Home Minister Shivraj Patil" who was requested to ask the governor to meet the President "to justify his decisions." Attorney General Milan Banerjee reportedly told the government that it would be difficult to justify the governor's action in the Court (*Times of India*, 2005). The Supreme Court took strong view of these unconstitutional misadventures.

Two decades after the Sarkaria Commission submitted its report, the central government has set up a four –member commission headed by former Chief Justice of India, Justice Madan Mohan Punchhi. The commission has been asked to submit its report within two years. The Terms of Reference of the Commission are alive to the challenges before the Indian federation in an era of profound changes marked by greater federalization, globalization, terrorism, natural disaster largely caused by climate change. Some important specific tasks assigned to the Commission include assessing the impact of the recommendation of the Eighth to Twelfth Finance Commissions on fiscal relations between the two orders of governments, and the continuing over dependence of the states on the center: a federal investigative agency to cope with inter state and international ramifications of crime; amendment of Article 355 allowing sue motto deployment of central forces in states in exceptional circumstances, and effective devolution of powers and autonomy to city councils, panchayati raj and autonomous tribal bodies under the Sixth Schedule of the Constitution (*Commission on Centre State Relations*, 2006).

CONCLUSION

With the growing regionalization within the Indian federation and in the supranational regional context, the intergovernmental interactions are coming under pressures for associating concerned sub national governments in the exercise of the treaty making power of the Union Executive. Similar pressures are evident from sub national governments for involving them in the process of treaty making in the context of increasing globalization of the Indian economy with the emergent world capitalist system. The challenges of mega city governance in Delhi and Mumbai and increasingly elsewhere for a similar place under the sun are also building up.

If we look at the changing scenario of intergovernmental interactions, especially in the context of the process of treaty making, the changes are not dramatic. Yet they are quite remarkable. New demands have been accommodated informally rather than through formal constitutional amendments, legislations, or parameter-altering case laws. This is well and good. For flexibility is preferable unless there is precipitous breakdown of mutual trust or crisis-caused new constitutional compact. The creation of federal consensus was previously made within the one-party dominant Congress system. Now it is the artifact of the coordination committees of the ruling coalitions or multiparty coalition governments. The latter paradigm has increased the maneuverability of the sub national governments. But it is still conducted mostly behind the scene, especially if the matter requires a formal treaty with a foreign power. The typical forums are the same as before, i. e. the conferences of the Prime Minister with the Chief Ministers, ministerial or secretarial conferences and the NDC and ISC, when it comes to domestic affairs. A suggestion for reform I put forward with arguments is the merger of the formal constitutional forums of the NDC and ISC. When it involves treaty making, the matter is largely handled by the Ministry of External Affairs or the Prime Minister himself/herself in consultation with the concerned state governments.

NOTES

The first draft of this paper was presented in an international conference on "Mechanisms of Intergovernmental Relations," organized by the Forum of Federation, Ottawa held in Brazil from 17-18 Sept. 2003. I would like to express my thanks to Professor M.P. Singh and Professor Richard Simeon for their valuable comments that helped me in revising the paper.

1. For example, at least three states—Tamil Nadu, Orissa, and Rajasthan—filed cases in the Supreme Court questioning the union's right to enter into treaties without consultation with, if not consent of the states especially in areas that fell in the exclusive jurisdiction of the states like agriculture. See Rajiv Dhavan, "Treaties ad People: Indian Reflections," *PILSARC Working Paper* No.131,Old Series,1996 and Rajiv Dhavan and Rekha Saxena, "Republic of India," *A Global Dialogue on Federalism, Legislative, Executive , and Judicial Governance in Federal Countries*, eds. Katy Le Roy and Cheryl Saundes, Vol.3, Quebec: McGill Queens University Press, 2006, p.178.
2. The term "executive federalism" was first used in Canadian federal studies by Donald Smiley. This means conduct of intergovernmental relations by the executive heads from federal and regional governments in conferences representing, in the case of India, all the chief ministers, lieutenant governors of the Union Territories chaired by the Prime Minister at levels lower than the first ministers.(D.V. Smiley, *Canada in Question: Federalism in the Eighties*, Toronto: McGraw Hill Ryerson Ltd., 1980, 3rd edition, chapter 4).
3. Balveer Arora is also of the opinion that there has been no serious effort to reinvent this House as a truly federal second chamber. Roundtable on mechanisms of Intergovernmental Relations organized by the Forum of Federations, Ottawa and Institute of Social Sciences, New Delhi in April 2002.
4. Although the first non-Congress government in New Delhi of the Janata Party (1977-79) was formally one-party majority dispensation, astute observers of the Indian political scene have generally interpreted it as a *de facto* coalition. This is because the five parties that hurriedly merged around the 1977 Lok Sabha elections in the backdrop of the internal Emergency (1975-77) never really completed the process of merger to its logical conclusion and its politics revolved around intense factional rivalry among the pre-merger constituent parties i.e. Congress (Organization), Bhartiya Lok Dal, Bhartiya Jana Sangh, the Socialists and the Congress For Democracy.
5. There are also some National Councils representing the Union and State governments in different policy areas like the National Council on Water Resources, National Urban Development Council, National Council on Local Government, National Council on Health etc. In addition, there are several other institutions/ agencies as well which are not intergovernmental in scope but they do facilitate articulation and harmonization of intergovernmental policies, e.g., the Finance

Commission, National Human Rights Commission, National Minorities Commission, Scheduled Castes and Scheduled Tribes Commission, and the Official Language Commission that are Union agencies with provincial implications. For a detailed discussion on Union agencies with provincial implications see Rekha Saxena, *Situating Federalism: Mechanisms of Intergovernmental Relations in Canada and India*, New Delhi: Manohar, 2006.

6. The term Secretary in India designates the bureaucratic head of the Ministry/ Department who is next only to the Minister, the political executive.
7. Prior to S.R. Bommai case, the court gave the Union Executive practically a free hand in determining whether the constitutional machinery in a State had broken down in terms of Article 356 for proclaiming a President's rule there. It had reasoned that it was a "political thicket" best left to the Union Executive. For the first time, the court reversed its earlier rulings in the Bommai judgement, saying that the power to declare President's rule was of course to be exercised by the President on the advice of the Union Cabinet but this power was not absolute; rather it was one which the Union Executive ought to exercise on the basis of certain determinable criteria that should bear relationship with the objective realities of the case concerned. The court in fact went ahead to establish its power of judicial review in the matter and ruled that the Assembly of the State in which a government is dismissed should not be dissolved until at least the approval of the presidential proclamation by the Parliament. The Bommai judgement thus in effect has become the new constitution so far as the President's rule is concerned until the Supreme Court itself reverses that ruling. In a recent ISC meeting it was also decided to incorporate the Bommai judgement in the constitution.(Rekha Saxena, ed., *Mapping Canadian Federalism for India*, Delhi: Konark, 2002, p. 33).
8. An IAS officer who has served alternately the Government of Orissa and the Government of India told this author that in the mid-1980s sometimes the Orissa delegation used to consist of nearly a hundred persons who came to New Delhi for 3-4 days for discussion with the Planning Commission. In more recent years, the number has considerably come down due to financial crunch. (Interview with A.R. Nanda, a former Health Secretary, Government of India, in New Delhi on 24 August, 2003).
9. For example, the Inter-State Council approved the alternative scheme of devolution of share in central taxes to States. A bill for giving effect to this decision was passed by the Parliament with effect from April 1, 1996, as the Constitution's Eightieth Amendment Act 2000 (internet).
10. In the past, during the period of one-party majority governments, Prime Ministers Morarji Desai and Indira Gandhi had started the practice of visiting different State capitals where they wanted to discuss performance of some centrally sponsored developmental plans with the State governments. Whenever they visited a State capital, Chief Minister and major officials of State concerned would meet the Prime Minister in a conference to monitor the progress. But now in the era of multi-party coalition governments with regional parties as partners ruling in some states, the

Prime Ministers do not find it politically feasible (Interview with A.R.Nanda cited earlier and M. P. Singh in Delhi on 1 Sept. 2003).

11. The tenth meeting of the ISC was held on 10 December 2006 with an agenda to discuss atrocities on Scheduled castes and tribes and status of implementation of the SC/ST Prevention of Atrocities Act, 1989.The Council was informed by the Union government that by the Home Ministry records there were 26127 incidents of crime against scheduled castes in the year 2005 and 5713 such incidents against scheduled tribes in the year 2005. Among the 12 States about whom data were presented, U.P and M.P had largest percentage of such incidents against SCs in 2005 (around 17%) whereas Kerala and Haryana presented a more optimistic scenario with 1.7% and 1.3% respectively. The condition of STs was most alarming in the same period in M.P (28.3%) and much better in Kerala and Bihar (both 1.4%).(*The Agenda paper*, courtesy The Inter-State Council Scretariat, pp. 3-5). The ISC meeting endorsed the proposal of Union Minister of Social Justice and Empowerment Meira Kumar that the plan to rid the country of atrocities on dalits and tribals by 2010 should be targeted. The Council also resolved in favour of making FIR obligatory by the police, setting up special courts and prosecutors to ensure speedy and time-bound disposal of cases. (*Indian Express*, New Delhi, December 11, 2006).

12. The 52nd meeting of the NDC was held on December 9, 2006, to approve the Approach Paper for the Eleventh Five-Year Plan prepared by the UPA government led by Manmohan Singh (Congress) which aimed at giving greater priority to agriculture and nine percent annual economic growth overall. While the Council approved the Approach paper, chief ministers of several states used the forum to articulate their demands and anxities. The BJP chief minister of Rajasthan, Vasundhara Raje Scindia, suggested that the NDC could be reformed as a Federal Council operating along the lines of the intergovernmental forums in Canada and Australia that provide greater opportunities for holding an 'open dialogue'. She was critical of "excessive control" over financial management ,recovery of loans from the states, and less than full implementation of the recommendations of the Eleventh and Twelfth Finance Commissions. The Congress chief minister of Uttaranchal, N.D. Tiwari, demanded that the centre consider setting up some special economic zones particularly for the hill states. The Nagaland Chief Minister also pleaded for opening avenues of trade with south Asian economies for the north-eastern states. (*The Hindu* and the *Hindustan Times* both Delhi,10 December 2006).

REFERENCES

Dhavan Rajiv. "Treaties ad People: Indian Reflections," *PILSARC Working Paper* No.131, Old Series, 1996 .

Dhavan, Rajiv and Rekha Saxena, "Republic of India," *A Global Dialogue on Federalism, Legislative, Executive , and Judicial Governance in Federal Countries*, eds. Katy Le Roy and Cheryl Saundes, Vol.3, Quebec: McGill Queens University Press, 2006.

Government of India, Commission on Centre-State Relations, *Report,* Parts I and II, Nasik: Government of India Press,1987-88 (Chair Justice R.S. Sarkaria).

Government of India, Commission on Centre–State Relation, Annexure n.d.

Government of India, *Report of the National Commission to Review the Working of the Constitution*, Delhi: Universal Law Publishing Co. Vol. 1, para 8.12.4, p. 164.

Guidelines for Identifying and Selecting Issues to be brought before the Inter-State Council, Inter-State Council Secretariat, 22 January 1999, Section I, Clause (i), (ii) and last paragraph.

Indian Express, New Delhi, March 21,1988.

Majeed, Akhtar. paper prepared for roundtable on Mechanisms of Intergovernmental Relations in India held on 22 April 2002 and organized by the Institute of Social Sciences, New Delhi, p.10.

Nanda, A.R in an interview in New Delhi, note No.12.

Saez, Lawrence. *Federalism Without a Centre: The Impact of Political and Economic Reforms on India's Federal System,* Delhi: Sage, 2002.

Saxena, Rekha, *Situating Federalism: Mechanisms of Intergovernmental Relations in Canada and India*, New Delhi, Manohar, 2006.

Saxena, Rekha. "Strengthening Federal Dialogue: Role of NDC & ISC," *Contemporary India*, Vol.1, no. 3, July-September, 2002.

Saxena, Rekha. "Treaty–Making Powers: A Case for "Federalisation and Parliamentarisation," *Economic and Political Weekly*, Vol. XLII, No. 1, January 6-12, 2007.

Saxena, Rekha. *Intergovernmental Relations in India,* Federal Studies Orientation Series, Center for Federal Studies, New Delhi, 2006.

Saxena, Rekha. "Role of Intergovernmental Agencies," *The Hindu*, 29 January, 2001.

Singh, B. P, former Home Secretary, Government of India in an interview in New Delhi on 29 August, 2003.

Singh, M. P. "A Borderless Internal Federal Space? Reorganization of States in India," *India Review*, vol. 6, no. 4, October-December, 2008.

Singh, M.P. Economic Liberalization and Political Federalization in India: Mutually Reinforcing Responses to Global Integration in *The Impact of Global and Regional Integration on Federal Systems: A Comparative Analysis,* (eds.) Harvey Lazar *et al.*, Queen's University, School of Policy Studies, Montreal: McGill Queen's University Press , 2003.

Singh, B.P and A.R. Nanda in an Interview in New Delhi, note nos. 9 and 12 above.

Smiley, D.V. *Canada in Question*: *Federalism in the Eighties*, Toronto: McGraw Hill Ryerson Ltd., 1980.

Supreme Court. Kuldip Nayar vs Union of India, 2006, *All India Reporter*, Supreme Court Section: 3057.

Supreme Court, S.R. Bommai and Others vs Union of India and Others, *Judgements Today*, Vol. 2, No. 8, March 1994.

The Hindu, October 14, 2008.

The Times of India, March 3, 2005.

Theodore, Caplow. Principles of Organization, New York: Harcourt, Brace and World, 1964.

UPA, *Common Minimum Programme of the United Progressive Alliance,* New Delhi, May 2004.

Verney, Douglas. V. "Responsible Government and Responsible Federalism—Parliamentary Government in Plural Societies," *Typescript* (Department of Political Science, York University, Toronto, 1990).

VIII

Cultural Politics and Contestations in India's Foreign Policy Making: Some Observations

A. K. Ramakrishnan

Introduction

Indian foreign policy is becoming a realm of increasing contestations. State's positions on a wide range of issues from the World Trade Organisation to the United States to Iran are intensely being interrogated. At last foreign policy looks like any other arena of public policy. The so-called 'consensus' culture of foreign policy nurtured by various political entities in the past now seems to be outmoded. Diversity of opinion and debates on the very political notions that govern foreign policy seem to be the order of the day.

Cultural aspects of India's foreign policy are traditionally discussed by experts as diplomatic endeavours involving the propagation of the civilizational heritage and the historical significance of India. There are not many works that throw light on the cultural contours of India's foreign policy. This chapter tries to look at the linkage between culture and foreign policy in a cultural perspective, or rather a cultural studies perspective. Such a perspective offers a critical reflexive analysis of cultural politics of foreign policy. Many analysts of foreign policy share elite anxieties about state power and insecurities and state's constraints in public policy making, including the making of foreign policy.

This is a preliminary attempt to problematize the linkage between culture and foreign policy in the Indian context by going beyond the instrumentalist notion of culture as a tool of external conduct. Here, culture is not only discussed in the limited realm of cultural diplomacy but also covering the realms of the culture of foreign policy, ideas, values and orientations that inform policy decisions from time to time. The civilizational and ideological domains of culture are also significant.

In traditional International Relations, the political and the cultural are viewed in a disconnected fashion. Foreign policy making is invariably discussed as involving security, strategy, decision-making and economy. It is also true that the domestic/international divide is stressed beyond a point due to versions Realist perspectives that dominate the field of study. As Gramsci has shown, culture cannot be separated from political and economic power, as it is a constitutive realm of such power (Halliday, 2000: 67). A cultural perspective enables one to politically engage with cultural practices of public policy realms including foreign policy. Domestic/international linkages are also significant in this cultural study.

Various ideological and political developments have created an increased concern for culture. The day in and day out discourses on terrorism, clash of civilizations, religious wars, etc. on the one hand and the ascendancy of values and ideas of identity, citizenship, community, civil society and social movements on the other hand provide abundant vistas of cultural analysis of international relations. Only a few contemporary arenas of cultural politics and political culture are taken up here for a brief discussion.

CULTURE AND FOREIGN POLICY

Niranjan Khilnani traces cultural elements of India's foreign policy in a fairly detailed manner. Describing the nature of intersection between tradition and modernity in Indian politics and finding their reflection in foreign policy, he wrote in the early 1980s that Gandhi's principles have a deep impact on Indian foreign policy.

> The present tenets of Indian Foreign Policy revolve around his three fundamental concepts: (i) Right means to achieve right ends; (ii) Never close the door of negotiation and conciliation even if an individual or nation attacks you; (iii) What is morally wrong is also politically wrong (1981: 123).

A. Appadorai also enlists three traditional values that have implications for India's foreign policy: 'tolerance, the equation of means and ends, and non-violence (1981: 29). One may immediately find this marriage of ethics and foreign policy in trouble in a number of contemporary foreign policy initiatives: strategic, nuclear, trade, etc. In another book, N.M. Khilnani gave more nuanced descriptions of cultural dimensions of India's foreign policy. He points out that 'newly-emergent independent countries utilized their "cultures" to overcome their respective crises of identities and to assert their nationhood' (1984: 89). Gayatri Spivak on the other hand talks about the problematic of culture in such a context: 'There is often a certain loss of style in the descent or shift from the high culture of nationalism within territorial imperialism to that search for "national identity" that confuses religion, culture, and ideology in the newly independent nation' (1999: 64). The use of culture for construction of national identity and foreign policy on the one hand, and the very implications various identity assertions have on culture on the other hand render this instrumentality more problematic. Defining oneself as a nation and projecting oneself as a nation involves problems attached with monocultural and representational practices. The structural logic of modern nationalism and the national assertions in post-independent situations giving way to oppressive new national projects make cultural projections of the nation abroad a contested, problematic realm. As Etienne Balibar so clearly states,

> the very category of nationalism is intrinsically ambiguous. This has to do, first of all, with the antithetical nature of the historical situations in which nationalist movements and policies arise.

> Fichte or Gandhi are not Bismarck; Bismarck or De Gaulle are not Hitler. And yet we cannot, by a mere intellectual decision, suppress the effect of ideological symmetry which imposes itself here on the antagonistic forces. We have no right whatsoever to equate the nationalism of the dominant with that of the dominated, the nationalism of liberation with the nationalism of conquest. Yet this does not mean we can simply ignore the fact that there is a common element—if only the logic of a situation, the structural inscription in the political forms of the modern world—in the(se) nationalism(s) (1991: 45).

Jawaharlal Nehru's view on nationalism in the context of India's role in the world was that narrow nationalism has no place here. While nationalism as such has a place in each country, 'it must not be allowed to become aggressive and come in the way of international development' (1983a: 303). The growth of aggressive nationalism in India's domestic political and particularly in the cultural front was bound to spill over overtly and covertly in the foreign policy dynamics of the government.

N.M. Khilnani points out that if colonialism was significant in the cultural renaissance and Indian national identity assertion, partition was significant in making the Indian leadership aware of the importance of shaping and maintaining cultural relations with neighbouring Asian regions, particularly West Asia and Southeast Asia (1984: 91). He offers the broad motivations and mechanics of the use of culture as an instrument of diplomacy in the following scheme:

- To ensure the flow of ideas, information, scientific and technological data between States;
- To foster (to the extent possible) an objective and realistic perception of values, influences and domestic, social and ideological compulsions between societies and peoples;
- To ensure international cultural and intellectual cooperation to meet economic and social problems which affect more than one country and transcend the framework of bilateral concerns;

- To create a climate of understanding, and to influence the decision-making sections of other societies in one's favour;
- To influence the academic, intellectual and cultural processes in other States which would bring them closer to the ideology and technology of one's own country;
- To sustain an interest in, and to preserve and create, academic, artistic and literary activities which would contribute to friendship and goodwill between countries; the overall objective being to create a favourable political climate which would contribute to the fulfilment of mutual interest, friendship and influence (Ibid: 89).

To undertake all these tasks, apart from the political ones, is no easy matter. This is why Nehru said that '(i)n the key places of the world the ideal ambassador must be some kind of a superman' (1983b: 205). But his superman cannot speak. To him, '(t)he first thing that an ambassador of ours has to learn is to shut his mouth and give up public or even private speaking', because a 'false step, a false phrase, makes all the difference' (Ibid: 206). As famous cartoonist and author O.V. Vijayan used to tell this writer that foreign policy is that which is not spoken. Obviously there are abundant documents in the written form. But texts are useful to the extent that one can decipher that which is not uttered. The problem that the foreign policy elite confronts, therefore, is to speak for the nation without speaking at all! This would not only mean not merely that there are umpteen structural and circumstantial constraints within which the foreign policy makers and advocates function, but also that the traps of the discursive realm are many and varied. In a way, cultural and political discourses involving foreign policy are fraught with *realpolitick* insularities rather than them being enabled by the abundance of cultural riches.

Also noteworthy is that the major instrument of cultural diplomacy still remains to be the Indian Council for Cultural Relations (ICCR), in spite of significant global changes and the range of tasks that have to be carried out. The ICCR was founded in 1950 as wing of Department of Culture, Ministry of Education. It subsequently came under the administrative control of the Ministry of External Affairs (Bandyopadhyaya: 229-32). ICCR's objectives are

- To participate in the formulation and implementation of policies and programmes relating to India's external cultural relations
- To promote cultural exchange with other countries and peoples
- To promote and strengthen cultural relations and mutual understanding between India and other countries
- To establish and develop relations with national and international organisations in the field of culture (ICCR, 1999).

The exchange of performing arts groups, academics, artists, administering scholarship schemes of foreign students in India, conduct of the activities of cultural centres abroad etc. are the work undertaken by the ICCR. What is striking is the gap between ICCR's organisational apparatus and the increased realms of cultural interaction required at the international level. The general context and the nature of contemporary international cultural relations is captured well by Mark Alleyne in the following words:

> Institutionalized international cultural relations became a regular means of conducting international relations for an elite club of states after the Second World War. The capital-intensity of international cultural relations has kept the number of states in this elite club small. They benefit from the power of communication and are positioned, therefore, to exercise the power of information (1995: 112).

It is almost like joining the nuclear club. Technologically, India has forged ahead in the realm of communication, but in the related cultural sphere, questions remain.

NATIONAL IDENTITY AND NATIONAL INTEREST

We all agree that national imagination involves the invoking of myths and history. Foreign policy making as a historical act does utilise national imagination to pursue what is referred to as 'national interest'. The mythology of national interest is projected both within and outside the territorial state as the cornerstone of foreign policy making. The act of policy making in this realm is more 'national' in character than such an endeavour in other public policy avenues. Invoking the myth of national interest involves the presupposition of a well-defined meta-conception of national identity. Culture works here in three ways: one, as a monolithic value of the nation; two, as a tool for the creation of national power that in part constitutes national interest; and three, as an element that can be projected beyond the boundaries as an instrument of diplomacy.

As Gyanendra Pandey suggests, 'the nation was, and continues to be, the outcome of many different visions and the struggle between them' (1990: 261). When the diplomats represent 'our' nation in 'foreign' lands, they in a way represent 'their' nation, as there is no singularity of national imagination. T.K. Oommen classifies the defining of the Indian 'nation' into seven ways:

> as (1) an ancient civilisational entity; (2) a composite culture; (3) a multi-national polity; (4) a religious entity; (5) a geographical/territorial entity populated by a a multiplicity of religious communities; (6) a collectivity of linguistic communities; and finally as (7) a unity of great and little nationalisms (2003: 267).

The success of any cultural diplomatic effort would imply the strategic deployment of any or a combination of these national imaginations to one's advantage. It is not always possible to have that cultural-strategic gain as there are certain definitions that have an uncomfortable relationship with the 'national interest' project of foreign policy and there are certain imaginations that are mutually untenable beyond a point. The points of conflict between contemporary cultural nationalist assertions at home with its international spread and the multi-pronged imagination of a nation also put considerable stress on cultural diplomacy of the Indian elite.

Amartya Sen talks about an interesting aspect of the role of the state in nationalism:

> It is certainly true that in the emergence or consolidation of any national unity, the nation-state may well have an important instrumental role, but the state need not be central to the conceptual foundation of this unity, nor account for the constructive emergence of the *sense* of a national unity, and thus of 'nationhood' (1997: 25).

The state's attempt at externally projecting itself at the central stage of the nation falls into a dichotomy, one that involves the articulation of national interest as emanating from the nation, while the very imagination of nation is not within its control and purview. Invoking Morgenthau here, one can say, interest is defined in terms of somebody else's power.

CULTURAL STRATEGY AND STRATEGIC CULTURE

The nuclear era in Indian politics coincides with a period of greater vulnerability of the population to insecurities emanating from new cultures of violence and increasing inequity (Ramakrishnan, 2004: 68-70). There is the securitization of more and more arenas of human life on the one hand and the increasing social and human security concerns on the other. The national security/national interest paradigm has asserted itself at one level and the criticism and challenges to it have emerged from various quarters. The classical Realist foreign policy doctrines are still in vogue as far as the elites are concerned. The Hobbesian state of nature is still valid for policy makers. How can one expect culture as a significant entity in foreign policy in such a milieu?

The emergence of nuclear India meant the assertion of a national security state, a process that involves changes in the cultural practices of the nation-state. Raja Mohan sees 'the nuclear leap forward' in 1998 as an extremely significant development in the positive direction. 'More fundamentally', he says, 'the nuclear tests and the post-Pokhran diplomacy changed the way the Indian elite began to think about external relations and diplomacy' (2005: 27). As Arundhati Roy sharply put it, "these are not just nuclear tests, they are nationalism tests," we were repeatedly told' (2001: 18). If for Raja Mohan, the decisiveness of Indian elite is more appealing from a state strategy perspective. From a cultural angle, questions of hegemony, life, and alternatives are significant. After all, culture, for the state elite is only a realm of 'soft power'. The changing strategic culture was twinned with the assertion of the monocultural power of the nation, particularly by Hindu nationalism. Nuclear capability was seen as part of a strong national and state entity. Their definition of Indianness presumed a strong state instrument for identity assertion (Sunil Khilnani 1998: 190). But, as Gayatri Spivak points out, there results a disjuncture between nation and state here, rather than the strong bond between them: 'Fundamentalist nationalism arises in the loosened hyphen between nation and state as the latter is being mortgaged further and further by the forces of financialization' (1999: 364).

THE CHANGING CULTURE OF FOREIGN POLICY MAKING

The culture of foreign policy making is undergoing tremendous changes due to the powerful blow of global winds through the corridors of South Block and beyond. The diplomatic preponderance in foreign policy making has, at least partly, given way to economic and commercial entities. Economics and politics of foreign policy making cannot be at odds anymore, says the new political class. It is good that there are more players now. It is also true that adjusting the rules of the game at a rapid pace might have even altered the very nature of the game itself. The values and orientations of foreign policy making by the Indian elite have to be rethought not only due to the entry of other elements into the process, but also due to the heaviness of influence of neoliberal market values. Long-term political calculations and the sneezy fluctuations of stock market need not always intersect. The new value orientation and value additions have created a cultural shift in the making of foreign policy by the Indian elite.

In a way Nehru anticipated the vagaries of time and compulsions in foreign policy making. He wanted to break the realist-idealist dichotomy by pointing towards both the momentariness and the futuristic elements of foreign policy. In a speech in Parliament in 1950, Nehru said:

> We have to deal with matters as they come up. In matters of foreign policy especially, one has to decide almost every hour what has to be done.... It is this spirit of realism that I want you to approach the question of our foreign policy.... What exactly is idealism? ... Idealism is the realism of tomorrow. It is the capacity to know what is good for the day after tomorrow or for the next year and to fashion yourself accordingly (1982: 26).

The Nehruvian notion of foreign policy involves a belief that

> foreign relations, though they involve trade, business, etc., are not like opening a branch of a business firm, as sometimes some of our business magnates seem to imagine. It is a very intricate and very difficult business dealing with the psychology of nations, involving considerations of their background and culture, language and so on (Nehru, 1983c: 241-42).

Nehru has also considered the new and the ancient character of Indian polity. Both the characters, of being young and being ancient impose opportunities and constraints. Recognising the nation's young character in the foreign policy field, he argued for a culture of foreign policy that gradually develops and unfolds (1983d: 259). The value and ideological power of non-alignment as a central stance in foreign policy was seen as integral in such a development. Not only the 'tradition of tolerance', but also 'practical considerations' were stated to be the thrust of Indian non-alignment (Appadorai and Rajan, 1985: 15 and Jaisingh 1983: 1-6). Nehru stood for the development of a political culture that combined elements of Western liberal citizenship-oriented political system that combines values of equity and justice. The reflection of such a political culture was embodied in the policy of non-alignment. It was 'the best of both worlds (liberal capitalist and socialist)' kind of non-alignment. The value of non-alignment as foreign policy vision and ideology was that it could mediate between the contradictions of liberty and control, and freedom and equity.

Many foreign policy analysts understood the change in India's foreign policy in the 1990s in terms of a transformation from idealism to pragmatism (Raja Mohan 2005: xxi). This author believes, as presented in an earlier work, that the shift in the sphere of India's foreign policy, as to be seen in other realms of public policy, is not from ideology to pragmatism, but from a developmental statist ideology and practice to a neoliberal ideology and practice (Ramakrishnan 2005: 27). Along with nuclear and other strategic orientations, this new dimension of foreign policy change projects a new image of the nation-state in global affairs. This would also entail questions of political legitimacy within the state. This is where the 'consensual' character of foreign policy is giving rise to more and more contestations.

The antidote to monocultural and market-oriented cultural practices in politics and foreign policy is sought in multicultural and democratic practices. As Jan Aart Scholte made it clear,

> The quest for multiculturality takes place in a contemporary world system suffused with capitalist expropriation, democratic deficits, environmental degradation and dogmatic belief—all of which work against its realisation. Hence the project of multicultural community cannot be pursued successfully on its own, emancipation in the realm of identity has to parallel, and be part of, concurrent emancipation in the areas of production, governance, ecology and knowledge (1996: 71).

Such a task necessitates a political and foreign policy transformation.

NOTE

An earlier version of this chapter was presented at the National Seminar on *Culture and Identity in International Relations: Impact on Foreign Policy* at the School of International Studies, Jawaharlal Nehru University, New Delhi, 16-17 March 2006.

REFERENCES

Alleyne, Mark D. (1995), *International Power and International Communication*, Basingstoke: Macmillan.

Appadorai, A. (1981), *Domestic Roots of India's foreign Policy, 1947-1972*, Delhi: Oxford University Press.

Appadorai, A. and M.S. Rajan (1985), *India's Foreign Policy and Relations* (New Delhi: South Asian Publishers.

Balibar, Etienne (1991), "Racism and Nationalism," in Etienne Balibar and Immanuel Wallerstein, *Race, Nation, Class*, London: Verso.

Bandyopadhyaya, Jayantanuja (1979), *The Making of India's Foreign Policy*, New Delhi: Allied Publishers.

Halliday, Fred (2000), "Culture and International Relations: A New Reductionism?," in Michi Ebata and Beverly Neufeld (eds.), *Confronting the Political in International Relations*, Basingstoke: Macmillan.

Indian Council for Cultural Relations (ICCR) (1999), "About the ICCR" [Online: Web] Accessed 29 June 2008, URL: *http://education.vsnl.com/iccr/aboutus.htm.*

Jaisingh, Hari (1983), *India and the Non-Aligned World*, New Delhi: Vikas Publishing House.

Khilnani, N.M. (1981), *Panorama of Indian Diplomacy*, New Delhi: S. Chand and Company.

Khilnani, N.M. (1984), *Realities of Indian Foreign Policy*, New Delhi: ABC Publishing House.

Khilnani, Sunil (1998), *The Idea of India*, New Delhi: Penguin Books.

Nehru, Jawaharlal (1982), "Speech in Parliament on 7 December 1950," in A. Appadorai, *Select Documents on India's Foreign Policy and Relations, 1947-1972, Vol. 1*, Delhi: Oxford University Press.

Nehru, Jawaharlal (1983a), "Inaugural Speech at the Asian Relations Conference, New Delhi, 23 March 1947," in *Jawaharlal Nehru's Speeches,* 1946-49, Vol.1, New Delhi: Publications Division, Ministry of Information and Broadcasting, Government of India.

Nehru, Jawaharlal (1983b), "Speech in the Constituent Assembly, New Delhi, 4 December 1947," in *Jawaharlal Nehru's Speeches*, 1946-49, Vol.1, New Delhi:

Publications Division, Ministry of Information and Broadcasting, Government of India.

Nehru, Jawaharlal (1983c), "Speech in the Constituent Assembly, New Delhi, 8 March 1949," in *Jawaharlal Nehru's Speeches*, 1946-49, Vol.1, New Delhi: Publications Division, Ministry of Information and Broadcasting, Government of India.

Nehru, Jawaharlal (1983d), "Speech at the Indian Council of World Affairs, New Delhi, 22 March 1949," in *Jawaharlal Nehru's Speeches*, 1946-49, Vol.1, New Delhi: Publications Division, Ministry of Information and Broadcasting, Government of India.

Oommen, T.K. (2003), "Demystifying the Nation and Nationalism," in Geeti Sen (ed.), *India: A National Culture?* New Delhi: Sage Publications.

Pandey, Gyanendra (1990), *The Construction of Communalism in Colonial North India*, Delhi: Oxford University Press.

Raja Mohan, C. (2005), *Crossing the Rubicon: The Shaping of India's New Foreign Policy*, New Delhi: Penguin Books.

Ramakrishnan, A.K. (2004), "Conceptualising Security," in Purusottam Bhattacharya, Tridib Chakraborti and Shibashis Chatterjee (eds.), *Anatomy of Fear: Essays on India's Internal Security*, New Delhi: Lancer's Books.

Ramakrishnan, A.K. (2005), "Neoliberal Globalism and India's Foreign Policy: Towards a Critical Rethinking," in Rajen Harshe and K.M. Seethi, (eds.), *Engaging with the World: Critical Reflections on India's Foreign Policy*, Hyderabad: Orient Longman.

Roy, Arundhati (2001), *The Algebra of Infinite Justice*, New Delhi: Viking.

Scholte, Jan Aart (1996), "Globalisation and Collective Identities," in Jill Krause and Neil Renwick (eds.), *Identities in International Relations*, Basingstoke: Macmillan.

Sen, Amartya (1997), "On Interpreting India's Past," in Sugata Bose and Ayesha Jalal (eds.), *Nationalism, Democracy and Development: State and Politics in India*, Delhi: Oxford University Press.

Spivak, Gayatri Chakravorty (1999), *A Critique of Postcolonial Reason*, Cambridge, Massachusetts: Harvard University Press.

IX

Transnational Neighbourhoods, Subnational Futures: Reimagining North East India

Nimmi Kurian

The ordering of space, both subnational and transnational, stands at the core of how a border is imagined as well as contested. State borders defined predominantly in territorial terms sit uneasily with the derritorialised agendas that globalisation brings in its wake. These hold important implications for new subregional initiatives that are in the process of reconnecting Northeast India with its transnational neighbourhood. The chapter argues that the shifting border discourse provides an interesting template for bottom-up approaches to India's foreign policy formulation with the potential for a subnational future for the Northeast. This in turn will hinge on the capacity to decenter participation by framing a subregional governance agenda and creating alternative discursive spaces. Together, these will form the twin constitutive strands of an integrative narrative about reimagining the Northeast as an actor with agency. The manner in which these difficult transformations are negotiated will in turn decide the success of India's subregional imaginary.

National Borders, Transnational Neighbourhoods

National borders situated in transnational neighbourhoods will wrestle with many inherent contradictions and tensions between national and transnational interpretive lenses. This, as James Anderson and Liam O'Dowd note, is inevitable since 'the nation-state ideal of cultural homogeneity and centralised political control is both confirmed and disrupted at the border' (Anderson et al., 1999: 596). In the national narrative, the Northeast appears as the periphery - the outer limits of the state's absolute sovereignty, a space that is territorially organised, patrolled, enforced and enclosed. The accompanying burden of marginality has shunted the Northeast to the edges in discourses of power and representation.[1] But seen in a transnational frame, the border becomes not quite the margin but the centre of a vast and bustling network of social and cultural flows. Along with Sikkim, the Northeastern region shares more than 99 per cent of its 5000 km long international border with China, Bhutan, Myanmar and Bangladesh. Given this compelling geographic location, it is not surprising that the Northeast has always looked outwards, the ethnic makeup of its peoples reflecting centuries-old processes of co-mingling and migrations. Typical of this has been the metamorphosis of faiths as they crossed borders and returned, enriched with local flavours. Thus, Tibetan Buddhism and Tai-Ahoms each brought its distinctive variant to the land of its origins. In this sense, the Northeast, as Sanjoy Hazarika notes, qualifies as 'one of the earliest "globalised" places in South Asia' (Hazarika, 2006). The 300 ethnic groups that trace their ties across the border and the powerful tug of shared history, geography and languages such as the Mon-Khmer and Tibeto-Burman family of languages that are spoken across Southeast Asia, southern China and the Northeast, impinge on daily consciousness in a manner that cannot be captured within territorial frames. It is this traffic that has been so vital to and an integral part of the everyday existence of border communities and which operate despite the exclusionary nature of territorial mapping of borders. Take this away and what emerges is an entity uprooted from its moorings, which has to unwittingly disown not just this intimate past but to

[1]Northeast India refers to the easternmost region of India consisting of the states of Arunachal Pradesh, Assam, Meghalaya, Manipur, Mizoram, Nagaland, Tripura and Sikkim. The region borders Bhutan, Nepal, China, Myanmar and Bangladesh.

foreswear a shared present as well as future. The discontents, which the region has experienced, originate in this inheritance of loss.

The securitisation of borders following Partition in 1947 created new geographical realities which all but partitioned the vast heartland of India from the seven states that now lay beyond Bangladesh. The disruption of historic routes of communication condemned the Northeast to geographical isolation as a distant outpost. Verghese ruefully notes India's inability to seek 'historic uses' employed effectively by Pakistan to secure rights over the Indus, Chenab and Jhelum during the negotiations over the Indus Treaty in the 1950s. India, he notes, never asserted a similar user right either to transit through East Pakistan or to Chittagong which was the traditional outlet to sea for the Northeast (Verghese, 2003:5). By abrogating the Barcelona Convention in 1956, India also voluntarily surrendered the right to inland navigation recognised under international law. Thus, what had once been one seamless transport corridor now became segmented with stiff barriers to trade and traffic. Contesting the characterisation of borders as 'spatial fixtures, lines in the landscape, separators of societies- the passive pre-given ground on which events take place', Schendel rightly argues that spatiality, be it at the local, national and global scales, should be recognised as socially constructed (Schendel, 2005:9). For instance, it is curious that the present political discourse on the Northeast as gateway rests critically on the proximity factor that is used to make the case for reconnecting India with the eastern neighbourhood. But this natural advantage was conspicuous by its absence during the long decades of its isolation from the very same neighbourhood–further reiterating the fact that the isolation and landlocked status of the Northeast is first and foremost a political construct which in turn calls for a political solution.

Thus, although knit together by geography, the new geopolitical realities went on to magnify distances and constrict connectivity (Kurian, 2002). For instance, the distance between Agartala, the capital of Tripura and Kolkata through Bangladesh is 400 kms. Take this connectivity away and the distance suddenly multiplies to 1,645 kms. The flow of goods and traffic ground to an abrupt halt and the subregion as a whole collectively bore the brunt. An illegal, crossborder trade has taken its place and assumed a formidable size, further draining the exchequer. Since India and Bangladesh do not have an agreement to move container traffic this entails inordinate delays, expense and time. A container from Delhi, bound for Dhaka could cover the distance of 2000 kms by rail in two to three days. Lacking this crucial facility, the container now makes a circuitous journey that takes 45 days. From Delhi, it moves to Mumbai, thence to Singapore, onto Chittagong port from where it is finally transported to Dhaka.

Today, the talk of reopening borders is misleading, for it conveys the impression that one is talking of reopening a dormant border. Far from it. The thriving of what is euphemistically referred to as informal trade attests to the fact that the border continues to be a zone of brisk trade and commerce with the crucial difference that much of it bypasses the official channel. What could not come in officially and legally came in unofficially and illegally. In the Northeast particularly, the existence of illegal cross-border trade shows the blurring of the external-internal divide wherein efforts to maintain an artificial distinction between the two have become untenable and clearly defy existing ground reality. A fortress mentality and sealing of borders has not deterred flows of all kinds which flow as if the barriers never existed and are as clear an indication as any of the considerable potential that exists for cross-border commerce. Studies reveal that informal trade with Myanmar through the border town of Moreh in Manipur is estimated at Rs 2000 crores a year (Singh, 2002:193). Goods from Myanmar, China and Thailand find their way to India, and Indian commercial presence is visible across the borders. A whole range of goods cross through these borders, which do not get reflected in official trade figures.

It is thus clear that the starting point for any exercise on rethinking borders by default has to be their sheer diversity and complexity. The politico-military understanding of borders as being mere geographical markers masks the enormous complexity and diversity that a border region encompasses. Seen in this limited manner, their understandings have been grossly generalised without reference to the multiplicity of meanings that they embody, all of which points to the need to contextualise and locate each border within its own political, economic, social and cultural specificities. Such a deliberately simplified categorisation robs the border of its rich and varied cultural, historical and social layers of identity. When the state seeks to 'close' its borders through formal measures, informal processes go on to 'open' the same border. Thus the border bears daily witness to a multiplicity of crossings which while not being 'official' or 'legal' are very much real in every sense. For those living on the frontiers, the border is far from the line of control that the centre constructs it to be. Paradoxically, for them the border is both an invisible as well as an integral aspect of their social existence. It is invisible because much of the transactions that are not 'authorised' by the state take place anyway, despite the state. As Schendel notes, border regions resonate with stories of how unsuccessful states are in 'enclosing people bent on crossing' the border (Schendel, 2005: 202). Integral to the way a border is imagined or reimagined will be the practices, perceptions of those who negotiate it in their daily lives imbuing it with a dynamic character. It is this constitutive nature of border regions that assumes a centrality in the lives and experiences of communities, which typically can be understood only within a transnational frame of reference. It will be this 'capacity to organise space and cross-border relationships' as Anderson and Dowd note, which will constitute 'a key to power in the contemporary global system' (Anderson et al., 1999: 598). As Rabinowitz asserts, 'Studying communities which live across borders, survive despite them, routinely cross them and constantly network around them has become an indispensable aspect of the discourse' (Rabinowitz 1998:142). Therefore, it is vital that the discourse on the Northeast as gateway is imagined not merely as an economic initiative. That will be too restrictive a vision. It is above all also about reconnecting lives sundered by rigid territoriality which is one of the most defining realities facing the region. It is this rupture that the discourse most urgently needs to engage with. The following section offers a critical assessment of this discourse and debates whether the Northeast will be in a position to take advantage of the opportunities opening up.

THE PERIPHERY AS HUB: THE DISCOURSE ON THE NORTHEAST AS GATEWAY

If policy statements proclaiming its new status are any indication to go by, the Northeast now stands elevated to the highest rhetorical levels of importance in state policy. Placing the Northeast at the centre of the country's eastward orientation, India's Prime Minister Atal Behari Vajpayee in his inaugural speech at the Second Northeast Business Summit in 2004 noted 'When I look at the North-East, I also naturally look at India's extended neighbourhood in South East Asia' (www.ibef.org, 2004). In the same vein, Prime Minister Manmohan Singh, during his maiden visit to Arunachal Pradesh in 2008, described the border state as the land where the 'sun kisses India first' and waxed eloquent on how it 'will rise from the east as a new star and become one of the best regions of our country' (*Indian Express*, 2008). While the metaphor may be a trifle trite, it reflects the growing priority India attaches to several subregional initiatives taken in recent years. Sub-regional economic zones envisage geographically proximate sub-regions within two or more countries as important sites of transnational economic exchange (Thant et al., 1994). Sub-regional initiatives like the Bay of Bengal Multi-Sectoral Initiative for Technical and Economic Cooperation (BIMSTEC), the Mekong-Ganga Cooperation (MGC) and the Kunming Initiative hold the potential of galvanising the entire eastern region of India by integrating it with the fast growing economies of Southeast Asia and beyond. The MGC, consisting of Cambodia, India, Laos, Myanmar, Thailand, and Vietnam was established in Vientiane in 2000 to boost cooperation particularly in the fields of tourism, culture, human resources development and transportation linkages. The BIMSTEC established in Bangkok in 1997 aims at closer economic cooperation through harmonisation of customs procedures, banking facilities and other trade facilitation measures. A Free Trade Agreement was signed during the BIMSTEC ministerial meeting in February 2004 in Phuket, Thailand, which also saw the inclusion of Nepal and Bhutan as new members. These are expected to considerably boost inter-regional and intra-regional trade. The Kunming Initiative which seeks to strengthen regional economic cooperation and cultural exchange between the contiguous regions of Eastern/Northeastern India, China's Southwest, Myanmar and Bangladesh. The initiative came to be so called since China chose Kunming as the venue for a Track II conference in 1999 to launch the regional economic forum. Such a sub-regional zone according to Che Zhimin will be 'at the centre of three markets of China, Southeast Asia and South Asia as well as the bridge and link for mutual radiation, permeation and exchange of the three markets. The zone can closely connect the two major markets of China and India and even the markets in the whole Asia and can quicken the economic integration of Asia so as to promote the speedy economic development of Asia and the world' (Che,1998:2).

The Centre has also been responding gradually to long standing demands from within the Northeast to reconnect the region with its eastern neighbourhood. Illustrative examples serve to highlight the well-articulated demands and activities that are beginning to successfully exert pressure on the Centre on a range of local issues. In particular, these have tended to coalesce around the demands to reopen border trade and improve both physical and institutional infrastructure for the free movement of people, goods and services. A case in point is the reopening of the Nathu La Pas trade route between India and China. The Nathu La pass linking Sikkim with Tibet had been central to the larger Eastern Himalayas region including West Bengal, Arunachal Pradesh and neighbouring areas of China. The Nathu La Study Group, commissioned by the Sikkim Government projected a \$4.57 million trade flow by 2007, \$78 million by 2010 and $127.5 million by 2020 (Hasan 2006). Based on the recommendations of the Study Group, the Nathu La pass was formally reopened for trade in 2006 after more than four decades of closure. There is also a growing demand to follow this up by connecting Kalimpong in West Bengal to Tibet via another alternate all-weather pass, the Jelep La. This route, at the India-Tibet-Bhutan tri-junction, had been an ancient trade route used by Indian and Tibetan traders and had seen brisk trade in silk, spices, musk, wool and textiles. There are also plans to promote tourism by connecting the Northeast with the well-established tourism network of Southeast Asia. Steps are being mooted to institutionalise cross-border cooperation in marketing, transit, research, training and a variety of imaginatively conceived package tour programmes (Bhuthalingam, 2003). Such an integrated approach can be extended to cover the entire region including Bhutan, Nepal, Sri Lanka. The Greater Mekong Sub-Region represents an example of a successful transnational tourism regime. Free and easy movement of tourists will however call for a review of restrictive regulatory regimes such as the Inner Line Permit for domestic tourists and Restricted Area Permits for foreign tourists. There have also been growing demands for opening more border trade points with Myanmar so as to provide states in the Northeast with more economic options. Following the opening of the Moreh-Tamu point along the border between Manipur and Myanmar, Nagaland and Mizoram too have been raising demands for additional trading points. During his visit to Myanmar in October 2008, India's Minister of State for Commerce and Power, Jairam Ramesh put forward the proposal for two additional border trade points in Avangkhu in Nagaland and Zowkhathar in Mizoram. The proposal also includes moves towards an expansion of the number of items to be traded.

Improving border infrastructure has been another long standing demand from within the region. The reopening of the Nathu La has also acted as a spur for demands from state governments in the region to reopen the Stilwell Road. The 1,726 km long road that runs from Assam through Pangsau Pass in Myanmar to Kunming in Southwest

China is seen as being critical for facilitating trade with Southeast Asia. The demand has enjoyed widespread support across the region with symbolic marches being held with thousands demonstrating for the reopening of the thoroughfare. Signalling its willingness to reverse long years of resistance, New Delhi has made significant moves to reopen the route. In November 2007, a border trade centre was opened at Nampong on the same road at a short distance away from the international border. Arunachal Pradesh governor Gen (retd) J J Singh recently announced that consultations were going on with the Centre to upgrade the road to international standards. Similarly, there have also been long standing demands for facilitating people to people contacts between India and Bangladesh. The deep-rooted historical, cultural and linguistic ties have led to demands for resuming road and rail links. These have seen gradual moves to re-establish connectivity on both sides. In addition to the bus services that connects Kolkata to Dhaka and Agartala to Dhaka, a passenger train service connecting Kolkata to Joydebpur, near Dhaka was resumed in 2007. Among the several cross-border infrastructure projects it is involved in, India is also pursuing an East to West Corridor through Myanmar to integrate the Northeast with the economies of Southeast Asia. The Indian Border Roads Organisation built the 165km long Tamu-Kalemyo highway in Myanmar that connects Moreh in Manipur in India to Kalemyo in Myanmar. India, Myanmar and Thailand have also commenced work on the Trilateral Highway project that will link Moreh through Pagan in Myanmar to Maesot in Thailand. The trilateral agreement also includes the highway from Kanchanaburi on the Thai border with the deep- sea port of Tavoy in Myanmar, which is expected to appreciably reduce shipping distances between India and Thailand.

While external connectivity will undoubtedly be essential, intra-connectivity within the Northeast will also form a critical corollary. The challenge will be to remove several formidable roadblocks to mobility, which is absolutely vital if there is to be a seamless flow of people, goods and services. Far more forbidding than the landlocked status of the Northeast is the sobering fact that each of these states suffers the double disadvantage of being "internally locked" on account of poor or non-existent transport linkages. Compounding these barriers to mobility has been the lack of institutional connectivity which has also worked to keep levels of border trade considerably below their potential. Complicated procedural requirements and paper work have resulted in higher transaction costs and diverted trade to informal private channels at the cost of the exchequer. Multiple handling and transhipment of goods are common resulting in mindless duplication of procedures. Single window clearance, harmonisation of tariff and customs procedures point the way forward, complemented by facilities such as banking facilities, warehouses, power supply. Recently, steps are being taken to develop 14 land customs stations along the border, eight of which are to be along the border with Bangladesh, four along the border with Nepal and one each with Pakistan and Myanmar. Integrated checkposts being planned aim at coordinating the movements of both trade cargo as well as passenger movements across the land border is expected to give a considerable fillip to regional trade (Ministry of Commerce, 2006).

While locating the Northeast at the core of India's Look East policy holds promise, what will be of critical importance will be the implications these hold for the economic future of the Northeast itself. The promise of trade-fostering industrialisation will depend on the region being able to realise its own potential based on its indigenous resource endowments. For the Northeast to benefit therefore, products in which the region enjoys a comparative advantage must find a place in the export basket. The manner in which this aspect is managed will make all the difference between the Northeast being either a production centre or ending up as a mere conduit for goods produced elsewhere. If one looks at the current export basket of India's border trade, the Northeast as a region does not enjoy a comparative advantage in any of the products being traded (Barua, 2005:441). For instance, products such as wheat, steel, treated steel, electronic goods which feature in India's exports to Bangladesh do not originate in the Northeast but are sourced from other domestic locations in India. The Northeast also does not find a presence in India's export basket to Southeast Asia which includes products such as shrimp, granite, cotton and aluminium ingots. If the region remains a mere conduit for exports on account of its location, the Northeast will only gain minimal benefits. From being on the margins of closed borders, it will be far more tragic if the Northeast is reduced to being on the edges of an open economy. Atul Sarma strikes a much-needed note of caution when he notes that while India's trade with both China and ASEAN have grown dramatically, trade volumes through continental routes have only trickled in comparison and 'has almost bypassed North-East' (Sarma, 2006: 44). He compares this anomaly to Assam's economy during the colonial period when gains from trade were negligible despite the overt internationalisation of the economy. Internationalisation operated in splendid isolation from the indigenous economic activities of the economy thereby passing the region by in the quest for external markets. This was in sharp contrast to the pre-colonial period which was marked by 'a long history of internationalisation' and high degrees of integration with the economies of the region.

DECENTERING PARTICIPATION: TOWARDS SUBNATIONAL FUTURES

A subnational future first and foremost speaks to a bottom up vision of foreign policy formulation by decentering participation at the constituent levels. Such a discourse would help shift the focus to local sites and towards issues that have a direct bearing on those living on the frontiers. A coequal focus on both agency and process will be decisive by opening the space for direct stakeholder participation and institutionalising mechanisms of cooperation by addressing issues of governance, livelihood and resource sharing among others. These find no place within politico-military frames of decision making which can at best only offer suboptimal solutions for issues that are essentially deterritorialised in nature. These can have knock-on effects on the borders by building trust and paving the way for issue-based linkages within the neighbourhood. These will be particularly valuable in situations marked by high levels of public alienation and resistance to linear modes of problem solving such as the Northeast.

While the existence of such areas provides incentives for cooperation, mechanisms that actualise it need to be conceived and challenges tackled. The first challenge will be to redress the subliminal democratic deficits that persist and shadow the highly visible focus on formal processes. Stressing the importance of participatory innovations at the local level, Dryzek points the need to step beyond a fixation on formal political institutions which can serve as alternative sites of deliberative capacity. Questioning the viability of the democratic experience in a militarised society, Dolly Kikon notes, 'the consequences of state policies where the language of rights and justice are abused, unresolved political conflicts are handed over to the army, and people are collectively clubbed under anti-democratic laws and regulation does not yield in the end, sustainable meaningful political settlements' (Kikon, 2005:2835). The ensuing popular alienation and resistance that steps into the void only prompts another cycle of back-sliding with the space for popular participation being pushed back even further. Popular mobilisations including the dramatic expression of dissent by Manipuri women who marched naked holding banners that read "Indian Army Rape Us" serve as a telling metaphor of human life stripped of dignity.

A second challenge will be the constitutionally weak positions of the Northeastern states that have translated into weak voices when it comes to effectively participating and influencing foreign policy formulation on critical issues such as immigration and development. The lack of effective asymmetric powers and effective jurisdiction over these critical issues, Sanjib Baruah feels has contributed to the emergence of an exclusivist, violent assertion of ethnic nationalism in Assam. While conceding that there is ample evidence of de facto asymmetry as well as 'some nods to asymmetry' in the constitution, Tillin argues that these have 'not been central to India's ability to "hold together' and should not be read as an official commitment to constitutional asymmetry as a principle of federal governance across India (Tillin, 2007:61). A successful example of differential provisioning is that of Quebec, which has negotiated considerable jurisdictional authority over issues such as immigration, employment and pension plans than other provinces. For instance, Canada's Immigration Act of 1976 introduced the requirement of planning and consultation with provinces on issues relating to immigration (Kelley et al., 1998).

A third challenge will be the lack of viable domestic sources of revenue generation considerably compromises local initiative and in the long run any prospects for meaningful autonomy. As Special Category States, the Northeast receives 90 per cent as grants from the centre and 10 per cent as in the form of loans whereas other states receive 30 per cent as grant and 70 per cent as loans. The problem with resource-flow based growth strategies is that they can end up being double-edged swords. On their own, huge fund transfers can at best only be a partial solution but can often end up being part of the problem itself. In the Northeast, financial transfers from the centre to the tune of Rs 20,000 crores annually has gone on to create its own constituency of vested interests among politicians, expatriate contractors and extortionists. For funds to be effective it is imperative that they are conjoined with capacity building so as to absorb the resources in generative ways. In the absence of attention to the latter, the funds will only serve to sustain the self-serving cycle of corruption, militancy and underdevelopment. Unless institutional entry points are created for local inputs within a participatory ethos, public perception of funds would tend to veer between indifference and a lack of ownership, furthering feelings of alienation (Baruah, 2007). Commenting on this disconnect, Hiren Gohain notes, 'Little wonder then that actions taken by its ruling class appear as an "act" more to convince its political masters in faraway Delhi than to benefit the region' (Gohain, 2006: 4109).

Subregional Governance Agenda

Central to unpacking the emancipatory potential that subnational futures promise will be the framing of a subregional governance agenda. The reality of fungible borders calls into question territorial modes of governance and control and throws up cross-border governance dilemmas. Such challenges arise as Susan Clarke notes, when 'interdependent, complex, loosely linked actors and institutions with shared purposes but no shared authority' are required to coordinate their efforts (Clarke, 2002:2). The fact that many of these challenges are experienced at the local level, will as Brian Hocking argues make 'localisation of foreign policy' a compelling reality (Hocking, 1993). Local frames of agency would, as he argues, contribute towards a broadening of foreign policy as local level participation becomes both possible as well as necessary. Such innovative frameworks will be particularly critical for addressing challenges in the subregion such as water management, climate change, and biodiversity. Ecological imbalances in the form of rising temperatures, retreating glaciers and droughts caused by indifferent rainfall are finding their way to parts of the extended region. The Tibetan 'water bank' for instance, constitutes Asia's water bank and the environmental sustainability of Tibet means the environmental sustainability of much of Asia (Kurian, 2004). Many of these rivers flow into some of the most populous regions of South and Southeast Asia. Very little research has as yet been done to monitor the extent of these changes to the ecosystem in the Tibetan plateau or in the Northeast. The manner in which these waters are used upstream will thus decide both the quality and quantity of the flows that are received below. The looming sustainability crisis as Roy Hudson notes creates the imperative for reworking conventional notions of region and place. Rethinking regions as 'sustainable economic spaces' can,

Hudson argues, help maximise intra-regional flows and secure major eco-efficiency gains (Hudson, 2007).

The complex nature of these multi-layered processes is increasingly bringing diverse actors into successful cross-border governance arrangements. A case in point are the spatial networks spanning the US and Canadian border that are responding to the need for cross border cooperation on issues such as immigration, transportation and security in the cross-border region. These issue-based coalitions have seen the subnational region of Cascadia emerge as a collective political actor creating effective coalitions and networks to articulate demands and interests. Similarly, community participation in the planning and implementation of water, irrigation and sanitation projects in Brazil and Taiwan offer successful examples of what Ackerman calls as 'co-governance', with the 'pro-accountability role' that society can play being compatible with a strong state apparatus (Ackerman, 2003; Ostrom, 1996).

Towards Alternative Discursive Spaces

Spaces have to be rethought and boundaries crossed in the field of knowledge creation also. The shifting boundaries of the state are bound to also call for a rethinking of the traditional boundaries of the discipline devoted to its study (MacMillan et al., 1995:2). IR as a discipline will increasingly struggle with the contradictions of maintaining its analytical focus on relations between territorially bound sovereign states as it faces the reality of social, economic and cultural flows that bear declining relevance to territory. Schendel rues the fact that scholarship has become captive to the dominant statist interpretations within their respective countries and has been unable to break free from its stranglehold. Contending intellectual epistemologies have ended up mirroring contending nationalisms which have in turn fed into each other and produced a 'veritable epistemological and historiographical minefield' (Schendel, 2005:30). The Partition and the academic discourse that emerged thus tended to be "convoluted" in the sense that it absorbed many of its partitioned frames into its analytic frames. The often uncritical intellectual tolerance and acceptance of this unwittingly effectively diminishes the space for alternative viewpoints. The cumulative result has been a straitened intellectual discourse that has turned its back on social processes that could only be understood within a necessarily regional and transnational framework. Unless these dominant interpretations are called into question and debated, extant categories and conventional imageries will only be reified over time without respite. These will however be problematic as any attempts at questioning triggers panic attacks and yet another bout of what Sankaran Krishna refers to as 'postcolonial anxiety' and 'cartography becomes nothing less than the social and political production of nationality itself' and the 'physical preservation of the borders' became 'metonymous with the state of the union' (Krishna, 1999: 200).

One of the effects of this fixation on the state has been the questions IR refuses to ask which are conspicuous by their absence. A spatial focus would in fact enable to think out of what Agnew terms the 'territorial trap' and come up with actionable ideas that can create bottom-up, inclusive approaches to regional development. Pointing that IR is in urgent need of 'socialising' with more meaningful engagement with other disciplines, Stephen Hopgood notes, one of the biggest disadvantages of IR has been that it has been a 'self-conscious discipline' which has not chosen to analyse what happens in international politics 'as people experience it every day' (Hopgood, 2003). For instance, poverty as a subject area remains largely ignored by IR theorists. Barring the work on underdevelopment and the North-South disparities, there is theoretical silence on questions of inequality and social exclusion that afflict individuals and situating micro-poverty within the processes of world politics. On the need for more sophisticated frameworks to study the international system than those offered in parsimonious models of inter-state relations and limiting politico-military constructs, Buzan and Little argue that new disciplinary inquiries have the potential to position IR to become 'a kind of meta-discipline, systematically linking together the macro-sides of the social sciences and history' (Buzan et al., 2001: 22). These emerging areas of scholarship also hold out the promise of exciting new conversations with other disciplines such as history, sociology and anthropology.

Dedicated border research centres and research programmes could be so designed so as to interrogate shared concerns within transborder terms of reference. It is essential that scholars from within the region should speak to a common set of issues that they have hitherto looked at within national and statist frames. Even more important than the need to establish common institutions it is imperative that we share what Dryzek refers to as 'a particular kind of language when talking about events, which in turn rests on some common definitions, judgements, assumptions, and contentions' (Dryzek, 1997: vii). In the absence of certain common denominators, there will be no scope for theory to project alternative scenarios and represent a wide cross section of views and perspectives. A related issue that needs to be addressed will be to explore if we can arrive at a common language of dialogue. Can scholars work towards a common understanding on certain basic norms and values? For instance, the repeated invocation of rigid notions of territoriality clearly stands to unravel the scope that alternative border discourses hold to transcend this logic to mutual benefit. These two contradictory norms hold out two vastly different futures for the border. While the logic of the former would imply little more than a military line, the latter would reconstruct the same as a dynamic gateway. While one would stimulate wariness, the other would help create joint stakes in peace.

CONCLUSION

The Northeast as 'periphery' presents a classic instance of reflexivity where a constructed image and its iteration becomes a social reality. Seen thus, the burden of location becomes one that the periphery is condemned to permanently suffer. The portrayal of the region in such terms and acceptance of this image in public discourse creates its own legitimising stamp and in time becomes the reality. The chapter has argued that India's new subregional imaginaries can offer creative ways of reimagining the Northeast and reclaiming its distinctly different past. Rethinking India's diplomacy with its transnational neighbourhood will be incomplete without rethinking the Northeast and its role in this reorientation. This will offer policy makers a richer and wider repertoire of alternative learning processes to experiment with.

REFERENCES

Anderson, James and Liam O'Dowd (1999) "Borders, Border Regions and Territoriality: Contradictory Meanings, Changing Significance," *Regional Studies*, vol. 33, 7, October, pp. 593-604.

Ackerman, John, (2003) "Co-Governance for Accountability: Beyond 'Exit' and 'Voice,'" *World Development*, vol. 32, No. 3, pp. 447-463.

'Arunachal is "our land of rising sun," says PM', *Indian Express*, 1 February 2008.

Barua, Alokesh, (2005) *India's North-East Developmental Issues in a Historical Perspective* New Delhi, Manohar.

Baruah, Sanjib (2007) *Postfrontier Blues: Toward a New Policy Framework for Northeast India*, Policy Studies no. 33, East-West Center.

Bhuthalingam Ravi (2003) "Around the Bend: Creating Prosperity through Tourism in the Bangladesh-China-India-Myanmar Region," Country Paper on Tourism presented at the Fourth Meeting of the BCIM Forum, Yangon, Myanmar, 19-21 March.

Buzan, Barry and Richard Little, (2001) "Why International Relations has Failed as an Intellectual Project and What to do About it," *Millennium-Journal of International Studies*, 30; 19, pp. 19-39.

Che, Zhimin (1998) "Proposition on Formation of Sub-Regional Cooperation Zone of China, India, Myanmar and Bangladesh," Mimeo, August.

Clarke, Susan E., (2002) "Spatial Concepts and Cross-Border Governance Strategies: Comparing North American and Northern Europe Experiences," Paper Presented at the EURA Conference on Urban and European Policies, Turin, 18-20 April.

Dryzek, John, (1997) *The Politics of the Earth: Environmental Discourses*, Oxford University Press.

Durfee, Mary and James N. Rosenau, (1996) "Playing Catch-Up: International Relations Theory and Poverty," *Millennium: Journal of International Studies*, vol. 25, no. 3, pp. 521-545.

Gohain, Hiren, (2006) "Governance as Theatre," *Economic and Political Weekly*, 30 September, pp. 4109-4110.

Hazarika, Sanjay, (2006) "India's Northeast: Looking Within: Stretching Eastward" in Manmohan Malhotra ed., *India: The Next Decade, Academic Foundation*, New Delhi.

Hopgood, Stephen, (2003) "Socialising IR," *GSC Quarterly* 10, Fall.

Hudson, Roy, (2007) "Region and Place: Rethinking Regional Development in the Context of Global Environmental Change," *Progress in Human Geography* 31 (6), pp. 827-836.

Kelley, Ninette and Michael Trebilcock, (1998) *The Making of the Mosaic: A History of Canadian Immigration Policy* (University of Toronto, 1998.

Kikon, Dolly, (2005) "Engaging Naga Nationalism: Can Democracy Function in Militarised Societies? *Economic and Political Weekly*, 25 June, pp. 2833-2837.

Krishna, Sankaran, (1999) *Postcolonial Insecurities: India, Sri Lanka and the Question of Nationhood*, University of Minnesota Press.

Kurian, Nimmi, (2002) India-Bangladesh Relations: Transcending the Transit Hurdle," *South Asia Politics*, May pp. 41-42.

Kurian, Nimmi, (2007) "Mainstreaming Margins: India, China and the Promise of Subregionalism" Paper presented at the Ninth Annual Tufts University Cross-Cultural Leadership Symposium on *Asia's Rising Giants: China and India* Tufts University, Boston, 22-25 February.

Kurian, Nimmi, (2004) "Takes Two to Solve a Water Crisis," *Indian Express*, 17 August.

MacMillan, John and Andrew Linklater ed., (1995) "Introduction: Boundaries in Question" in *Boundaries in Question: New Directions in International Relations*, London.

Ministry of Commerce, (2006), Government of India, Ministry of Commerce, "Centre to Spend Rs 850 Crore to Develop Infrastructure for Regional Trade, says Jairam Ramesh," *Press Release by the Department of Commerce*, 29 September.

Ostrom, Elinor (1990), *Governing the Commons: The Evolution of Institutions for Collective Action*, Cambridge: Cambridge University Press.

PM's Inaugural speech at the 2nd North-East Business Summit, 20 January 2004, accessed at http://www.ibef.org/.

Rabinowitz, Dan (1998) "National identity on the frontier: Palestinians in the Israeli education system" in Thomas M Wilson and Hastings Donnan (eds.), *Border Identities: Nation and State at International* Frontiers, Cambridge.

Sarma, Atul, (2006) "The North-East as Gateway to Southeast Asia: Big Dream and Home Truths," *Man and Development*, June, pp.35-50.

Schendel, Willem van (2005) *The Bengal Borderland: Beyond State and Nation in South Asia* London, Anthem Press.

Hasan, Shehla Raza (2006) "The India-China Road to—Somewhere," *Asia Times*, 29 August.

Singh, N Mohendro (2002), *Development Experience in Manipur*, Imphal: Institute of Development Studies.

Tillin, Louise, (2007) 'United in Diversity? Asymmetry in Indian Federalism', *Publius: The Journal of Federalism*, vol. 37, no. 1, pp. 45-67.

Thant, Myo, Min Tang and Hisoshi Kakazu, ed., (1994) *Growth Triangles in Asia: A New Regional Economic Cooperation* (Oxford, OUP.)

Verghese, B G, (2003) "The Northeast and its Neighbourhood: Remembering the Future," The Twentieth C.D. Deshmukh Memorial Lecture, 13 January, New Delhi.

X

Foreign Policy Making in India in the Pre-Liberalization and Coalition Era: Unit Level Variables as Determinants

Paul Staniland

INTRODUCTION

India's foreign policy has undergone dramatic changes in the wake of economic liberalization and coalition governments at the centre. Since 1991, domestic forces have fundamentally shaped India's interests and capabilities, from a surging economic sector to powerful regional parties. Yet it is important to understand this change in a broader historical perspective. This chapter makes two simple claims. First, I argue that since independence Indian foreign policy has had important domestic determinants. I focus on two topics in particular—the role of ideological beliefs in Indian alliance strategy between 1947 and 1972 and the importance of regional politics in shaping foreign policy towards Sri Lanka in the 1980s. The alliance formation question determined India's place in the Cold War world and the Sri Lankan intervention was a costly and frustrating failure abroad. Second, I argue that analyzing the post-liberalization era is best accomplished by focusing not on the question of "does domestic politics matter?" but, instead, "does domestic politics matter in ways different from the pre-liberalization era? And, if so, why?" This allows scholars to explore similarities and differences between the two periods that can explain variation in policy decisions.

I adopt a fairly broad understanding of domestic politics in this study, focusing on struggles for power and wealth within India. This includes the dominant ideologies of political elites, the activities of economic firms and organizations, the electoral incentives of politicians, and the interests of state bureaucracies (Milner 1988; Moravcsik 1998; Schweller 2004). These domestic variables played an important role, alongside structural pressures, in determining the broad contours of Indian foreign policy in the 1947-1991 period, as well as in influencing specific policies. In many respects, India was not as tightly constrained as other countries during the Cold War. It had options about how to ally and where to intervene. This means that studying the post-1991 period is an exercise in specifying what *changed* domestic ideas and interests from their prior, and then asking whether these changes operate through different mechanisms than previous domestic processes. Put simply, the theoretically informed study of Indian foreign policy can accommodate both the pre- and post-1991 periods.

The article proceeds in four sections. First, I discuss ideological influences on alliance decision-making, with an emphasis on the Nehruvian approach to strategic alignment in the wake of independence. Second, I show how the domestic politics of Tamil Nadu combined with geopolitical interests to encourage Indian intervention in Sri Lanka. Third, I offer tentative conclusions about mechanisms through which domestic politics influenced India's foreign policy before 1991, and how the consequences of these policies then interacted with new structural conditions to drive change in the post-1991 world.

OVERCOMING THE LEGACIES OF EMPIRE: NON-ALIGNMENT AND THE NEHRUVIAN WORLDVIEW

'Among the major sources of India's external policy the ideas and power of Jawaharlal Nehru have no real competitor' (Power, 1964: 259).

Alliances are fundamental to the fashioning of foreign policy.

Indian decisions about alignment in the period from 1947 to 1972 were critical to the shape of Indian international posture. I argue in this section that, broadly speaking, alliance decisions combined both international structural incentives with domestic ideological beliefs. The pressures of security competition with Pakistan and, later, China created geopolitical, structural needs for balancing that were met in the form of alliances and arms deals, primarily with the Soviet Union. There were certainly system-level causes of alliance decision-making in this period. But these pressures were weak (especially before 1962) compared to those facing states like West Germany or Japan. India had significant potential flexibility in the world of diplomacy.

I argue that Nehru's ideology had two specific effects on Indian alignment. First, it significantly delayed the fashioning of a coherent strategy towards China, despite a significant and growing imbalance of power between the two countries over the course of the 1950s. Second, it profoundly influenced decisions about how to approach the broader global Cold War. When the stakes were highest and clearest, in regional security competition, structure appears to be largely dominant in explaining decision-making. But when threats and opportunities were more ambiguous, domestic ideologies played a crucial role in guiding policy, perhaps to an even greater extent than we see in the post-1991 period. The ability of Congress to maintain a stranglehold on power at the Centre, even in periods of internal friction, allowed the pursuit of a certain idea of Indian foreign policy. The structural environment, while influential, was far from determinative, particularly in the 1950s. Though there were changes in Indian foreign policy after 1972, the outlines of India's global posture remained largely static until the collapse of the Soviet Union abroad and liberalization at home two decades later, so I focus on 1947-1972.

Room to Move: India and the World, 1947-62. The crucial first question for a study of domestic politics is whether there was space for domestic variables to make much of a difference. If structure was highly constraining and determining, then we can largely dismiss or downgrade the causal power of domestic politics. I argue here that, with the crucial exception of Pakistan, India had significant room to move in the international sphere. Scholars often look to the balance of threats and power in a state's security environment to explain its decisions about alliances (Waltz, 1979; Walt, 1987). In the late 1940s through early 1960s, Pakistan was the major apparent threat due to the conflict over Kashmir (Ganguly, 2001). Pakistan did devote massive effort to its defence expenditures, but remained dwarfed by India (Jalal, 1990). A much more distant second place in terms of structural threat was China, but its chaos and poverty in the wake of the civil war and the mountainous, conquest-averse nature of the border areas made a less plausible candidate for armed conflict. Thus we should expect to find India aligning against Pakistan.

But other than Pakistan, and more distantly China, there is little at the structural level that would allow us to definitely predict choices between alignment with the US-led western bloc, alignment with the Soviet-led eastern bloc, or neutrality and non-alignment. All of these were plausible options in terms of hard power politics—alignment with the west to keep China at bay and weaken Pakistan's ties to the US and UK, alignment with the east to counter Pakistan and to maintain good relations with China, or an attempt to thread the needle by mobilizing the developing world into non-alignment. Furthermore, India had extremely limited security interests outside the subcontinent—unlike the US, UK, France, and USSR, it lacked power-projection capabilities, troop deployments abroad, or colonial possessions on the periphery. As such, India in the 1950s had extraordinary flexibility in its choices. Finally, India was a sought-after partner on both sides of the Cold War fence. American administrations in both the 1950s and 1960s looked to democratic India as a potentially appealing ally (Kux, 1992), while the Soviets saw it as a socialist state with an anti-imperialist orientation.

Thus, India had expansive room to move in the international sphere. Though militarily weak, it nevertheless occupied time and attention among the superpowers and had plausible structural reasons for choosing an alignment with either side. Instead, India pursued an alternative course in the 1950s—generally more sympathetic to the Soviets and confident of friendship with China, but not tightly tied to either pole in the Cold War competition. The Non-Aligned Movement was the signature public manifestation of this project, with Nehru occupying pride of place as a face and voice of the former (Tharoor, 2003). Nehru coined the phrase "non-alignment" in 1954 and played a crucial role in organizing conferences, outlining an ideological framework for the movement, and determining India's foreign policy. India in this period forsook the opportunities for wealth and power that could be offered by both superpowers in favor of trying to forge its own unique place in the world. There were various plausible options—none were intrinsically more determined than the others by international structure.

To what can we trace the origins of this pivotal decision? Haas suggests that in indeterminate structural conditions, states tend to rely on ideology in making their decisions about alliances (Haas, 2005). I argue here that the combination of anti-imperialism, socialism, and nationalism that characterized the dominant Congress ideology (which, it should be noted, was often fractious or inconsistent) provided the framework for India's approach to alliances in the 1950s. Due to a perceived solidarity with other states in the developing world, conflicts of interest were downplayed. Pakistan, as always, stood as an exception to this, framed in popular discourse as an artificial, arbitrary creation of colonialists. Regarding China, Nehru felt that there would be mutual solidarity in struggle for development and respect within the international system. He also saw Egypt, Indonesia, and the other new nations as sharing with India a common set of objectives and worldviews that would provide the basis for sustained cooperation.

In addition to providing a favorable view of other post-colonial states, Nehruvian ideology involved a sustained suspicion of the West's intentions that was further heightened by US alignment with Pakistan. Willing to admire its science and technology, Indian elites in this tradition nevertheless assumed a certain fundamental degree of exploitative intent on the part of the capitalist West. This made alignment with the US and its allies a dubious proposition, a return to colonial dependence. Nehru and the strategic class may not have liked aspects of the Soviet Union's internal politics but perceived a less aggressive colonialist bent to its policies, thus making it a slightly more attractive partner within the broader context of non-alignment (Cohen, 2001: 38; Guha, 2007: 172-4). Kux quotes Nehru as writing "Personally I think that in this worldwide tug-of-war there is on the whole more reason on the side of Russia, not always of course" (Kux, 1992: 51). Nehru "found the United States too cocksure about the rights and wrongs of the Cold War, too insensitive to the aspirations of colonial peoples, and too patronizing in dealing with India" (Kux, 1992: 69). This "neutralist approach and chronic moralizing about US foreign policy, had by 1954 thoroughly tried the patience of top levels of the State Department, the Pentagon, and many in Congress" (Kux, 1992: 114). Mohan notes that "these ideas formed the keystone of mental architecture of many generations of the Indian elite, who grew up in the era of national movement and the early decades of independence" (Mohan, 2004: 31).

This ideological worldview had two major effects in the 1950s. First, it fostered poor understanding of Chinese power and intentions. As confrontation over the contested Indo-Chinese border escalated, a false sense of complacency endured about the prospects for cooperation and likelihood of Chinese retaliation (Guha, 2007:317-8). This was most striking among Nehru and his civilian advisers rather than the military, but Nehru and his Defence Minister Krishna Menon were the key actors driving Indian policy (Kavic, 1967; Kux, 1992; Garver, 2001). The consequences of these beliefs became quickly obvious as India suffered a humiliating defeat on the battlefield. Nehru himself painfully realized this as Chinese forces brushed aside the Indian Army.

Second, the move towards non-alignment and greater sympathy to the Soviets rather than the West securely established ties between Pakistan and the Anglo-American powers. By the early 1960s, Pakistan had positioned itself as an American ally on the troubled Cold War periphery (Jalal, 1990; Kux, 2001; Cohen, 2004; Nawaz, 2008). As discussed below, this reduced options for India in the post-1962 world—a rapprochement with the west remained possible (and briefly occurred), but broadly speaking Pakistan had found allies and there was little leverage India could bring to bear in changing this. The Nehruvian foreign policy ideology, whatever its strengths and weaknesses, fundamentally shaped and then constrained India's alignment options. This does not mean that Nehru represented a unanimous consensus—the Communists looked east, while the right wing of Congress was conversely much more uncomfortable with a leftward lean (Mohan, 2004: 34-35). But Nehru had primacy within the decision-making apparatus. There certainly was a consensus about the need to stand firm against Pakistan (Kux, 1992: 109). So, as long as Nehru's policy did not impinge on the crucial Pakistan question he had significant freedom to move at the broader strategic level—he "was not only India's chief foreign policy theoretician, he was its dominant, almost sole, practitioner for nearly twenty years" (Cohen, 2001: 37).

Scrambling to Catch Up: India's Constrained Quest for Power, 1962-72. Domestic ideology played a pivotal role in alignment decisions during the 1940s and 1950s, as the relatively loose demands of power politics gave India flexibility. However, the 1960s and early 1970s would see Indian elites trying to acquire material power in a much more constricted structural setting. The 1962 war with China ended in defeat and made very clear that India was a weak state living in a dangerous neighborhood (Garver 2001). The era of flexibility and ambiguity was clearly over, and structural pressures forced India to look to the superpowers for aid. India expanded its military and purchased arms from both east and west. Indian foreign policy in this era looks much more like what we would expect from threat—and power-based theories of alignment. Nevertheless, the legacies of the 1950s endured—alliances between Pakistan and the Americans and Chinese had already been forged during India's long flirtation with non-alignment, dramatically reducing India's options. As much as Indian elites understandably resent Pakistan's links to great powers, it is important to remember that Indian decisions, driven by a certain idea of how the world did and should work, shaped the circumstances under which these ties were established. India's ideology of non-alignment created a "path-dependent" (Pierson 2004) trajectory of alliance relations in South Asia that would serve it poorly in future.

For a short period following 1962, India engaged with both the US/UK and USSR for weapons while expanding the size of its armed forces. The build-up was a response to the obvious need for raw material power after the war. The 1965 Indo-Pakistan war reflected this strengthening—Indian forces blunted Pakistani offensives that had been launched in the hopes of catching a weakened India before she could re-arm. As so common, Pakistan miscalculated and India was able to decisively fend off the attack. The role of the US in the 1965 war, though not particularly dramatic, made India once again suspicious of the west's pro-Pakistan leanings. As Indira Gandhi rose to prominence in the late 1960s, the combination of her own leftist tendencies and the difficulty of balancing US and Soviet aid led to an increased emphasis on ties with the USSR. Mrs. Gandhi and US President Richard Nixon got along very poorly, their personal relations exacerbating the already tenuous grounds for security cooperation between the two countries (Bundy, 1998; Dallek, 2007).

The 1971 Indo-Pakistan war led to a final solidification of India's alliance position in the international system. The war resulted from the bloody struggle in East Pakistan between Bengali-speaking nationalists and a West Pakistan-dominated military establishment unwilling to countenance significant autonomy (much less independence) for East Pakistan (Sisson and Rose, 1992). As Pakistani counterinsurgency operations grew in scope and brutality, refugees streamed across the border into India. India began supporting Bengali insurgents (the Mukti Bahini) and Pakistani forces had little success in using mass coercion to bring sustainable order to East Pakistan. In anticipation of a major conventional push into East Pakistan, India looked to the Soviets for aid and alliance. The signing of the Indo-Soviet Treaty of Peace, Friendship, and Cooperation in August 1971 marked India's clear move to the Soviets prior to the 1971 Indo-Pakistan war. The contours of this policy, though susceptible to minor changes, would remain largely in the place until the collapse of the Soviet Union (Cohen, 2001; Mohan, 2006). By the time of the Janata Dal government, "there was now a broad consensus within the nation on a strong relationship with Moscow, which was based on the imperatives of the regional security environment" (Mohan, 2004: 35).

I have argued in this section that a domestic ideology, the Nehruvian worldview, played an important role in determining Indian alliance decisions. This was particularly true in the period before 1962 as India tried to keep the West and (to a lesser extent) East at bay while pursuing non-alignment. Beliefs in the solidarity of the developing world also encouraged undue faith in harmony between India and China. The importance of ideology would diminish in the wake of the 1962 war, but its influence persisted through the constraints operating on India—it emerged from 1962 militarily weak and with its primary foes (Pakistan and China) already in alliance with one another and Pakistan tied to the US. At this point both structure and ideology impelled a move eastwards in favor of tighter links with the Soviet Union. Indo-Soviet ties solidified as East Pakistan bled, and remained in place for nearly two decades afterwards.

II. INTO THE ABYSS: TAMIL POLITICS AND INDIAN INTERVENTION IN SRI LANKA

The 1980s was a period of turbulence in Indian foreign policy, including severe tensions with Pakistan over Operation Brasstacks, Sikh militancy in Punjab, and the Kashmir "compound crisis," an economic blockade of Nepal, and the further expansion of northeastern insurgencies into Myanmar, Bangladesh, and Bhutan (Kohli,1991; Hazarika, 1995; Bajpai et al., 1995). But one of the most traumatic experiences arose from Indian intervention in Sri

Lanka—first in support of Tamil armed groups, then in armed opposition to the Liberation Tigers of Tamil Eelam (LTTE) in support of the 1987 Indo-Lanka Accord. India's involvement in Sri Lanka was caused by the intersection of domestic politics with broader perceptions of strategic interest. During the period between 1983 and 1990 in particular, Indian policymakers pursued dual objectives with regard to Sri Lanka—limiting Sri Lanka's perceived tilt towards external powers, and mollifying outrage in Tamil Nadu over discrimination against Sri Lankan Tamils without encouraging Tamil separatism in India (Dixit 1998: 16-17). This combination of structural and unit-level pressures led to a series of dramatic, and ultimately failed, policies that embroiled India in Sri Lanka's ethnic conflict. Domestic politics mattered hugely in forcing the hands of elites at the Centre, who otherwise would have faced real but weaker and more flexible incentives for some form of intervention.

Disagreement between Sinhalese and Tamils over the central government's language policies and the appropriate extent of devolution to provincial governments became particularly heated following 1956. Competition between Sinhalese parties to reap the majority vote involved significant "outbidding" over the language issue, driving radicalization of Tamils (Tambiah, 1986; DeVotta, 2004). In 1972, a militant group was founded by Velupillai Prabhakaran on the Jaffna Peninsula that would become the LTTE. Low-level militancy grew during the 1970s, matched by growing demands for independence by Tamil politicians. Several other major armed groups emerged in northern and eastern Sri Lanka, including the Eelam People's Revolutionary Liberation Front (EPRLF), People's Liberation Organisation of Tamil Eelam (PLOT), Tamil Eelam Liberation Organisation (TELO), and Eelam Revolutionary Organisation of Students (EROS). All of these groups began began targeting pro-government Tamils and security forces. These organizations used Tamil Nadu as a sanctuary across the Palk Straits from the Sri Lankan government. They mobilized financial and logistical support among Indian Tamils, but prior to 1983 remained relatively small, both in India and in Sri Lanka.

Supporting Tamil Militancy: India and Sri Lanka, 1983-1987. This situation changed dramatically in 1983. In July of that year, the LTTE ambushed an army patrol in Jaffna, killing 13 soldiers. This attack triggered a wave of anti-Tamil riots, particularly in Colombo, that led to a massive increase in the extent and depth of Tamil militancy. Young Tamils began joining armed groups in large numbers and an escalation in violence ensued. The riots had a major effect on the politics of Tamil Nadu as well. Many Indian Tamils believed that a campaign to destroy the Sri Lankan Tamils was under way and demanded action by their representatives. This took two forms—one at the state level and one at the Centre. In Tamil Nadu, both the DMK and AIADMK began more actively supporting Tamil armed groups, with party leaders M Karunanidhi and M. G. Ramachandran liberally dispersing cash and political legitimacy for their activities. The parties also actively lobbied, along with mass demonstrations, in favor of the Centre taking action. Money was provided to the Tamil armed groups in large quantities, the state police either actively helped or ignored their activities, and Tamil Nadu became an eager sanctuary for the militants. Moreover, Indian Tamils looked to the central government to take action in the sphere of national security.

These domestic political pressures intersected with geopolitical incentives at the Centre. The Sri Lankan United National Party (UNP) government of JR Jayewardene had embraced economic liberalization and moved towards the West in its political alignment. Indian foreign policy-makers feared that the strategic harbor at Trincomalee would become a home to the American Navy and that Sri Lanka would more broadly be an outpost of the West in the subcontinent (Dixit, 1998; Bose 2007: 33-34). Indian elites felt that this was unacceptable—Sri Lanka was fundamentally part of India's sphere of influence and should stay that way. Though it's retrospectively dubious that the US had any great interest in Trincomalee or basing subversive radio stations on the island, at the time the Indian government appears to have sincerely feared this was indeed the case.

The mixture of political agitation in and pressure from Tamil Nadu with the fears of Indian policy-makers about Sri Lankan foreign policy changes was very powerful. J.N. Dixit, a senior Indian diplomat involved in Sri Lanka ascribes motivations for intervention to "the combination of the Tamil Nadu factor, and these patterns of international connections of Sri Lanla" (Dixit, 1998: 15). Sri Lanka received extremely extensive attention from politicians and bureaucrats at the Centre. The decision was made that Sri Lanka had to be taught a lesson, but that an independent "Tamil Eelam" was unacceptable because it might encourage India's Tamils to more seriously consider separatism (Smith 1999). Tamil Nadu politics cut both ways—they put pressure on India to do something but also limited how far central policy-makers were willing to go, for fear of an independent Tamil state fracturing the Union. Though it's frankly not clear that there was a serious risk of Indian Tamil separatism, it is clear that this fear was present in decision-making.

The first step was using RAW to train the Tamil armed groups between 1983 and 1987 (Gunaratna, 1993; Swamy, 1994. Extensive training programs were established, camps were used in Tamil Nadu and in north India for this purpose, and Indian security services largely looked the other way even as these groups engaged in troublesome behavior in Tamil Nadu. The hope was to use the groups to put pressure on the Sri Lankan government to arrive at a settlement. In retrospect, "all Tamil groups now assert that India was never serious about Eelam and gave them training and arms only to teach Colombo 'a lesson' for its pro-West foreign policy" (Swamy, 1994: 109). TELO in particular was seen as the Indian proxy army, while the LTTE pursued its own agenda with a focus on maintaining autonomy and independence in decision-making. Violence escalated in the north and east of Sri Lanka, also stretching into Colombo.

The Indian government attempted to facilitate negotiations between Tamil armed groups and the Sri Lankan government at

Thimpu in 1985. But these negotiations failed miserably and things began to spiral out of control. Feuding between the militants both in Tamil Nadu and northern Sri Lanka escalated, and in 1986 and 1987 the LTTE effectively wiped out TELO and PLOT, while driving EPRLF out of the Jaffna peninsula. The Sri Lankan government, meanwhile, launched large-scale offensives that put the LTTE on its heels and generated outrage over human rights violations among Indian Tamils. 1987's Operation Liberation in particular pushed deep into Jaffna, triggering panic in India that the government might be able to impose an armed peace on the north and east. Mass demonstrations once more rocked the streets of Madras as Tamil politicians vehemently argued that Sri Lankan Tamils were facing extermination at the hands of the Sinhalese-dominated army. Bose argues that "in mid-1987 the Rajiv Gandhi government, buffeted by growing domestic political troubles, decided to engineer a foreign-policy triumph to boost its sagging popularity" (Bose, 2007: 32).

The Origins of the Indian Peacekeeping Force. Rajiv Gandhi and his advisers decided that something needed to be done. A frenetic series of diplomatic sorties and explicit military threats (including the dropping of supplies onto Jaffna by Indian Air Force planes) ensued. Under massive pressure from India, Jayewardene agreed to allow an Indian Peace Keeping Force (IPKF) into the north and to devolve powers to provincial councils. This was extremely unpopular in Sri Lanka, leading to an assassination attempt against Rajiv Gandhi when he visited Colombo to sign the Indo-Lanka Peace Accord and helping to trigger a bloody armed uprising by the ultra-leftist/ultra-nationalist JVP in southern Sri Lanka (De Silva, 1998). The Indo-Lanka Accords represented an Indian-dominated attempt to broker a solution to the ethnic conflict, but it suffered from a fatal flaw—neither the Sri Lankan government nor the LTTE were really committed to the deal. The largely domestic compulsions that pushed Rajiv and his advisers did not take into account the realities of the situation in Sri Lanka. In Cohen's words, "the Sri Lankan intervention was laced through with party political calculations, both under Mrs. Gandhi's regime and that of her son" (Cohen, 2001: 151).

As chaos engulfed southern Sri Lanka, the Indian Army was hastily dispatched to the north. Civilian policy-makers did a remarkably poor job of preparing the army for its task, and over-confidence by senior army leadership contributed to a toxic web of confusion (Singh, 2007; Das and Gupta-Ray, 2008). Ultimately, the IPKF and LTTE went to a war, a grinding counterinsurgency campaign that lasted nearly three years. At the height of the campaign over 100,000 Indian forces were on the ground in the north and east, also using the EPRLF and remnants of other Tamil groups as "Tiger-hunting" paramilitaries. Yet the IPKF was unable to decisively break the Tigers and its presence generated resentment in both Sri Lanka and Tamil Nadu. By 1989, the IPKF was stuck in place, waging a bitter counterinsurgency campaign in the jungles of northern Sri Lanka—it had stumbled into "a military catastrophe" (Cohen, 2001: 60).

The end and aftermath of the IPKF. Domestic politics helps explain why the IPKF's mission was ended, just as it helps explain why it was launched. When Rajiv Gandhi's government fell in 1989, a new Janata Dal-led coalition government arrived in power with a distinctly more skeptical view of the IPKF. Not only had the IPKF become unpopular among many Indian Tamils, but in the eyes of Prime Minister V.P. Singh it represented Indian meddling in areas outside of its real realm of responsibility. Sri Lankans would have to find Sri Lankan solutions—India would not commit its men and treasure to fighting the LTTE. This became a particularly compelling argument when the new Sri Lankan regime of President Ranasinghe Premadasa turned on the IPKF, fearing that it represented an Indian armed presence that would never leave. This perception of Indian expansionism led Premadasa to embark on an ultimately ill-fated rapprochement with the LTTE, most dramatically in the form of arms transfers to the Tigers. This combination of domestic and foreign factors led Singh to pull the IPKF out. Indian security services attempted to prop up the EPRLF in the north, but the EPRLF's use of forced conscription caused it to disintegrate under the weight of LTTE hammer blows in 1990 (Swamy, 1994). The Tigers emerged victorious with control of large swathes of territory.

A tragedy in 1991 made Indian elites even more reluctant to become seriously involved in Sri Lanka. Rajiv Gandhi was on the campaign trail trying to return Congress to power. LTTE leadership feared that he might send the IPKF back in, or at least crack down very hard on Tiger operations in India, and so targeted him for assassination (Kaarthikeyan and Raju, 2004). His death at the hands of a suicide bomber triggered a shift in Tamil views of the LTTE. While many remained unwilling to categorically condemn the LTTE, the vigorous demands for Indian action in support of the Tigers disappeared. Sri Lanka largely dropped off the Indian domestic-political radar screen. Along with the easing of Cold War-era tensions that made Sri Lanka's strategic position less important, the lack of domestic support for more assertive involvement in Sri Lanka led to a dramatic shift in India's approach to the conflict— India would not support the LTTE anymore, but it also would not engage in direct combat with the organization. The "island of blood" (Pratap, 2003) was left to its own devices as India has only occasionally launched diplomatic initiatives, primarily acting in a behind the scenes role.

III. DOMESTIC POLITICS AND FOREIGN POLICY IN PRE-LIBERALIZATION INDIA: EXPLANATIONS OF THE PAST, LESSONS FOR THE FUTURE?

India's foreign policy has always been shaped by the vicissitudes of domestic politics, whether the ideas of Nehru or the passions of Tamil Nadu. In this sense, there is nothing *conceptually* different about the post-1991 world - domestic politics, broadly defined, mattered on both sides of that year. Yet the pre-1991 period, and especially the pre-1971 world, impelled India in a very different direction than what would follow. Explaining the contours of the new trajectory of Indian foreign policy is the challenge taken up by the other chapters in this volume. But it is worth considering how some of these changes happened, and what they might say about the sources of change in Indian foreign policy more broadly. We can see a broad pattern in which shocks have reshaped the domestic circumstances that led to the original policies, leading to the creation and endurance of both new ideas and new political coalitions.

Interestingly, despite all of the (understandable) lamentation about the myopia, short-sightedness, and ignorance of Indian bureaucrats and politicians, the lessons learned in response to these shocks appear to have actually "stuck" to some degree. Indian foreign policy thus resembles a series of critical junctures (Collier and Collier 1991), at each of which domestic coalitions and beliefs determine policy but are then later forced back to the crossroads as a result of an interaction between the feedback (often unexpected) from the original decision and new structural circumstances. Elite consensus is an important aspect of foreign policy decision-making (Schweller, 2004; Legro, 2005), making the construction and adaptation of this consensus critical to understanding India's path in the world.

I have already explored how the Sri Lankan crisis bloodily exploded back into Indian politics—the balance between the demands for and costs of intervention shifted dramatically away from an active role. The IPKF disaster convinced strategic elites in Delhi to avoid Sri Lanka, while the tumult of Tamil politics and aftermath of Rajiv Gandhi's assassination shattered any pro-LTTE consensus in Tamil Nadu. Neither bureaucrats nor politicians any longer had powerful incentives to take a potentially costly stand on Sri Lanka. The political class learned the hard way about the complexities of that country's war, and the policy learning has largely endured and even been institutionalized in the corridors of power. This is important—it is clear that the lessons of Sri Lanka and legacy of the Rajiv assassination have not been forgotten by myopic elites or re-molded by cunning politicians. It is now nearly two decades after the assassination but the direction of policy has not dramatically changed even as various governments and parties have risen and fallen in power.

My analysis of alliances largely stopped in 1972. This is because the period between 1972 and 1990 was not one of dramatic shifts in alignment. I argued that the power of Nehruvian ideology was extremely powerful before 1962, and had created a path-dependent structural environment that newly-power-seeking Indian elites were forced to operate in between 1962 and 1972. From 1972 to 1990, the alignment game was largely, though not wholly, static—there were no major external shocks, though an even-closer relationship between Pakistan and the US in the 1980s was most unwelcome. The collapse of the Soviet Union in the early 1990s dramatically changed the structural situation. As Mohan puts it, India then had to "cross the Rubicon" into a new post-Soviet foreign policy (Mohan, 2004). The lessons of the Soviet collapse were more ambiguous than those driving shifts in Sri Lanka policy. Indian elites learned the dangers of an overly-close reliance on one major ally, creating a greater interest in strategic independence. Significant domestic anti-Americanism made the US an unlikely substitute for the Soviets, and the bitter legacies of 1962 made a move to China unlikely. But neither of these countries were actively threatening, and both have made at least gestures of friendship, as have Japan and Europe.

Thus, the international structure facing India has been fairly open, if confusing, while domestic politics offered little clear direction—some anti-American and anti-Chinese sentiment, certainly, but nothing dramatically negative. Moreover, those feeling strongly anti-Chinese (primarily on the Hindu right) are opposed ideologically to the most vitriolically anti-American (the Communist left). Unlike the creation of new coalitions favoring economic liberalization and opposing intervention in Sri Lanka, domestic politics offer no clear prediction of alliance behavior. As such, Indian alliance policy, particularly regarding the US, has proceeded somewhat fitfully and unpredictably (Kapur and Ganguly, 2007). The battles in 2007 and 2008 over the Indo-US civil nuclear deal make this lack of domestic consensus clear. This is likely to continue until India is forced to commit to a rigid alignment by some unforeseen, perhaps very distant, event that will leave the country once more facing a critical juncture in its quest for wealth and power. Until then, it is free to choose.

Acknowledgments: I thank Happymon Jacob, Vipin Narang, and Adam Ziegfeld for their helpful comments.

REFERENCES

Bajpai, Kanti, P.R. Chari, Stephen P., and Sumit Ganguly (1995), *Brasstacks and Beyond: Perception and Management of Crisis in South Asia*, New Delhi: Manohar Publishers.

Bose, Sumantra (2007), *Contested Lands: Israel-Palestine, Kashmir, Bosnia, Cyprus, and Sri Lanka*, Cambridge: Harvard University Press.

Bundy, William (1998), *A Tangled Web: The Making of Foreign Policy in the Nixon Presidency*, New York: Hill and Wang.

Cohen, Stephen P. (2001), *India: Emerging Power*, Washington, DC: Brookings Institution Press.

Cohen, Stephen P. (2004), *The Idea of Pakistan*, Washington, DC: Brookings Institution Press.

Collier, Ruth Berins and David Collier (1991), *Shaping the Arena: Critical Junctures, the Labor Movement, and Regime Dynamics in Latin America*, Princeton: Princeton University Press.

Das, Gautam and M.K. Gupta-Ray (2008), *Sri Lanka Misadventure: India's Military Peace-Keeping Campaign, 1987-1990*, Colombo: Vijitha Yapa.

De Silva, K.M. (1998), *Reaping the Whirlwind: Ethnic Conflict, Ethnic Politics in Sri Lanka*, New Delhi: Penguin.

DeVotta, Neil (2004), *Blowback: Linguistic Nationalism, Institutional Decay, and Ethnic Conflict in Sri Lanka*, Palo Alto: Stanford University Press.

Dixit, J.N. (1998), *Assignment Colombo*, New Delhi: Konark.

Ganguly, Sumit (2001), *Conflict Unending: India-Pakistan Tensions since 1947*, New York: Columbia University Press.

Garver, John (2001), *The Protracted Contest: Indian-Chinese Rivalry in the Twentieth Century*, Seattle: University of Washington Press.

Guha, Ramachandra (2007), *India After Gandhi: The History of the World's Largest Democracy*, New York: Ecco.

Gunaratna, Rohan (1993), *Indian Intervention in Sri Lanka: The Role of India's Intelligence Agencies*, Colombo: South Asian Network on Conflict Research.

Haas, Mark (2005), *The Ideological Origins of Great Power Politics, 1789-1989*, Ithaca: Cornell University Press.

Hazarika, Sanjoy (1995), *Strangers in the Mist: Tales of War and Peace from India's Northeast*, New Delhi: Penguin.

Kapur, Paul and Sumit Ganguly (2007), "The Transformation of U.S.-India Relations," *Asian Survey*, 47(4): 642-656.

Jalal, Ayesha (1990), *The State of Martial Rule: The Origins of Pakistan's Political Economy of Defence*, Cambridge: Cambridge University Press.

Kavic, Lorne (1967), *India's Quest for Security: Defence Policies, 1947-1965*, Berkeley: University of California Press.

Kohli, Atul (1991), *Democracy and Discontent: India's Growing Crisis of Governability*, Princeton: Princeton University Press.

Kux, Dennis (1992), *India and the United States: Estranged Democracies, 1941-1991*, Washington DC: National Defense University Press.

Kux, Dennis (2001), *The United States and Pakistan, 1947-2000: Disenchanted Allies*, Washington, DC: Woodrow Wilson Center Press and Johns Hopkins University Press.

Legro, Jeff (2005), *Rethinking the World: Great Power Strategies and International Order*, Ithaca: Cornell University Press.

Milner, Helen (1988), *Resisting Protectionism: Global Industries and the Politics of International Trade*. Princeton: Princeton University Press.

Mohan, C. Raja (2004), *Crossing the Rubicon: The Shaping of India's New Foreign Policy*, New York: Palgrave Macmillan.

Mohan, C. Raja (2006), "India and the Balance of Power," *Foreign Affairs*, 85(4): 17-32.

Moravcsik, Andrew (1998), *The Choice for Europe: Social Purpose and State Power from Messina to Maastricht*, Ithaca: Cornell University Press.

Nawaz, Shuja (2008), *Crossed Swords: Pakistan, its Army, and the Wars Within*, Karachi: Oxford University Press.

Pierson, Paul (2004), *Politics in Time: History, Institutions, and Social Analysis*, Princeton: Princeton University Press.

Power, Paul (1964), "Indian Foreign Policy: The Age of Nehru," *Journal of Politics*, 26(2): 257-286.

Pratap, Anita (2003), *Island of Blood: Frontline Reports from Sri Lanka, Afghanistan, and Other South Asian Flashpoints*, New Delhi: Penguin.

Schweller, Randall (2004), Unanswered Threats: A Neoclassical Realist Theory of Underbalancing," *International Security*, 29(2): 159-201.

Singh, Harkirat (2007), *Intervention in Sri Lanka: The IPKF Experience Retold*, New Delhi: Manohar Publishers.

Smith, Chris (1999), "South Asia's Enduring War," in Robert Rotberg (ed.), *Creating Peace in Sri Lanka: Civil War and Reconciliation*, Washington DC: Brookings Institution Press. pp. 17-40.

Swamy, M.R. Narayan (1994), *Tigers of Lanka: From Boys to Guerrillas*, New Delhi: Konark.

Tambiah, S.J. (1986), *Sri Lanka: Ethnic Fratricide and the Dismantling of Democracy*, Chicago: University of Chicago Press.

Tharoor, Shashi (2003), *Nehru: A Biography*, New York: Arcade Publishing.

Walt, Stephen (1987), *The Origins of Alliances*, Ithaca: Cornell University Press.

Waltz, Kenneth (1979), *Theory of International Politics*, Reading, MA: Addison-Wesley.

XI

India's Engagement with the World Trade Organization: The Role of Non-State Agents

Reji K Joseph[1]

There has been a perceptible change in the conduct of foreign trade policy of India with the emergence of the multilateral framework of World Trade Organization (WTO). The commitments that the country makes in the WTO would have its impacts on various segments of the society and hence the decision making requires continuous inputs from the concerned stakeholders. The non-state actors have, in the process, become important pressure groups airing the national interests whom the state finds it difficult to ignore. This paper is an analysis of the contribution made by the civil society groups and political parties in protecting the national interest while making India's intellectual property rights law in conformity with the WTO framework.

1. The Background

India's decision to be a party to the Uruguay Round of trade negotiations and to become a Member of the World Trade Organization (WTO) has led to a paradigm shift in the trade policy

[1]I am grateful to Biswajit Dhar, Professor and Head, Centre for WTO Studies and B K Keayla, convener of National Working Group on Patent Law for their comments on the draft of this paper.

from being purely a domestic concern to a subject of intergovernmental disciplines and scrutiny. The commitments under various WTO Agreements necessitated the expansion of scope of the trade policy from hitherto objective of import substitution to other areas such as reduction in subsidies, reduction of tariffs, abolition of non trade barriers, protection of minimum intellectual property rights (IPR) standards, etc. which have implications on protection of livelihoods, protection of industry and access to medicines, among others. Formulation of WTO consistent trade policy, which has implications on various segments of the society, requires the involvement of various stakeholders and this is in sharp contrast to the pre-WTO scenario where the Ministry of Commerce and Industry (MoCI) enjoyed a privileged position to make trade policy largely in isolation without consulting the stakeholders. Now, while the consultation process of the Department of Commerce (DoC) helps garnering the views and concerns of stakeholders especially the organized sector like the industry, the consultation of different bodies under the Parliament becomes a channel for airing the concerns of the non-organized stakeholders like civil society groups, farmers groups, health activists, etc. which do not have otherwise direct involvement in the trade policy making. Further, the increased clout of small political parties at the central level, like the left parties in the United Progressive Alliance (UPA) Government, forces the government to take into consideration their concerns and interests as well in the making of WTO consistent trade policy in India.

There are a few studies on the role played by different agencies in shaping India's engagement with the WTO. Jenkins (2003) has dealt in detail how the federal structure has influenced the trade policy especially in the area of agriculture. The state governments and a number of regional parties have attempted through various channels-through judiciary, through setting up WTO Cells, through making it an electoral issue, etc., to influence the decision making. He has identified three factors contributing to the friction between the states and the government of India (GoI) on WTO related issues: (a) the commitments that GoI has made under the WTO Agreement on

Agriculture (AoA) is perceived by the states as usurpation of their rights over agricultural policy, forcing some states to go to the extent of taking the matter to the court, (b) the economic impact of WTO rules vary among states as these effects are sector specific and those states which have a concentration of adversely affected sectors would protest strongly against the fashion in which GoI engages with the WTO, and (c) the independence of states in matters of foreign direct investment (FDI), aftermath of economic liberalization since 1991, and the resultant competition among the states for courting FDI requires them to stake out extreme position on policy questions that are beyond their own administrative competence, like international trade which is in the domain of central government. The study, however, observes that the state governments have only been marginally influential in shaping India's approach to the WTO. Interestingly, the study finds that the regional parties have been quite successful in pressurizing the GoI to make certain initiatives[2]; but it is not clear to what extent these tactics were successful in addressing the apprehensions of the states. The study by Dhar and Murali (2007) has made an in-depth analysis of the structure of WTO consistent trade policy making in India and the government machineries involved—various Ministries, the Upper and Lower Houses of Parliament and the consultation process of the Department of Commerce (DoC). The study also captures the contribution of non-state agents—the industry and the civil society groups, in shaping the WTO related trade policy in the country. The industry associations, though a non-state entity, have become part of India's official delegation for WTO negotiations since the Seattle Ministerial Conference in 1999 and therefore have become the only non-state agency with direct access to the trade policy making machinery.[3] The study finds two reasons for the engagement of the

[2]The pressure exerted by regional parties representing well off farmers resulted in the central government organizing a series of federally organized consultations on the WTO AoA.

[3]Recently, the DoC has conducted consultations with industry on sectoral proposals under WTO NAMA negotiations with focus on the sectors of chemicals, electronics/electrical products and industrial machinery at Delhi, Ahmadabad, Chennai,

industry and the government: (a) industry associations made some attempt to assess the importance of various issues covered by the WTO Agreements from the point of view of their members, and (b) industry associations consistently demanded, for a meaningful participation in the consultation, GoI to encourage the emergence of independent view points on some of the more contentious issues which would help in making decisions based on holistic view and consultations should take place based on an understanding of the issues involved. The study also shows the contribution made by civil society groups in helping the GoI to incorporate flexibilities in the Trade Related Aspects of Intellectual Property Rights (TRIPS) Agreement while amending India's Patents Act 1970.

While these studies have covered the major actors involved in the process of WTO related trade policy making, it is essential to understand the channels through which these agencies exert pressures and the causal effects of their interventions. Two non-state actors which have decisively intervened in shaping India's engagement with WTO in the area of intellectual property rights are the left political parties and the civil society groups. This paper is an analysis of the contribution of left political parties and civil society groups, their modus operandi and their interplay between them and with the government machineries, when India fulfilled its obligations under WTO agreement on TRIPS by amending its Patents Act of 1970. The paper is structured as follows: section two gives a brief of structure of trade policy formulation in India, section three gives a background to the TRIPS agreement and the amendments to India's Patents Act 1970 and section four is the analysis of the interventions of left political parties and the civil society groups.

2. STRUCTURE OF TRADE POLICY MAKING

The DoC of MoCI is the nodal agency responsible for formulating WTO consistent trade policy in India. The Director General of

Hyderabad, Kolkata, Mumbai, Pune, Bangaluru and Ludhiana from 28 August to 18 September 2008. These consultations were conducted by the Centre for WTO studies, DoC.

Foreign Trade (DGFT) and Trade Policy Division (TPD) are the two divisions under. These two departments engage in consultations at the inter-ministerial level and with the stakeholders on WTO related issues[4] (Dhar and Murali, 2007). Following Diagram shows the agencies involved directly and indirectly in the process of India's engagement with the WTO.

Agents in WTO Consistent Trade Policy making

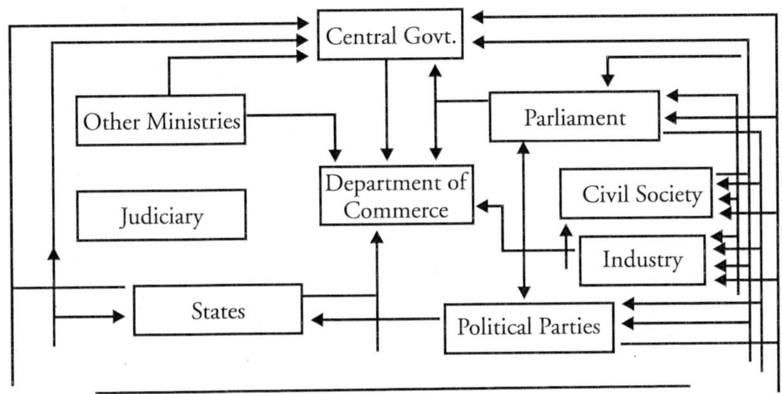

The two houses of the Parliament, the Rajya Sabha (Upper House) and Lok Sabha (Lower House) intervene decisively in the policy making though its Departmental Standing Committees, Joint Committees and the debates in the Parliament. The Departmental Standing Committees[5] in the process of making its reports seek the views of all the stakeholders and hence their reports are quite

[4] Commitments under various WTO Agreements require involvement of various Ministries and Departments in the process of trade policy formulation. Commitments under the AoA bring various organizations within the Ministry of Agriculture and DoC into the focus. Similarly, commitments under the agreement on TRIPS require the involvement of ministries of Agriculture and Health and the Departments Commerce and Industrial Policy and Promotion within MoCI.

[5] They are Parliamentary Standing Committees of the Houses related to concerned Ministries/Departments and its membership spread across a number of political parties. The current Standing Committee on Commerce have 30 members from 13 political parities of which nine are members of Rajya Sabha and 21 are members of Lok Sabha. Functions of the Committee include examining of Bills, pertaining to the related Ministries/Departments and consideration of national basic long term policy documents presented to the Houses, among other things.

influential in the policy making.[6] The reports of a Standing Committee have a persuasive value; Rule 277 of 'Rules of Procedure and Conduct of Business in the Council of States' specifies that report of standing committees 'shall be treated as considered advice given by the Committee'. A Parliamentary Joint Committee is a Committee consisting of members from both the Houses to look in detail into different aspects of a proposed Bill. Amendments can be moved to the various clauses of the Bill by members of the Committee. The Committee can also take evidence of associations, public bodies or experts who are interested in the measure. After the Bill has thus been considered, the Committee submits its report to the House which considers the Bill again as reported by the Committee. The debates in the Parliament are very important because they provide a mechanism through which the decisions made by administrative ministries are reviewed. The level on intervention in the Parliament on the trade policy issues has been significant. While in Rajya Sabha, 192 Members raised 511 questions during the period between 1995 and 2004, in Lok Sabha 330 Members made 2900 interventions between 1999 and 2004 (Dhar and Murali, 2007).

The industry and their associations in India play a critical role in the making of WTO related trade policies in the country. It is already mentioned in the previous section how the industry associations have become officially recognized as stakeholders in trade policy making.

Judiciary is another important machinery that intervenes in the policy making. Judiciary have been involving in issues of patent disputes, pharmaceutical pricing policy and import of genetically modified food products and in some of these cases forcing the government to review its policy. The involvement of judiciary is dealt in detail in section three. The civil society groups resort to judicial proceedings quite extensively, apart from banking on other forums such as parliamentary committees, to get their views heard.

[6] The Departmental Standing Committee on Commerce, while preparing its 1993 report (Parliament of India, 1993) had held 39 meetings with civil society organizations, industry associations and administrative ministries (Dhar and Murali, 2007).

With the small political parities becoming the king makers at the central level, their interests have become one of the crucial factors influencing the direction of trade policy. This has become very clear during the third amendment in 2005 of India's Patents Act 1970 when the UPA government conceded to most of the demands raised by the left parties.

3. TRIPS Agreement and India

At the Ministerial conference held at Marrakesh in 1994, the GoI ratified the Final Act of 1986-1994 Uruguay Round of trade negotiations establishing the WTO and it became obligatory for India to implement various Agreements incorporated in the Final Act. TRIPS Agreement, an important agreement of WTO covering various forms of IPRs, had to be implemented by amending various IPR laws of the country. The IPR laws covered by TRIPS relate to:

(a) Copyrights and related rights
(b) Trademarks
(c) Geographical Indications
(d) Industrial Designs
(e) Patents (also includes sui generis protection for plant varieties)
(f) Layout Designs of Integrated Circuits
(g) Protection of Undisclosed Information.

While the Members are obliged to enforce the minimum standards of IPR protection prescribed by the Agreement, they have considerable freedom in framing the working of IPR provisions such as scope of patentability, compulsory licensing provisions, etc. based on the interests of each Member. All the laws on IPRs in India except Patents have been amended without much debate in the Parliament or protests from the public.[7] Amendment of the Patents Act 1970 has

[7]There have been concerns expressed from various corners (Industry Association Indian Pharmaceutical Alliance, CSOs, Health Activists, Academics, etc.) in the case of protection of pharmaceutical test data. GoI appointed an inter-ministerial Committee to study the issue and the Committee submitted its report in 2007. GoI is yet to take an official decision on the issue.

been crucial issue especially for the general public and the pharmaceutical industry (NWGPL, 2003). It was feared that the implementation of product patent rights in pharmaceuticals would give monopoly rights to the innovators of new medicines for a period of 20 years, resulting in sharp increase in the price of medicines. The new patent regime under the TRIPS was also perceived as a threat to the sustenance of Indian generic pharmaceutical industry, which supplied cheap and quality medicines to patients in India as well as foreign countries. This industry, which has thrived under the process patent regime under the Patents Act 1970, would no longer be able to continue with their modus operandi of reverse engineering and continue the production of cheap medicines. Thus, amending the Patents Act of 1970 was the most important hurdle in making Indian IPR system, TRIPS compliant.

TRIPS Agreement provided some transitional arrangements to developing country Members. Though the provisions of the Agreements are expected to be in force by 1st January 1996, developing countries which had process patent regimes were given time, if they wanted, to extend the period for further four years, i.e., till 1st January 2000.[8] However, the Agreement required these Members to make provisions for receiving patent applications.[9] And for developing countries which are obliged to extend product patent protection to areas of technology not so protectable in its territory on the general date of application of the Agreement, i.e., 1st January 1996, could delay the application of the provisions for an additional period of five years, i.e., till 1st January 2005. India was having process patent regime in pharmaceuticals and agro-chemicals and had the time till 1st January 2005 to extend product patent rights in pharmaceuticals and agro-chemical products, though in other areas it had to meet its obligations by 1st January 2000.

India complied with its obligations under the TRIPS Agreement in three steps. The first step was the Patents (Amendment) Act of

[8]Article 65.2 of TRIPS Agreement.

[9]Article 70.8 of TRIPS Agreement.

1999, which provided for receiving of patent applications (mail-box applications) and for exclusive marketing rights.[10] The Patents (Amendment) Act 2002 introduced comprehensive amendments to bring together various provisions of the Patents Act 1970 into conformity with the TRIPS Agreement.[11] For the third and most important amendment aimed at introducing product patent rights along with already existed process patent rights in pharmaceuticals and agro-chemicals, a Bill amending the Patents Act was introduced in 2003 by the National Democratic Alliance (NDA) government led by the Bharatiya Janata Patry (BJP). The Bill lapsed owing to a change in government at the centre and the consequent dissolution of the Lok Sabha. The new Congress-led UPA coalition government, established with the external support of left parties, pushed the 2003 Bill to amend the Patents Act so as to meet the TRIPS time line of 1st January 2005.[12] But the UPA could not gather the necessary support particularly owing to the disagreement of left parties on the provisions of the Bill and hence passed as a Presidential Ordinance on 26th December 2004 to meet the deadline. The government had six months to codify this Ordinance by obtaining the approval of the Parliament. Owing to pressure from various corners especially the Left parties, substantial changes were made to the Ordinance and cleared by the Parliament in the third week of March as the Patents (Amendment) Bill, 2005. After receiving Presidential assent and being published in the official gazette, it finally came into force as Patents

[10]An ordinance was issued on 31st December 1994 amending the Patents Act 1970 to introduce the mail-box provisions. But the amendment was not passed by the Parliament. The United States dragged India into a dispute in the WTO (WT/DS50) on the failure of providing mail-box facility where the decision went against India. Exclusive Marketing Rights brought with them a five-year, patent-like monopoly for products covered by the product patent applications made under the mailbox system. The company securing an exclusive marketing right has the exclusive right to sell or distribute the article or substance covered in a patent application in a country.

[11]It introduced 64 amendments (Basheer 2005).

[12]For details see Basheer (2003) and 'Brief History of National Working Group on Patent Laws: Activities During Past 20 Years', report by B K Keayla, Convener of NWGPL, 2008.

(Amendment) Act 2005 with retrospective effect from 1st January 2005.

4. Role of Political Parties and Civil Society Groups in Amending Patents Act in 2005

The political view of the left parties on the TRIPS agreement played a critical role in enacting various provisions of the Patents (Amendment) Act in April 2005. The left parties, i.e., CPI(M), CPI, Forward Block and RSP said "the left parties have been consistently of the view that TRIPS was and continues to be an iniquitous agreement balanced heavily in favour of multinational corporations" (People's Democracy, 2005). The interventions that these parties made were based on this perspective. The left parties intervened in a major way in the third amendment of the Patents Act.

There were eight areas where the left parties wanted the Government to review the provisions in the Ordinance. The eight areas are: (1) patentability criteria, (2) pre-grant opposition to patent applications, (3) compulsory licensing provision, (4) export of drugs produced under compulsory license, (5) production of drugs for which applications were pending in the mail-Box, (6) patenting of software, (7) exclusion of micro-organisms from patenting, and (8) defining what is a new chemical entity (people's Democracy, 2005).

There were serious concerns that a narrow definition of what is patentable (patentability criteria) would lead to 'evergreening' of patents, that is the continuation of patent rights beyond the stipulated 20 years by acquiring patents on small changes made to the original invention. The third amendment restricted the chances of 'evergreening' by defining pharmaceutical substance and clarifying what is meant by an 'inventive step', which is the most important criterion determining the patentability of a subject matter.

The Ordinance had in fact restricted the ability of any entity to oppose the grant of a patent. If an entity finds on valid grounds that patent should not be granted on a patent application, it could raise that matter with the Controller of Patents. The ordinance had reduced the number of grounds under which the grant of a patent could be opposed from 11 to two and had also deleted the clause which provided for a hearing in person to the person making the opposition. The third amendment restored all the original grounds in the Patents Act 1970 for opposing grant of a patent.

Compulsory licensing, which allows third parties to produce and market patented medicines on certain grounds and the Government to override patent rights in situations of national emergency or other circumstances of extreme urgency or for public non-commercial purposes, was another issue of concern. In the case of a third party, it was required before making an application to the Controller of Patents for compulsory license, to enter into negotiations with the patent holder for a license on reasonable terms and conditions and such efforts have not been successful within a reasonable period. But, the Ordinance did not specify what is the reasonable period within which such negations should be completed, resulting in widespread concerns that compulsory licenses may take too long and thus defeat the whole purpose of the vary provision. The third amendment addressed this concern by specifying that the reasonable time period is six months. The other issue in this context was the export of medicines from India produced under compulsorily license to other countries which do not have manufacturing capacities. The TRIPS Agreement (Article 31.f) originally provided that compulsory license can be used predominantly for the supply of the domestic market of the Member authorizing such license. This required domestic manufacturing capacity as a pre-requirement for the exercise of compulsory license and a number of developing and least developed countries raised this matter in the WTO ministerial and the Doha Declaration clarified that countries without sufficient or no manufacturing capacities can import from any country which has issued a compulsory license. Import from India of medicines produced under compulsory license was a major concern for the health activists and governments in developing countries because these countries benefit from import of cheap and good quality medicines from India. The ordinance had provided that patented drugs, which are produced through compulsory licenses in the country, can be exported to developing countries with in insufficient or no manufacturing capacity subject to the condition that the importing country grants a compulsory license. Globally this clause had attracted widespread criticism owing to the procedural hurdles for such countries to grant compulsory license. The third amendment clarified that the country can import from India if 'provided compulsory license has been granted by such country or such country has by notification or otherwise allowed importation of the patented pharmaceutical product from India'.

Possibly the biggest concern expressed after the Ordinance was on the continued production of drugs for which applications were pending in the mail-box. It was apprehended that generic medicines that are already produced and marketed in India for which patent application are pending in the mail-box, would go off the market once the patent is granted, leading to a quantum jump in drug prices. The Glivec case, the anti-cancer drug (Imatinib mesylate) for which the Swiss MNC Novartis obtained exclusive marketing rights in 2003 would be the best pointer to the concerns on the drug price. The price of Glivec was more than 10 times higher than that of its generic counterparts: Novartis charged Rs 130000 per person for one month whereas the price of Indian generic equivalents was Rs 10000 per person for one month.[13] These generic drugs going off the market would mean that patients have no other choice but to buy highly expensive patented medicines or continue with the disease without taking required medication. The third amendment clarified that those Indian companies already producing medicines for which applications are filed in the mail-box can continue to produce them even after patent is granted to the drug, after paying a royalty to the patent owner.

[13]See http://www.centad.org/download/centad%20Oct%202007%20Hyd.pdf, accessed on 27th October 2008.

Patenting of software was permitted in the ordinance by providing that computer programmes with technical applications and those that are combined with hardware could be patented. Software patents would give large corporations a strategic advantage over small and medium-sized ones, and a potentially destructive weapon against open source. The Third Amendment has withdrawn this provision and has maintained what was there in the Patents Act 1970.

Two of the amendments recommend by the Left parties—exclusion of micro-organisms from patenting and definition of new chemical entities were not accepted by the Government. However, the Government appointed an expert committee to look into these matters.

To a large extent, the changes made to the Ordinance were made to appease the left parties without whose support the UPA could not have survived at that time. A case in point is the 'inventive step' clause, which was copied verbatim with an addition of just two words from the list of recommendations by the CPI(M), which in turn appears to be based on a report by a prominent civil society initiative—the National Working Group on Patent Law (NWGPL). Section 2.j of the Patents Act after the third amendment defines an inventive step as "a feature of an invention that involves technical advance as compared to the existing knowledge or having economic significance or both and that makes the invention not obvious to a person skilled in the art." The recommendations sent by CPI(M)[14] to GoI defined an inventive step as "a feature of an invention that involves technical advance as compared to the existing knowledge or having economic significance and that makes the invention not obvious to a person skilled in the art" and the CPIM has copied this verbatim from the Report of the Fourth Peoples' Commission on Review of Legislations Amending Patents Act 1970, commissioned by NWGPL.[15]

[14]Communist Party of India (Marxist), Left Parties on Amendments to the Indian Patent Act, at http://www.cpim.org/upa/2004_patents.pdf, accessed on 11th October 2008.

[15]Report of the Fourth People's Commission on Review of Legislations Amending Patents Act 1970, at http://www.who.int/entity/intellectualproperty/documents/Report4thCommission.pdf, accessed on 11th October 2008.

Civil Society Groups

The civil society groups like the NWGPL, Medicines San Frontiers (MSF), Gene Campaign, etc. have been a decisive force in the formulation of WTO consistent domestic policies from a perspective of protecting the interests of the people of the country. These organizations though do not have any official representation, act as pressure groups. The role played by the civil society groups especially the NWGPL during the final amendment of Patents Act is praise worthy and would be the best example of civil society groups successfully pressurizing the government to review its stance.

The NWGPL, which is a network of 12 organizations,[16] began its work on WTO issues as early as 1988 during the mid-term review of Uruguay Round negotiations. The positive impact of the Patents Act 1970 was widely visible at this time as India had a vibrant generic pharmaceutical industry which brought down the prices of medicines in India from one of the highest in the world[17] to one of the lowest in the world in a matter of few decades. The Ayyangar Committee Report and the Report of the Patents Enquiry Committee which formed the basis of the Patents Act 1970 had already generated a lively discussion in India and other developing countries about the merits of the process patent regime. So it was quite natural for the people working in this area to come together in a group to convince the government on the importance of continuing with the Patents Act 1970. NWGPL held that India should continue with protecting the

[16]The 12 organizations are: (a) Public Interest, Legal Support and Research Centre, (b) CSIR Scientific Workers Association, (c) Delhi Science Forum, (d) Academy of Young Scientists, (e) Consumers' Forum, (f) National Confederation of Officers' Association of Public Sector Undertakings, (g) Forum of Financial Writers, (h) All India Drug Action Network, (i) Forum for Preservation on Indian Patents Law, (j) National Campaign Committee on Drug Policy, (k) All India Lawyers Union, and (l) Indian Drug Manufacturers Association.

[17]The United States' Senate Committee on Drug Prices, the 'Kefauver Committee' reported in 1962 that 'in drugs, India ranks amongst the highest priced nations of the world'.

processes and not the products and there should be a strong compulsory license system (Dhar and Murali, 2007).

The NWGPL established Peoples' Commissions, members of which constituted eminent personalities from diverse fields in the country like bureaucracy, academics, industry, law, etc., to study various facets of new patent regime and come out with reports. The Fourth Peoples' Commission established in 2003 to study the provisions of the '2003 Bill' with I.K Gujral, former Prime Minister of India as Chairman and Prof. Yaspal, former chairman of University Grants Commission, Prof. Muchkund Dubey, former Foreign Secretaty, B.L Das, former India's ambassador to GATT, Dr. Yusuf Hamied, Chairman and MD Cipla, S.P Shukla, former member, Planning Commission, Prof. Prabhat Patnaik, Professor in Jawaharlal Nehru University, Dr. Rajeev Dhavan, senior advocate at supreme court of India and Prof. Ashok Parthasarathi, former secretary of GoI as members and B.K Keayla, former commissioner of payments as convener submitted its report in October 2004. The Recommendations of the Commission became the breeding ground for the protests from various corners when the UPA attempted to introduce the final amendment Bill in December 2004.

The report of the Fourth Peoples' Commission has dealt with each of the important provisions of the proposed Patents (Amendment) Bill and made concrete recommendations for the consideration by the GoI. The report clearly states the objective of the exercise. It says:

> "... we must ensure that the exercise of making our Patent Act WTO – compliant does not end up contravening or jeopardizing the fundamental rights that the Constitution guarantees to our people.... A sound and balanced national patent system is of crucial importance for the autonomous development of any economy and for meeting public demand for drugs, pharmaceuticals and other essential commodities. It is, therefore, extremely important that every provision of the amending Bill

should be formulated with utmost care and attention and with clarity and precision" (pages 6,14).

The recommendations of the Peoples' Commission were spread into six broad areas; most of them were raised also by the left parties. The major issues raised by the commission were: (a) Scope and Patentability, (b) Compulsory licensing, in order to enable the domestic enterprises to ensure abundant availability at competitive prices, of pharmaceuticals and other products covered by the patent regime, (c) The terms of patent i.e. period of patent and licenses, (d) Royalty parameters, (e) Export of patented products; and (f) Pre-grant opposition to patent claims. Most of these recommendations were accepted by the GoI, as we have seen earlier in this section. One specific issue which the Commission raised was to limit the reasonable period after which the applicant can approach the Controller of Patents for compulsory license to 150 days.[18] The third amendment clarified it by saying that "reasonable period shall be construed as a period not ordinarily exceeding a period of six months." A brief analysis of the working of NWGPL, which is given below, would show the efforts of the Group in sensitizing the policy makers and concerned stakeholders the method adopted by them for the sensitization.

When the NWGPL was formed, the first task they undertook was to evolve some kind of a program. They focused on sensitizing the people on the impact of changes in the patent law by organizing national and international conferences. The first national seminar organized by the group in 1998 was attended by eminent scientists, jurists, economists, technocrats, industrialists, journalists, representatives of government and various organizations. A clear cut position got established with the unanimous adoption of a resolution in the concluding session of this conference which was addressed by K R Narayanan, then Minister of State for Science and Technology, P N Haksar, former vice Chairman, Planning Commission, Justice V R Krishna Iyer and Justice D A Desai, former judges of Supreme Court, Dr Surendra Patel, world known economist and senior

[18]See page 27 NWGPL (2004).

scientists like Dr Nitya Anand. The resolution became the basis for the national campaign against change to the patent law.[19] After the seminar, representatives of the Group led by Justice V R Krishna Iyer met then Prime Minister Chandra Shekhar to appraise him of their serious concern and the need to protect the national interest during the GATT negotiations. In 1993, an International Conference on Patents Regime proposed in the Uruguay Round of GATT negotiations was organized by NWGPL jointly with ALIFAR (Asociación Latinoamericana de la Industria Farmacéutica or the Latin American association of the pharmaceutical industry) of South America, Canadian Drug manufacturers Association and IDMA. New Delhi Declaration and New Delhi Statement were issued, which became landmark documents for further campaign. Arising out of this conference, a delegation of these industries associations was led by NWGPL to Geneva and met the officials at GATT.

The second major initiative of the Group came in the wake of Dunkel Draft in December 2001. A Peoples' Commission on constitutional issues of Dunkel Draft Text with the Chairman and Members of former Judges of Supreme Court was established in November 1993. The Commission submitted a detailed report which was submitted to the Prime Minister and circulated extensively. The report had looked into the constitutional issues arising out of GoI holding negotiations in the Uruguay Round on agricultural issues without consulting the state governments. The group members approached a number of state governments and held discussion with them about the implications of Dunkel Draft Text. Some of the state governments—Tamil Nadu, Rajasthan and Orissa agreed to file petitions in the Supreme Court.[20] These petitions were drafted by Dr. Rajeev Dhavan, a member of NWGPL.[21]

[19]See 'Brief History of National Working Group on Patent Laws: Activities during Past 20 Years, report by B K Keayla, Convener of NWGPL, 2008.

[20]In the course of time there were changes in the leadership in these state governments and the writ petitions were withdrawn.

[21]Supra note 18.

NWGPL took the lead in establishing a Forum of Parliamentarians on patent law and WTO Issues in 1995. The core group of the forum included Dr. Murli Manohar Joshi as Convener and Dr Ashok Mitra, A B Bardhan, Jaipal Reddy, George Fernandes and Prithviraj Chauhan as members and B K Keayla as convener, S P Shukla as forum advisor. NWGPL and the Parliamentarians Forum jointly organized an international Conference of Parliamentarians in 1996, attended by a number of Parliamentarians from South America, Pakistan, Bangladesh, Sri Lanka, Nepal, etc.

NWGPL established the second Peoples' Commission in 1998 to examine the transitional period obligations in the TRIPS agreement and implementation of the obligation in the TRIPS agreement and submitted its report of the government with recommendations. The Third Peoples' Commission was established during the course of introduction of second amendment. A large number of experts and stakeholders numbering 25 appeared before the commission. The Commission has also received nine detailed papers from various experts, who could not personally appear before the Commission.[22] The Commission submitted its report in 2003 for the consideration of the Government and Members of Parliament. In December 2003 the Government introduced the final Patents (Amendment) Bill, prompting NWGPL to set up the Fourth Peoples' Commission on Review of Legislations Amending the Patents Act 1970. This Commission went into the depth of various amendments already carried out and the proposed amendments in the final amending Bill. In order to put their views upfront, NWGPL co-ordinate with the left parties, the king maker of UPA coalition government. S.P Shukla of NWPL acted as the coordinator with left parties during the course of third amendment to the Patents Act 1970.[23]

We have already seen that there are commonalities in the contents of interventions of the left parties and NWGPL in the context of

[22]Supra note

[23]This point came out during my conversation with B K Keayla, convener of NWGPL.

making Indian patent regime compatible to the WTO. These two groups were quite successful in exerting pressure on the government. What is more important is that there is a commonality in the ideology representing both these groups-the left parties and the NWGPL believed that the TRIPS agreement had sought to strengthen the monopoly position of multinational companies.[24] These two non state actors led by a common ideology turned out to be the most important pressure group in directing India's relations with WTO in the area of IPRs.

The other area of concern under TRIPS was patents for plant varieties. Article 27.3.b of the TRIPS Agreement provides that "members shall provide for the protection of plant varieties either by patents or by an effective *sui gneris* system or by any combination thereof." In meeting India's obligation to provide plant breeders rights, it had the option of joining the UPOV (international union for the protection of new plant varieties) a readily available international framework, like many developing countries did. But, UPOV provides for only breeders rights and there is no recognition of farmers' rights. The most recent UPOV Convention (1991) requires that member countries provide a monopoly of limited duration to reward the development of new plant varieties by way of an exclusive property right, without giving any recognition to farmer's rights. The civil society groups held that the role of farmers as creators of land races and traditional varieties which form the foundation of modern plant breeding and their contribution in the identification, maintenance and refinement of germplasm have to be acknowledged. The dominant view of these groups was that the legislation that India needed to adopt should recognize the rights of traditional farmers who are involved in plant breeding activities and should not be based on the UPOV model. Two CSOs, the Gene Campaign and the Centre for Environment and Development proposed an alternative treaty to UPOV- Convention of Farmers and Breeders (CoFAB), which sought to strike a balance between the interests of farmers and breeders. After

[24]See page 9 of NWGPL (2004) and Peoples Democracy (2005).

a series of internal deliberations,[25] the government introduced a uniquely framed Bill on the Protection of Plant varieties and Farmers Rights in 1999, which aims to protect the rights of the plant breeders and farmers.

The Bill contained provisions for protecting farmers' rights, but its articulation of farmers' rights was limited to a single article (Article 31), which read: 'nothing contained in this Act shall affect the right of a farmer to save, use, exchange, share or sell his farm produce of a variety protected under this Act: Provided that a farmer shall not be entitled for such right in case where the sale is for the purpose of reproduction under a commercial marketing arrangement.' The wording of this article was highly criticized because the term 'produce' was thought to give Farmers' rights to their crops, but not to the seeds of those crops (Cullet, 2000). This was also a time when farmers groups in various parts of the country initiated movements against seed MNCs and to assert the rights of farmers to produce, improve, exchange, and sell seeds, against the perceived threat to these practices posed by the entry of multinationals into the Indian economy and Article 27.3(b) of the TRIPs Agreement. In one such cases in early 1990s, members of the Karnataka Rajya Ryota Sangha (KRRS), a farmers' organization in the state of Karnataka, raided the offices of Cargill Seeds India, a subsidiary of the US multinational in December 1992. Speaking on this occasion, Professor M.D. Nanjundaswamy, the leader of the KRRS commented that 'We are going to launch a one-point programme—to drive out the multinationals. Our genetic resources are our national property'.[26]

[25]The Departmental Standing Committee on Commerce while preparing its report (parliament of India, 1998) had held 39 meetings with civil society organizations, industry associations and administrative ministries (Dhar and Murali, 2007). The report brought out the demand of private and public seed companies to have plant breeders' rights, the concern of Department of Biotechnology on in-house research and development and the apprehension of civil society groups on farmers' rights.

[26]See Shaila Seshia, 'plant Variety Protection and Farmers' Rights in India: Law Making and the Cultivation of Varietal Control, accessed on 3rd October 2008 at http://unpan1.un.org/intradoc/groups/public/documents/APCITY/UNPAN021315.pdf.

The Bill was referred to a Joint Parliamentary Committee, which in the process had invited suggestions and comments on the bill by issuing notices to a wide cross section of stakeholders—farmers groups, seed companies, agricultural research centres, civil society organizations and academics—and using the mass media. The committee received 132 written submissions and 17 oral submissions by individuals and associations (Dhar and Murali, 2007). The most notable change made as a result of the Joint Parliamentary Committee process was the expansion of provisions on Farmers' Rights. Provisions from the 1999 Bill that pertained to Farmers' Rights such as benefit-sharing, and the National Gene Fund were consolidated in a separate Chapter (Chapter 6) on Farmers' Rights. Importantly the Committee eliminated the fears of farmers on their rights over the seeds by specifying that a farmer 'shall be deemed to be entitled to save, use, sow, resow, exchange, share or sell his farm produce including seed of a variety protected under this Act in the same manner as he was entitled before the coming into force of this Act Provided that the farmer shall not be entitled to sell branded seed of a variety protected under this Act' (Chapter 6.1(iv)). Section 39.1(iv) of The Protection of Plant Varieties and Farmers' Rights Act, 2001 is a verbatim reproduction of Chapter 6.1(iv) of the Committee report.

Using of Parliamentarians Forums is a strategy used by civil society groups to raise an issue of concern in the parliament. Recently, during the brainstorming discussion on implications of the new definition of counterfeit medicines by the International Medical Products Anti-Counterfeiting Taskforce, organized by the Centre for Trade and Development, it was felt that there needs to be generated a discussion urgently on this issue at the official level. The strategy evolved was to generate a discussion in the Parliament on this issue by raising it with Indian Medical Parliamentarians' Forum.[27]

CONCLUSION

The formulation of India's trade policy is no longer an easy task as it used to be in the pre-WTO era where the MoCI had the freedom to

[27] I participated in the meeting.

frame such policies depending on the domestic requirements. Now the trade policy is evolved after a series of consultations among various government bodies as well as with the non state-agents like the civil society groups and the industry. The process of making India's IPR laws in conformity with the WTO has shown how important are the non-state agents in shaping the WTO consistent trade policy in the country. The civil society groups and the left political parties, led by the ideology that TRIPS agreement is iniquitous in nature and caters to the monopoly interests of foreign MNCs, became the most powerful force in directing the terms of the new law.

REFERENCE

Basheer, Shamnad (2005), 'India's Tryst with TRIPS: The Patents (Amendment) Act 2005', The Indian Journal of Law and Technology, Vol 1, pp 15-46.

Cullet, Phillipe (2000), Farmers' Rights in Peril', Frontline, Vol 17, Issue 7, 1-14 April.

Dhar, Biswajit and Murali kallummal (2007), 'Trade Policy Off the hook: The making of Indian Trade Policy Since the Uruguay Round' in Mark Halle and Robert Wolfe (Ed.), Process Matters: Sustainable Development and Domestic Trade Transparency', International Institute for Sustainable Development, Manitoba, Canada.

NWGPL (2004), Report of the Fourth Peoples' Commission on Review of Legislations Amending patents Act 1970, available at http://www.who.int/entity/intellectualproperty/documents/Report4thCommission.pdf

Parliament of India (1998); 'India and the WTO', Department Related Parliamentary Standing Committee on Commerce, 35th Report, Rajya Sabha Secretariat, New Delhi.

People's Democracy (2005), Weekly Organ of Communist Party of India (Marxist), Vol XXIX, No 13, March 27.

Sahai, Suman (2007), SC to Look Into Deregulation of GM Food Imports, Indiatogether, accessed on 27th October 2008 at http://www.indiatogether.org/2007/nov/agr-gmstay.htm

USTR (2006), National Trade Estimate Report on Foreign Trade Barriers, available at http://www.ustr.gov/Document_Library/Reports_Publications/2006/2006_NTE_Report/Section_Index.html.

ABBREVIATIONS

AoA	Agreement on Agriculture
DGFT	Director General of Foreign Trade

DoC	Department of Commerce
FDI	Foreign Direct Investment
GoI	Government of India
IDMA	Indian Drug Manufacturers Association
IPR	Intellectual Property Rights
MoCI	Ministry of Commerce and Industry
NWGPL	National Working Group on Patent Law
TPD	Trade Policy Division
TRIPS	Trade Related Aspects of Intellectual Property Rights
UPA	United Progressive Alliance
WTO	World Trade Organization

XII

Domestic Politics and India's 1998 Nuclear Tests

Deepa Ollapally

Introduction

At first glance, there are few issues more compelling for an external, international systems explanation than a nation acquiring nuclear capability. After all, whether in the conventional literature or popular mind, nuclear weapons are seen as the ultimate weapon, providing the highest level of security. Indeed, discussion of nuclear weapons are most often along the lines of deterrence and inter-state competition. This chapter investigates the role of domestic politics in India's 1998 nuclear tests in an attempt to assess the significance, if any, of the internal realm. Although many of the chapters in this book use the emergence of coalition politics as a reference point for assessing the impact of domestic politics on India's foreign policy, it may be noted that the nuclear tests occurred toward the beginning of coalitional governance.

The chapter begins by laying out the theoretical framework that would allow us to test for domestic factors versus the international system. It then sets up the international systems argument for why India conducted the five nuclear tests in Pokhran in 1998 and considers how well it stands up to scrutiny. I will then take up a domestic level explanation to see if it is able to fill the gaps of the external argument. In theory at least, the international systems approach has the home court advantage, and thus this could be viewed as a crucial case. Thus even if we were to discover that while the domestic level is not determining and that it is still a necessary explanation, it will call into question the dominant explanation for nuclear testing. In discussing the domestic level, three explanations will be considered: leadership; ideology and political compulsions.

THE INTERNATIONAL SYSTEM ARGUMENT

The presumption in the international relations literature is that decisions about high level security issues are determined by the anarchic nature of the international system. After all, in a situation where survival is determined by self help, why would any given state be driven by anything other than such basic pressures? The most compelling argument is made by Kenneth Waltz in his widely cited book *Theory of International Politics* (Waltz, 1979). The systems argument is however a deductive one—i.e., it begins with the assumption of anarchy which then leads to self help, forcing countries to engage in balancing behavior or at rare times, bandwagoning. While this is an elegant and parsimonious model offering crucial insight into the general behavior patterns of states, it has been repeatedly critiqued for being too broad (Keohane, 1982). The international systems argument with its focus on security is inherently problematic because security itself is infinitely stretchable: who is to say how much security is enough? Should worst case scenarios be a standard practice of security policymakers? Also, we see different decisionmakers take different decisions under similar threat scenarios, suggesting that short of responding to a military attack on the homeland, there is always room for choice. Most foreign policy decisions are made in conditions far less dire, and the international systems explanation leaves us without a clear enough guide as to why states choose certain foreign policies over others. This is a huge shortcoming if we are to understand short or medium term policy choices.

At the same time, if we can understand decisions at the level of the international system, it would be important in theory building in international relations following the dictum of 'explaining a lot with a little.' We also have to be mindful that except for the most compelling and pressing international threats which leaves little choice of action for states, state leaders are motivated by other pressures, from ideology, domestic politics, to economic considerations, and usually have a variety of ways to respond, well beyond simply balancing or bandwagoning for security reasons. In order to understand their specific choices, the international systems argument is likely to offer too little. Given this background, how can we understand India's nuclear tests in 1998? Can the international argument provide us with the full explanation or do we have to climb down to unit level variables?

INDIAN FOREIGN POLICY CHOICES AND THE INTERNATIONAL ENVIRONMENT

For the international systemic explanation of India's 1998 tests, we would expect to find the following condition: the security environment must have deteriorated prior to the test, with heightened threat perceptions. We should have seen conditions suggesting the need for enhanced nuclear capability rather than simply improving or expanding India's conventional military capacity. In determining the nature and level of threat facing India, it is difficult to find a simple one-to-one correspondence in threat elevation and a nuclear test response. Indian defense minister George Fernandez who had a reputation for outspokenness, was the most vocal in identifying neighboring China as the number one threat to India prior to the nuclear tests (*Economist*, May 9, 1998:86). After the tests, the prime minister himself put forth the strongest case for the tests as a response to rising threat from neighboring China. In prime minister Atal Bihari Vajpayee's much cited letter of May 13, 1998 to US president Bill Clinton (obtained by the *New York Times*), Vajpayee cast the argument squarely in security terms: "I have been deeply concerned at the deteriorating security environment, specially the nuclear environment, faced by India for some years past. We have an overt nuclear weapon state on our borders, a state which committed armed aggression against India in 1962" (*New York Times*, May 13, 1998). He went on to note this adversary's assistance to Pakistan in developing a covert nuclear capability, and in turn the terrorism and militancy of Kashmir fueled by the latter. The threats from China and Pakistan were laid out without mentioning either country by name. Interestingly, what was missing was any reference to the changed strategic landscape for India after the end of the Cold War and the collapse of the Soviet Union, a reliable ally since the late 1950s that had become even more important since 1971. The new Russia failed to renew the 1971 Treaty of Friendship and Cooperation whose article 9 approximated a semi-alliance between the two countries. The loss of Soviet power in 1991 that India could count on clearly created strategic anxiety, but then again, it had not gotten any worse by 1998.

The China Threat

A case may be made that the government's interpretation of the Chinese was credible. The declared Chinese nuclear doctrine was one of "no first use" and no use against non-nuclear powers. India's ambiguous nuclear status before 1998 could have placed it in either the nuclear or non-nuclear category in China's eyes. At the same time, China had developed medium range weapons which New Delhi perceived as India-targeted, had transferred M-11 missiles and sensitive technology to Pakistan, and was not in favor of including India in any discussions on global or regional nuclear arms control talks. The implication of the latter stand was perceived by India as Chinese unwillingness to see India as "a great power." By the same token, as of 1998, it is safe to say that India itself had not reached the level of seeing China as "a peer competitor," (as it currently seems to) as opposed to a major threat that India did not have the means to deter. China's continued strong ties with Pakistan was read by New Delhi as part of the Chinese objective of keeping India "contained" to South

Asia, something that riled Indian policymakers of all stripes. In addition, China was making inroads into Burma in a bigger way since the military coup of 1988, with stepped efforts in the early 1990s. There were some reports that in 1994, the Chinese had built up radar and electronic surveillance facilities on the Coco Islands leased from Burma, located just 30 kilometers north of Indian controlled Andaman Islands (Poon Kim Shee, p.36). The range of India's missiles at the time was only as far as western China; it was only in 1999 that Agni II, a missile that could reach Beijing was test fired successfully. Fernandez's declaration following the Pokhran II tests that "We have reached a point where no one any where can threaten us," (*Times of India*, April 12, 1999) bolsters the international security argument.

Against this stood the fact that beginning with Rajiv Gandhi's visit in 1988 (the first Indian prime ministerial visit in 34 years) and culminating in the agreement to set aside the border dispute in 1993, relations had been steadily improving between the two countries. Subsequent to the "Agreement of the Maintenance of Peace and Tranquility along the Line of Actual Control in the India-China Border Areas" signed in 1993, another key Agreement on Confidence Building Measures in the Military Field along the Line of Actual Control," was signed in 1996 during a visit of President Jiang Zemin to India (Ranganathan, p. 3). Thus it is not surprising that a number of analysts dispute the Indian government's rationale of the China threat as motivation for the nuclear tests. Eric Arnett goes the farthest by terming it "cynical" (Arnett, p. 11). Another analyst notes that while China had been perceived as a threat "on and off," China's 1964 test and subsequent 45 tests with the last ones in 1995, did not lead to alarm. Indeed, the 1998-99 Indian Defence Ministry's annual report stated that India does not view China as an adversary and favors developing friendly relations through bilateral negotiations as quickly as possible (Ali, p. 47).

The thaw in relations had indeed led to an equilibrium of sorts, but without dispelling all of India's fears. That New Delhi viewed the sensational rise of Chinese economic and military might since the

1980s with increasing concern is indisputable. Although relations had warmed, some on the Indian side liked to point out that while China had settled its border disputes with former adversaries Russia and Vietnam once and for all, the Sino-Indian border talks remained inconclusive with about 90,000 square kilometers of Indian territory being claimed by China. The assertion that China has accepted India's claim of Arunchal Pradesh being an integral part of India continues to be disputed by Chinese officials (*The Hindu*, November 12, 2008). In addition, the 1962 war with China which had not only caught India off-guard, but led to a humiliating rout, had given rise to a "never again" mentality. No matter the apparent progress in Sino-Indian relations, it seems that the 1962 residue lingers, to this day (See for example, B. Raman, June 22, 2007; Brahma Chellaney, "India Goes to China Hat in Hand," *Washington Times*, June 6, 2000). Apart from clearly identifiable left groups, especially the Communist Party of India-Marxist, China has not been above suspicion for most of India's political elite. Thus it is difficult to simply set aside the government's argument that the nuclear tests were motivated by a perceived threat from China. However, it still leaves open the question as to whether nuclear tests were necessary to meet the Chinese threat when India had already demonstrated its nuclear capability, and why the tests were conducted when they were. In order to address these questions, we need to climb down from the international systems level to domestic politics and leadership levels.

DOMESTIC POLITICS

Those who see domestic politics as the driving force for nuclear tests invariably point to the ascendancy of the Bharatiya Janata Party (BJP) to national power. There are three different ways to assess the importance of this factor: political and ideological preferences of the BJP; rigors of a new brand of coalitional politics; and decisionmaking by the leadership. The importance of the political preferences held by the BJP is best supported by the party's electoral platform that had chalked out a new approach, if not a new policy, on India's nuclear capability. Soon after its victory, the BJP along with its alliance partners (numbering up to 17 parties) released the National Agenda for Governance of March 18, 1998 that enunciated the following under the category of National Security, and it is worth quoting at some length:

> The state of preparedness, morale and combat effectiveness of the Armed Forces shall receive early attention and appropriate remedial action. We will establish a National Security Council to analyse the military, economic and political threats to the nation, also to continuously advise the government. This council will undertake India's first ever Strategic Defence Review. To ensure the security, territorial integrity and unity of India we will take all necessary steps and exercise all available options. *Towards that end we will re-evaluate the nuclear policy and exercise the option to induct nuclear weapons* (Emphasis added) (Available at www.indianembassy.org/special/nafg.htm).

The reference to a strategic review suggested that there would be no precipitous moves in national security re-formulations. Indeed, Bill Richardson, US ambassador to the United Nations who met with Prime Minister Atal Bihari Vajpayee a month prior to the nuclear tests apparently came away satisfied that no major changes would take place in the near future given that the Indian government had just appointed a high level task force to consider the composition of a national security council which would then enunciate a nuclear doctrine (Chengappa, 2000:30-31. Chengappa uses extensive interviews with key decisionmakers to chart the government's path to nuclear testing). Still, the document gave a strong signal that the government was prepared to break with the time honored practice of "keeping the nuclear option open."

IDEOLOGY, COALITIONAL AND ELECTORAL POLITICS

The BJP's political ideology could certainly have predisposed the party toward exercising the nuclear option. Along with its strident Hindutva philosophy, was a nationalism underscored by military hard power and economic self-sufficiency. This was a studied contrast to the Congress Party's Nehruvian secularism, multilateralism and economic developmentalism that had been the dominant political ideology since independence. But then how do we explain Congress Prime Minister P.V. Narasimha Rao's apparent decision to test nuclear weapons in 1995? According to a variety of sources, Rao rescinded the decision only because the US got wind of it thanks to satellite imagery and confronted the Indian government with the evidence. This indicates that political ideology does not seem to be a strong predictor for preferences on nuclear testing.

Another domestic political factor to consider is the nature of coalitional politics—a newly emergent governance structure for India after 1995. There is some evidence that Prime Minister Vajpayee did not want to appear a "weak" leader this time around, having been unable to keep a governing coalition afloat two years earlier when the BJP came to power for a mere 13 days in 1996. But he seemed to be coming under pressure more from his friends in the Rashtriya Swayamsevek Sangh (RSS) outside the coalition. Vajpayee's reputation in the BJP (viewed as the political face of the RSS) was one of a moderate and pragmatic politician, which did not sit well with RSS hardliners. For example, Vajpayee had apparently faced stiff opposition from the RSS for choosing centrist Jaswant Singh for his cabinet. Perhaps the Prime Minister decided to test to demonstrate his hardline credentials, but this cannot be traced to coalition politics.

There was no clamoring from the coalition partners to test; nor had two other coalitions that had preceded Vajpayee's government (United Front coalitions) tested. Besides, none of Vajpayee's coalition members were even informed prior to the tests, something that could potentially have backfired politically. Although exercising the nuclear option was noted in the election manifesto, so were three other controversial issues: enacting a uniform civil code; building a Hindu temple at Ayodhya and repealing article 370 giving special status to Kashmir. None of these were followed through once in power, likewise there is no evidence that lack of nuclear testing would have created any extra pressures either.

Still, perhaps the compulsions of consolidating electoral gains were a motivation. The nuclear tests could be used to enhance and solidify the BJP's standing and place it above all other parties in the popular mind. Indira Gandhi's peaceful nuclear explosion in 1974 supposedly increased her popularity. The large groundswell of popular support following the tests suggests the plausibility of this thesis. But as Neil Joeck asks: why would the same reasoning not have motivated Prime Minister Rao or his two successors? As Joeck puts it, "If electoral politics drove the BJP *after* it won an election, why didn't electoral politics drive the other parties and other prime ministers *before* an election?" (Joeck, 1999: 14). If consolidation of popular support was indeed the aim, it proved to be extremely short-lived. In the first big political test faced by the BJP just six months after the tests in November 1998, it lost elections in the critical states of Rajasthan and Madhya Pradesh, along with Delhi. Madhya Pradesh was especially surprising since the BJP had expected the Congress government to be unseated in the Indian electorate's usual anti-incumbency vote. As it turned out, national pride about the nuclear tests was not a match for the sudden skyrocketing price of onions at the grass roots. Of course this is an ex post facto observation, so we cannot make any definitive conclusions about what the BJP's expectations might have been. If popular support was a factor, it turned out to be a miscalculation, and even though it is not a fully satisfactory explanation, we cannot rule it out.

ECONOMIC LIBERALIZATION

Another question we have to address at the domestic level is how the new economic liberalization launched in 1991 might have affected the decision to test or not. The Narasimha Rao government and Vajpayee government operated under the new conditions, but one tested while the other did not. What does the evidence say about how economic liberalization may have constrained Rao and not Vajpayee? Both governments knew that testing would risk economic sanctions from the U.S. and other important industrial powers, but economic considerations might have been more critical for the Congress government. Liberalization had been introduced under Narasimha Rao in response to India's acute financial crisis in 1991 (foreign reserves had sunk to a shocking value of three weeks worth of imports). This was a bold step the government took, to high expectations abroad and high hopes at home. Given the singular importance of economic reform to the Narasimha government, it is not surprising that Rao stepped back from going ahead with the tests when faced with the certainty of U.S. economic sanctions and jeopardizing economic relations with key western countries. The fear of derailing the new economic experiment no doubt played an important part particularly when measured against the uncertain gains from conducting the tests.

Three years later, the BJP came to power even more committed to making India reach the ranks of developed countries (Baru, 2004). How did this objective not serve as a brake on testing? By the end of April 1998, India's foreign exchange reserve position was stronger, having grown to $26 billion, it equaled about six months worth of imports, which is considered very healthy (Morrow and Carriere,1999). The adequacy of reserves is an important indicator when assessing a country's ability to absorb external shocks such as sanctions. Also, India was still not overexposed internationally, and by then, there were important large Indian corporate houses (termed the Bombay Club) that seemed to welcome a slowdown in openness in light of international competition they would face. As it turned out, many of these companies have successfully managed competition from abroad, but at that time it was not clear that India would be a net beneficiary of globalization. This was in addition to some in the nationalist right wing of the BJP who believed that a possible forced return to more autarkic policies would have a salutary effect toward "self-sufficiency." This group had held reservations about liberalization which would lead to greater foreign capital control of the Indian economy (Joeck, 1999: 11). Over time, most of these groups in India have come to recognize that trading a measure of "sovereignty" for economic benefit can lead to a net gain in the current globalized system (Subramanian, 2007).

Moreover, India specifically stood little to lose economically by citing the China threat. In 1998, the two-way trade between India and China reached only $1.4 billion, a tiny fraction of each country's total exports (Srivastava, p. 9). This stands in stark contrast to the dramatically changed in the current environment in which China has become India's number one trading partner with trade reaching $30 billion in mid-2008 (overtaking India's trade with the US). Finally, although India's share of global trade between 1995 and 1998 had increased only slightly, it had become more interwoven into the international economic system and there was some sense that major companies in the U.S. in particular, that stood to gain from entering the Indian market, might even "lobby" against harsh and long term economic sanctions. The example of China was repeatedly cited in this connection in the run up to the tests.

PROXIMATE VERSUS LONGER TERM DRIVES TO TEST

Even if the BJP's cost-benefit calculus regarding testing versus sanctions was different from its predecessors, it could not have done the preparatory work for testing in the two months after taking power. This brings up the fact that the groundwork for carrying out the tests had long been in the making, crossing different parties and leaders. Moreover, since 1988, six governments drawn from different political parties had maintained nuclear weapons ready to be tested (Paul, 1998:2). This suggests that whatever the difference in the propensity to carry out the tests, there was a shared sentiment regarding the necessity for a nuclear option. Continuity has been the hallmark of

India's nuclear policy—indeed, the case for India having a nuclear capability was being articulated as far back as the 1950s by top political and scientific leadership. This was in part a function of India's goal to be a world-class industrial power, and in part in opposition to the extant global nuclear order.

The atomic energy program proceeded apace from government to government with hardly a break since the establishment of the Atomic Energy Commission (AEC) in 1948. The key architect of India's nuclear program, Homi Bhabha, enjoyed a close relationship with Prime Minister Jawaharlal Nehru. The administration of the nuclear program was entrusted to small high-powered group, answerably directly to the prime minister. Nehru remained opposed to nuclear weapons publicly and used this issue to attack US and Soviet policies. However, after the 1962 Sino-Indian war and the Chinese nuclear tests in 1964 and 1965, India became embroiled in a debate about appropriate Indian nuclear strategy, but without the benefit of Nehru's views (he had died before China went nuclear). Then AEC Chairman Vikram Sarabhai and the director of the newly set up Institute for Defence Studies ad Analyses, Major General Som Dutt, were among those unconvinced that India required nuclear weapons. However, in a speech to the International Atomic Energy Agency after the second Chinese test, Bhabha stated that it would be difficult to follow a policy of restraint given the introduction of nuclear weapons in the neighborhood. Soon after the Chinese thermonuclear test in 1967, a scientific effort was begun in India to study the nuclear design of an explosive (Ollapally, 2000:72). The era that followed until the 1998 tests was one of studied strategic ambiguity by successive Indian governments, with the official stand of keeping the nuclear option open.

Continuity and a shared outlook were the dominant features of India's nuclear posture, suggesting that governments of different stripes believed that security interests could be safeguarded thus. Pakistan's acknowledgement of its nuclear capability in 1987 (ironically to well-known Indian journalist Kuldip Nayar) had set the stage for a new element in their rivalry. Over a short period of time, the working assumption became that deterrence conditions existed between India and Pakistan, described variously as "recessed" to "existential" to "non-weaponized" deterrence. It proved to be an efficacious way to achieve deterrence without expending significant resources for a large nuclear stockpile or an open declaration of weaponization. What then motivated India to move from a recessed nuclear stance to testing? We need to explain the break from the past that the tests signified within this context. Looking at the time period leading up to the tests well before the BJP took power, what stands out is the renewed attention given to the status of India's nuclear capability since 1996—the type of attention that it had not received since the 1974 test. The trigger for a re-examination was the international dialogue on the Comprehensive Test Ban Treaty (CTBT) that had reached an unprecedented level at the Conference on Disarmament (CD) in Geneva.

THE CTBT DEBATE: TIPPING THE BALANCE

It is necessary to go into some detail on the CTBT debate in India because it sheds important light on the changes in domestic thinking that was occurring. While India had civilian nuclear capability, recessed deterrence and ultimately the nuclear weapons option, the Test Ban brought into sharp relief questions about the credibility of the so-called option. The CTBT which India had cosponsored in the UN General Assembly as late as 1994, came to viewed in an entirely different light after May 1995, when the Nuclear Nonproliferation Proliferation Treaty (NPT) Review Conference extended the treaty indefinitely and unconditionally. This came as a shock to most Indian analysts since it meant that there was no leverage to hold over nuclear weapons states on disarmament in the future. It meant that non-nuclear states were essentially destined to remain in the two-tier system indefinitely.

In the ensuing months and indeed over the next two years, a number of concerns converged that loudly questioned continuing

India's nuclear ambiguity. Indian diplomacy on security was faulted along several lines: the inability to change a persistent outside tendency to equate India and Pakistan and to denigrate Indian concerns vis-a-vi China; the failure to get external acknowledgement of India's broad restraint in the nuclear arena; the inability to put forth national interest in strategic, realpolitik terms as a result of being boxed in the with past "moralism;" the perception that the treaty was aimed specifically at India (the two other threshold states—Pakistan and Israel—were seen as having nuclear patrons in China and US respectively; and perhaps most importantly, the possibility that the nuclear option for all practical purposes, would be closed.

Between 1995 and 1998, despite the changeovers from one ruling coalition to another, there was a fairly steady questioning about India's traditional stand. The domestic debate came to a head with the sudden and unexpected imposition of the "entry into force" clause toward the end of negotiations at the CD. The clause held that the CTBT would not come into force for any state until India (and other states with nuclear power capability) ratified the Treaty. By then, Indian opinion had moved toward withdrawing from the CD and letting it run its course without participation. The argument was that just as India had stayed outside the NPT regime, it would simply remain outside the CTBT. The entry into force clause precluded that possibility which India saw as deliberately painting it into a corner. In the face of the new clause, there was a fairly swift closing of ranks across the political spectrum in India behind the Deve Gowda government's decision to cast a veto at the CD. Prime Minister Gowda, a highly unlikely candidate for bucking the international trend, ended up approving a veto, which was to prove a significant symbolic turning point. There was near unanimity among the political parties about the need to safeguard India's nuclear "option." A key question related to just how to protect it however, including whether testing was necessary or not to lend credibility to an option that had been kept open for twenty-four years without much public display.

On the question of credibility, the veto at the CD was presented as evidence of India's "resolve" to maintain the nuclear option and not give into international pressure. Indeed, in some quarters there was almost relief that by being "forced" to take such a strong action at the CD, India was able to establish the credibility of the nuclear option without having to test (Ollapally, 2000: 74-77). The debate over the CTBT had strengthened those who favored a stronger nuclear posture, but the question of testing remained fairly contentious. A strong argument for testing was found in the following question: If India did not test in a world without the CTBT, why would it test in a world with the CTBT? In other words, if India did not test, the nuclear option was for all practically purposes dead. There was a hint of a generational preference for and against testing, with some of the traditional Indian strategic and defense scientists being averse to breaking India's past behavior, with newer strategic analysts arguing that India needed to chart a bolder path.[1]

The credibility issue did not die down after India's veto at the CD, with the most convincing argument being made that while existing Indian capability would be credible against Pakistan, it did not reach that standard with China. The China factor began receiving greater attention than it had previously, though it was pitched mostly in future terms. Thus, while it is difficult to pinpoint an immediate rise in the threat level from China prior to India's nuclear tests, we can find a rising concern over the efficacy of India's nuclear capability in relation to China in general.

The scrutiny that India's nuclear capability received as a result of the CTBT negotiations and the domestic reactions to perceived international pressure goes a long way to explain the change toward a much more hospitable climate for testing, should any government had wanted to do so. The aftermath of the CTBT brought together fears of longer-term international security and a spike in popular nationalism. Both played directly into pre-existing BJP preferences, making it easier

[1]This is the impression of the author who held discussions with a cross section of strategic analysts and officials during the 1996-1998 period.

for the Vajpayee government to test. We may also postulate another tipping factor for the BJP unlike previous governments: diplomatic isolation might not have appeared as ominous as it would have been for Congress led governments. After all, Congress, with its multifaceted Nehruvian legacy of multilateralism, diplomatic activism and internationalism, no doubt would have had greater difficulty in becoming an international outcast. The BJP had no such legacy to live down. How much did Prime Minister Rao's reversal of his decision to test have to do with such a consideration? We cannot know for sure, but we cannot rule it out either.

One final domestic level explanation that has been put forward is that a small group of defense scientists with disproportionate power and influence, commonly referred to as "the strategic enclave," pushed the government to test. These analysts point to the way in which India's nuclear program managers operated from the 1940s onwards—direct access to the Prime Minister, lack of critical oversight and accountability, and the high national regard for their work. George Perkovich puts it rather bluntly, noting that "Their [defense scientists] influence peaked again in the 1995-1998 period, culminating in the test of a thermonuclear device that had no articulated strategic or doctrinal necessity but that capped the careers of retirement-aged scientists" (Perkovich, 2002: 447). This claim begs a number of questions. If the scientific elite held undue power during the entire post-independence period, why were they not able to press for nuclear tests earlier? Or put another way, how did India's political decisionmakers resist such pressure for more than two decades? Moreover, India's technical elite have not been a monolithic group historically, casting doubt on Perkovich's argument.

CONCLUSION

The fact that different Indian governments arguably faced similar security environments since 1991, but only one chose to go through with the conduct of nuclear tests, calls for an explanation that goes beyond the systemic level. From the discussion above, unit level factors seem to have some role in tipping the balance from sitting on the fence to actual testing. The simplest domestic explanation would be the ascendancy of the nationalist BJP as the critical causal variable. To attribute the tests to the BJP government would however be only getting part of the story. Domestic opinion along a wide spectrum had hardened on the nuclear issue by 1998, thanks ironically to perceived international pressure on India during the CTBT negotiations. Thus the BJP came to power at a time when the national sentiment on nuclear testing was more inflamed than it had been over the past 25 years. Domestic climate is an important intervening variable that needs to be taken into account.

But from a longer term perspective, without the buildup of India's nuclear program by each of the preceding governments, the BJP would not have been in a position to call for tests, no matter what the sentiment. Ultimately, what we see is an interaction of rising security concerns with a premium on meeting future security threats especially from China, coupled with the BJP government which was much more pre-disposed to testing and absorbing the negative international repercussions than any of its predecessors. What we cannot say with full confidence is that any other government in the BJP's place would have gone all the way to test, and hence the role of the BJP is important at minimum, in the timing of the tests. Thus to understand Pokhran II, it is not enough to understand what was occurring at the international level.

REFERENCES

Ali, M.M. 2000. "Has Pokhran-II Made India More Secure?" in A. Subramanyam Raju ed. *Nuclear India: Problems and Perspectives*. New Delhi: South Asian Publishers.

Arnett, Eric. 1998. "Nuclear Weapons and Arms Control in South Asia after the Test Ban," in Eric Arnett ed. Nuclear Weapons and Arms Control in South Asia After the Test Ban, Oxford: Oxford University Press for the Stockholm International Peace Research Institute.

Baru, Sanjaya. 2004. "Common Vision versus Common Practice: Defining the Partnership," paper presented at Conference on US-India Bilateral Cooperation: Taking Stock and Moving Forward, George Washington University, April 1.

Chengappa, Raj. 2000. Weapons of Peace, New Delhi: HarperCollins.

Raman, B. "Tawang: Some Indian Plain-Speaking at Last," South Asia Analysis Group, Paper No. 2273, June 22, 2007.

Joeck, Neil. 1999. "Nuclear Developments in India and Pakistan," Access Asia Review Vol. 2, No. 2 July 1999.

Morrow, Daniel and Carriere, Michael. 1999. "The Economic Impacts of the 1998 Sanctions on India and Pakistan." *The Nonproliferation Review Fall* (6) 2.

Perkovich, George. 2002. *India's Nuclear Bomb: The Impact on Global Proliferation.* California: University of California Press.

Ranganatha, C.V. 2001. "China Threat: A View from India," paper presented at the International Conference on China Threat Perceptions from Different Continents, Hong Kong Baptist University, January 11-12.

Shee, Poon Kim. 2002. "The Political Economy of China-Myanmar Relations: Strategic and Economic Dimensions," *Ritsumeikan Annual Review of International Studies* (1).

Srivastava, Anupam. 2000. "Living with the Dragon: Re-Calibrating India's Relations with China," in Kanti Bajpai and Amitabh Mattoo eds. *The Peacock and the Dragon: India-China Relations in the 21st Century*. New Delhi: Har-Anand Publications.

Subramanyan, Arvind. September 4, 2007. *India's Global Economic Policymaking.* Available online at casi.ssc.upenn.edu/iit

Waltz, Kenneth. 1979. *Theory of International Politics.* Reading, MA: Addison-Wesley.

Index